pig

King of the Southern Table

Other Books by James Villas

American Taste, 1982

The Town & Country Cookbook, 1985

James Villas' Country Cooking, 1988

Villas at Table, 1988

The French Country Kitchen, 1992

My Mother's Southern Kitchen, 1994

Stews, Bogs, and Burgoos, 1997

My Mother's Southern Desserts, 1998

My Mother's Southern Entertaining, 2000

Between Bites, 2002

Crazy for Casseroles, 2003

Biscuit Bliss, 2004

Stalking the Green Fairy, 2004

The Glory of Southern Cooking, 2007

The Bacon Cookbook, 2007

Dancing in the Lowcountry, 2008 (a novel)

pig

King of the Southern Table

JAMES VILLAS

Photography by Lucy Schaeffer

WILEY

JOHN WILEY & SONS, INC.

Published by John Wiley & Sons, Inc., Hoboken, New Jersey

Published simultaneously in Canada

For general information on our other products and services or for technical support, please contact our Customer Care Department within the United States at (800) 762-2974, outside the United States at (317) 572-3993 or fax (317) 572-4002.

Wiley also publishes its books in a variety of electronic formats. Some content that appears in print may not be available in electronic books. For more information about Wiley products, visit our web site at www.wiley.com.

Library of Congress Cataloging-in-Publication Data:

Villas, James.
Pig: king of the Southern table / James Villas.
p. cm.
Includes index.
ISBN 978-0-470-19401-0 (cloth)
1. Cookery (Pork) 2. Cookery, American—Southern style.
I. Title.
TX749.5.P67V56 2010
641.6′64—dc22
2009018557

Printed in the United States of America

10 9 8 7 6 5 4 3 2

To Kathleen Purvis, intrepid journalist,
ardent ham expert, and loyal Tarheel friend
who always comes to my rescue

CONTENTS

Preface:
A Passion for Pig

Crisply braised,
A paragon of fat and lean
Drips juicily upon the pit.
Sustainer of the South,
The Pig doth yearn to
Sacrifice and serve.
I eat it lustily,
Sauce-stained and smiling.

—Anonymous

I can't state it any more succinctly: Pork is and has been and always will be my favorite meat. But, after all, I was born and bred in North Carolina and have yet to meet a fellow Southerner who didn't love, respect, and, indeed, *understand* pig like no other American. I could almost say, in fact, that pork is my birthright, that I was virtually weaned on the inimitable sight, aroma, and taste of hog, and that no childhood memories are more indelible than those connected with the mighty pig.

Every other Saturday morning, for instance, it was a ritual for the whole family to pile into the car and drive out to the market on a huge working farm called Morrocroft so Mother could replenish our staples of fresh country bulk sausage, thick slabs of back bacon, souse, streak-o'-lean cooking meat, and satiny livermush. Come late summer each year, nothing was more exciting than making the trip up to W. G. Long's remote farm at Glendale Springs in the Blue Ridge Mountains to inspect, discuss, and eventually pick out two of the same hand-cured, slowly aged, moldy, luscious, 18-pound country hams that today Mother and I still travel two-and-a-half hours to procure.

And though it seems we were constantly attending one pork barbecue benefit or pig pickin' after another at churches, schools, country clubs, and private homes, what we awaited with utmost anticipation was the lavish extravaganza thrown in October (yesterday and today alike) out at Mallard Creek Presbyterian Church. There, the aroma of hickory-smoked meat that filled the air was intoxicating; the hog pits stretched thirty or more yards; volunteers stirred giant tubs of Brunswick stew with wooden paddles; hungry visitors at long, rickety tables piled their plastic plates with 'cue, stew, applesauce, tangy coleslaw, and slices of plain white loaf bread; and politicians up for election from all over the state circulated to hand out fountain pens and calendars and crazy little hats to pitch their campaigns.

Today, pig is as much king on the Southern table as when I took my first bites of juicy pork roast with sweet potatoes, fried salty country ham with red-eye gravy, and pickled pigs' feet. No matter where I travel in Dixie, there's never a moment when I'm not sniffing out a new brand of country sausage, a different style of pork barbecue or roasted spareribs, an intriguing country ham spread or bacon dip, or an increasingly rare but sapid hog's head stew. The state of Iowa might be up there in American swine production and distribution (by last report, North Carolina is now number one); Chicago may still be called by some the "hog butcher for the world"; and no doubt Texans and Kansas Citians can talk with some authority about Chester Whites, Durocs, spots, and other breeds of pig. But when it comes not only to the art of curing, smoking, pickling, seasoning, and cooking pig, but also to outright pork consumption, nobody—repeat, nobody—outperforms Southerners.

Even at a time when the popularity of pork nationwide is increasing (due primarily—for better or worse—to much leaner hogs), rarely in markets outside the South do you find much more than standard chops and rib roasts, smoked hams and bacon, frozen sausage rolls and revolting precooked links, and maybe a little salt pork. The meat departments in Southern stores, by contrast, boast vast sections devoted exclusively to pork products, a real pig spectacle that baffles the unenlightened and gives credence to the adage that Southerners eat every part of a porker but the oink.

In addition to all the ordinary cuts, there are gallon tubs of pork chitterlings (or chitlins, the small intestines) and lard; trays of fresh ears, jowls, snouts, liver, tongues, and knuckles; bags of bellies and brains; packages of meaty pigs' feet, country ham, fatback, ham hocks, and streak-o'-lean (lean salt pork); and containers of liver pudding, cracklin's (rendered, crisp skins), souse (head cheese), and scrapple. Up North, I gave up a long time ago trying to find superior, well-seasoned bulk sausage that contains just the right proportions of lean meat and fat, but the last time I was home to stock up, I counted in one grocery store case no less than nine different brands of fresh sausage just waiting to be pattied and fried for breakfast, or used in stuffings, coatings, spoon breads, sauces, and, yes, even pies and cakes. As for aged Southern country ham, this sublime delicacy may not be as readily available as it was just twenty years ago, but I still manage to find enough salty slabs to prevent utter deprivation off home territory if my own supply is exhausted.

Pork, of course, has been a primary food in the South since the earliest days of settlement. The first domesticated pigs in the United States were a herd of 13 brought from Spain to Tampa, Florida, in 1539 by Hernando de Soto, and since the animals proved to be so easily housed, fed, and cared for, they quickly became the region's main dietary staple. Not only was pork the most economical meat to produce, with a minimum of waste, it was also one that could be successfully salted, smoked, air-dried, and preserved in other ways for long periods of storage without losing its textural and palatable integrity.

Colonial Virginians ate such quantities of pig that William Byrd reported jestfully that they were "prone to grunt rather than to speak." So infatuated was Thomas Jefferson with the potential of swine that he imported Calcutta boars to crossbreed with his Virginia sows, and by the early nineteenth century, the exceptional hams produced in Smithfield from

shoats that foraged in the surrounding peanut fields had already gained such renown that even Queen Victoria had a standing order.

Throughout the South, "pork barrel legislation," "high on the hog," having "a hoggish temper," doing something "whole hog," and other such colloquial expressions became part of the vernacular. And there's more than a modicum of truth in the theory that the Confederacy lost the War Between the States partly because strategic pork rations dwindled to the point where the troops were literally half-starved.

From the bayous of Louisiana to the mountains of Tennessee and Alabama to the swampy Lowcountry of South Carolina and Georgia, the multiple ways that pig is utilized in the kitchen are staggering. All Southerners, naturally, love a traditional herby pork loin, shoulder, or fresh ham roasted with sweet potatoes or turnips; a plate of crispy spareribs; earthy pork stew with black-eyed peas or butter beans; and a regal baked country ham stuffed with any variety of greens or fruits. But move through the regions and you also find pork-studded Kentucky burgoos; spicy ham and sausage perloos in Charleston and Savannah; Cajun blood puddings; chitlin hash and crunchy fried pigs' ears throughout Mississippi; bacon and squash pudding; sausage spoon bread;

pork-pone pie; silky brains and scrambled eggs; crusty baked pigs' feet; and deviled pork liver.

What Rebel would dream of simmering "a mess of greens," peas, or beans without a ham hock or piece of side meat for flavor? Who can deny that even the most pristine cornbread is not enhanced by a few cracklin's? And just the idea of frying chicken in vegetable shortening or lard that doesn't contain a little bacon grease is, well . . . Yankee!

It has been said that Southerners never agree on religion, politics, and barbecue, and all you have to do to see tempers flare on this last subject is attend one of the outlandish barbecue champion cook-offs held annually in Lexington and Raleigh, North Carolina; Owensboro, Kentucky; Memphis, Tennessee; Vienna, Georgia; and Lord knows where else. It must first be understood that, in the South, genuine pit-cooked barbecue means pig and only pig, since pig is the one meat that can absorb flavorings and seasonings without losing its integrity—which is why Texans (with all their beef and chicken and goat roasts) have never been considered true Southerners.

Of course, every Southern state, indeed every region, county, and town, deems itself the world authority on barbecued pig, and in my home state of North Carolina alone, passions run so deep over the fine distinctions between eastern-style and western-style barbecue (as well as the different styles of sauce, coleslaw, Brunswick stew, and hush puppies served with the meat) that I learned never to air a preference on the complex and heated topic for fear of alienating family and losing friends. In my never-ending search for great barbecue (chopped with pieces of cracklin' mixed into the meat, if you please), I've eaten superior pig at Big Bob Gibson's in Decatur, Alabama; Maurice's Piggy Park in Columbia, South Carolina; Goldies Trail in Vicksburg, Mississippi; Wilber's in Goldsboro, North Carolina; and dozens of other such down-home digs. But far be it from me to make a definitive proclamation now or in the future on the national dish of the South.

For nearly five centuries, the noble pig has sustained the South through development and prosperity, grief and glory, and defeat and recovery, a veritable symbol not only of survival but also of the gastronomic excellence that has come to define so many of the distinctive dishes that grace the Southern table. President Harry S. Truman, from Missouri, may not have been a legitimate Southerner, but no doubt he won over the hearts of Rebs from Maryland to Mississippi when he once declared that "no man should be allowed to be president who does not understand hogs."

THE PIG

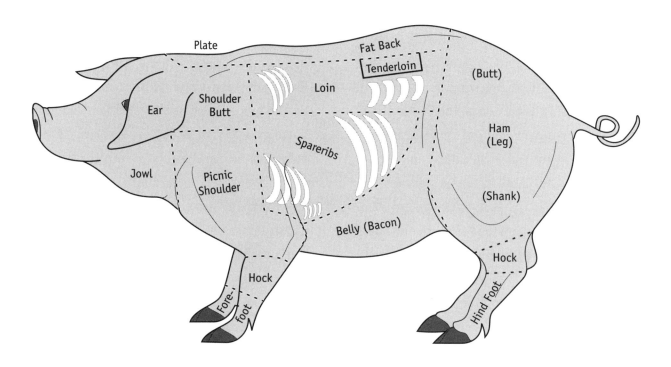

INTRODUCTION

A Southern Pig Primer: From Head to Tail

Hog's Head Used to make a pungent stew and, when the various parts are pickled in brine and laced with spices, molded into souse (head cheese).

Pig Jowl The fleshy, sweet cheek of the pig that is cured, smoked, and generally used to flavor boiled vegetables, stews, and puddings. Also known as Bacon Square.

Pigs' Ears Mild, sweet, gelatinous pork that is baked, broiled, battered and deep fried, or added to stews to enrich texture.

Pork Neck Bones Pieces of bone, cartilage, and meat used to give body and depth to long-simmered stews and sauces.

Pork Shoulder The upper, mostly lean section that provides Boston butt roasts, blade steaks, stew meat, and ground meat for sausage and other products. The lower, fattier section provides picnic roasts, arm steaks, canned luncheon meats, and ground meat for sausage.

Hocks (or Knuckles) The meaty but gristly upper portion of a pig's front legs and lower portion of its hind legs. Can be fresh, cured, or smoked. Hocks are either slowly braised on their own or used to flavor soups, stews, beans, and peas.

Pigs' Feet (or Trotters) Bony, sinewy, gelatinous feet and ankles that are available fresh, smoked, or pickled. They are stewed, deviled and baked; added to soups and stews; or used to make sauces.

Fatback The thick, fresh (unsalted and unsmoked) layer of fat that runs along the pig's back and encases the loin. Used to make lard, cracklin's, and some breads, and as a fat for shallow frying. Not to be confused with Salt Pork.

Pork Loin The leanest and most expensive cut that runs along the pig's backbone ("high on the hog") and provides loin and rib roasts, chops and cutlets, Canadian bacon, and the purest fatback.

Pork Tenderloin A boneless, lean, long muscle cut from the pig's loin end and equivalent to a filet. Expensive.

Country-Style Ribs Very meaty ribs cut from the end of a pig's upper shoulder butt.

Baby Back Ribs Meaty cut of ribs left after the loin is removed from the pig's back. Smaller than Spareribs.

Spareribs A long, narrow cut of fatty/meaty ribs cut from the pig's belly after the section used for bacon is removed. Larger than Baby Back Ribs.

Pork Belly A fatty/lean section of meat beneath a pig's loin and behind its ribs from which bacon and salt pork are cut. Whole, it can also be stuffed and braised or sliced and fried.

Bacon Cured and/or smoked meat cut from the pig's side and belly.

Salt Pork A fatty "side meat" cut, like bacon, from the pig's side and belly. It can either be sliced and fried or used to flavor boiled vegetables and some stews. Not to be confused with Fatback.

Streak-o'-Lean A popular term for salt pork streaked with lean meat that is used primarily to flavor boiled greens, beans, peas, and soups. Can also be sliced, fried, and served with boiled vegetables and cornbread.

Ham (Pork Leg) The hind leg of a pig that provides fresh, smoked, and cured country hams, as well as ham steaks. Fresh and smoked hams are generally marketed in shank and slightly meatier butt portions, while country hams involve the entire leg. A fresh ham is neither cured nor smoked and is cooked like a pork roast.

Pig Tails Slightly meaty, sweet, gelatinous cuts that are stewed, barbecued, or crumbed and grilled, and are also used to flavor boiled greens and field peas.

A Southern Pig Glossary

Blood Pudding (or Blood Sausage) A pork, rice (or oatmeal), and pig's blood link sausage popular in Appalachia and the Carolina Lowcountry. Similar to Cajun Boudin.

Boudin A Cajun pork and rice link sausage with pork liver or chicken, and possibly pig's blood. Similar to Blood Pudding and Blood Sausage.

Brunswick Stew A thick Virginia, North Carolina, and Georgia stew with ham hock, chicken, and vegetables, served at large outdoor gatherings and at pork barbecue houses.

Burgoo A thick Kentucky stew with various cuts of pork, other meats, and vegetables, served at large outdoor gatherings. Related to Brunswick Stew.

Chaurice A spicy, garlicky Creole sausage used to enrich gumbos, jambalayas, and bean dishes.

Chitlins (or Chitterlings) The small intestines of hogs that are washed, soaked for several days in salt water, scraped, and boiled till tender. Used to make hashes, loaves, casseroles, chilies, fritters, and gumbos.

Cochon de Lait Cajun roast suckling pig.

Country Ham Any ham that is cured by the dry-salt method, smoked with green hickory or other hardwood, and aged for at least six months.

Country-Style Bacon Cured, heavily smoked, salty bacon produced from the same hogs bred for Smithfield and other premium country hams. Rarely available outside the South.

Cracklin's Rendered, crisp morsels of pork fat used to flavor salads, stews, and breads. Also, the crisp skin of a barbecued pig.

'Cue A short term for barbecue in the Carolinas and Georgia used at least since the Civil War.

Drippings Rendered salt pork or bacon fat used for frying, as shortening in breads, and to flavor numerous Southern dishes.

Dutch Goose A whole roast pig belly.

Hash A South Carolina term for a thick pork gravy served over rice or grits as a main course.

Hog Pot A large pot of various pork cuts simmered with cabbage and other vegetables and served at large social, religious, and political gatherings in Appalachia and the Deep South.

Lard Rendered fresh pork fat. The finest lard, known as "leaf lard," is made from solid fat from around the pig's kidneys. Emulsified commercial lard, sold in cardboard containers, should be white and have a slightly oily aroma.

Livermush A Carolina breakfast dish that, by law, is at least 30 percent pork liver plus other pork meat that is ground, mixed with cornmeal and seasonings, chilled in a block, and pan fried. Also called Liver Pudding and Scrapple.

Middlings Any pork side meat used to flavor boiled greens, beans, and other vegetables.

Mountain Oysters Pigs' testicles that are breaded and deep fried. Considered a delicacy in West Virginia, Tennessee, and Arkansas.

Outsider An outside portion of barbecued pork that is dry, crisp, crunchy, and slightly charred.

Pickled Pork A shoulder cut of pork marinated in brine. Used in Louisiana to season gumbos and bean dishes.

Pig Pickin' An outdoor celebration where part of the meat of a whole barbecued hog is picked off with the fingers.

Pulled Pork Pork pulled in shreds off a whole barbecued pig at an outdoor Pig Pickin'.

Red-Eye Gravy A skillet gravy made by deglazing the debris of fried country ham with water or coffee. Served over ham, biscuits, and grits.

Sack Sausage Fresh bulk pork sausage that is sacked, smoked, and aged in country smokehouses alongside bacon and country hams.

Salt Pork Salt-cured, unsmoked pig belly and sides used primarily as a side meat to flavor boiled vegetables, stews, and casseroles. Not to be confused with Fatback. Also called White Bacon.

Scrapple A South Carolina mush of pork scraps and white cornmeal fried in bacon drippings. Also called Livermush and Panhas elsewhere in the South.

Side Meat Any form of fatty pork (bacon, salt pork, fatback, streak-o'-lean, belly, jowl, or ends of country ham) used to season boiled peas, beans, and vegetables.

Slab Bacon A whole cured and/or smoked slab of pork belly with rind and streaks of lean meat. The average ratio is about two-thirds fat to one-third lean meat. Can be double-smoked for more intense flavor.

Souse A chilled, jellied hog's head cheese traditionally served at Christmas.

Tasso A Cajun lean, cured, smoked, highly spiced pork used to flavor beans, eggs, and noodles throughout Louisiana. Rarely available outside the region.

Wets and Drys Memphis, Tennessee, terms for sauced and dry-rubbed barbecued ribs. Wets are spicy, sweet, and sticky; drys are pepper hot and cotton dry.

White Bacon Another Southern term for Salt Pork.

Smithfield: King of Southern Hams

Produced for over 300 years in Smithfield, Virginia, and beloved by Thomas Jefferson, Queen Victoria, Sarah Bernhardt, Woodrow Wilson, and epicures the world over, Smithfield hams are considered to be America's premier country-cured ham. Until about thirty years ago, all Smithfields were cut from carcasses of hogs fattened almost exclusively on local peanuts, a diet that produced sublime hams with translucent fat, deep amber color, and a distinctive oily, sweet flavor. Today, however, because of America's phobia over fats and demand for leaner pork, the age-old tradition of nut-fed hogs destined for Smithfield hams has ceased to exist, resulting in a product that is still tightly controlled and superior but decidedly different. In 1968, Virginia's General Assembly issued a statute that required all Smithfields to be made from "peanut-fed hogs"; today, the revised official decree reads as follows: "Genuine Smithfield hams are hereby defined to be hams processed, treated, smoked, aged, cured by the long-cure, dry salt method of cure and aged for a minimum period of six months; such six-month period to commence when the green pork cut is first introduced to dry salt, all such salting, processing, treating, smoking, curing, and aging to be done within the corporate limits of the town of Smithfield, Virginia."

Smithfield hams are available in many finer markets, or they can be ordered from Smithfield Foods, Smithfield, Virginia (800–926–8448; www.smithfieldhams.com), and Gwaltney of Smithfield, Smithfield, Virginia (800–292–2773). All Smithfield hams are expensive.

Southern Country Hams

The most exquisite peak in culinary art is conquered when you do right by ham. The making of a ham dinner, like the making of a gentleman, starts a long, long time before the event.

—ANONYMOUS SOUTHERN WRITER

In addition to the legendary Smithfield hams of Virginia, superior dry-cured, smoked, and naturally aged country hams are also processed elsewhere in Virginia, as well as in North Carolina, Georgia, Tennessee, and Kentucky, by relatively small producers whose families have been in the business for generations. Generally, the salty hams are available whole (12 to 18 pounds, cooked or uncooked) or in prepackaged slices. All whole aged country hams should be scrubbed thoroughly with warm water and vinegar to remove any mold, then possibly soaked briefly or longer in water to restore moisture and remove salt (according to individual taste). Any reliable butcher should be willing to slice a whole country ham (about ¼ inch thick) not intended to be baked. Wrapped tightly in freezer paper and plastic bags, slices of country ham can be stored in the freezer for up to six months without losing moisture or flavor.

Some of the South's finest country hams can be ordered from the following venerable producers:

S. Wallace Edwards & Sons, Surry, Virginia (800-222-4267; www.virginiatraditions.com)

Wayco Ham Company, Goldsboro, North Carolina (800-962-2614)

Meacham Country Hams, Sturgis, Kentucky (800-552-3190)

G & W Hamery Country Hams, Murfreesboro, Tennessee (615-893-9712)

B & B Food Products, Inc., Cadiz, Kentucky (502-235-5294)

The Gospel of Southern Barbecue

Barbecue is more than a meal;
it's a way of life.

—**Greg Johnson and**
Vince Staten, *Real Barbecue*

Southern barbecue is probably the most controversial and misunderstood subject on earth, and nothing stirs Rebel passions more. First, barbecue in the South always refers to a specific food or an event and *never* to the metal contraption with hot coals known only as a "grill." Hamburgers, hot dogs, and chicken are "grilled" in the South, never "barbecued."

Second, 99 percent of the time, Southern barbecue signifies one meat and one meat only: pork (which is one reason why Texans and western Arkansans, champions of "barbecued" beef brisket, goat, mutton, and who knows what else, are not considered by many to be Southerners). It also implies mostly the age-old method of cooking whereby a whole hog or specific cuts of a hog are roasted very slowly anywhere from several to 12 hours over glowing charcoal and/or hardwood (hickory or oak) coals, basted with a mopping sauce, possibly chopped or sliced, and enhanced with more sauce. Barbecue can be produced on grates over vast open pits in the ground, in special steel cookers or drums, or on a simple kettle grill; and while the cooking procedure is basically

the same all over the South, techniques vary slightly from region to region and from one pit master to the next. Some styles of barbecue can also be produced in an ordinary kitchen oven.

Third, what distinguishes one style of pork barbecue from another is not so much the cooking method as the different sauces, dips, and dry rubs used to flavor the meat and produce various wet and dry textures. Generally, sauces begin in the eastern mid-Atlantic states as spicy, vinegar-clear emulsions and gradually become thicker, more tomatoey and mustardy, and sweeter the farther south and west you go. (Just in North Carolina—the self-proclaimed "barbecue capital of the world"—the thin, peppery, vinegar sauces in the eastern part of the state can differ drastically from the tomato-based ones in the western part.)

Fourth, what is served with barbecue is as important as the barbecue itself. Coleslaw, baked beans, and French fries are almost universal, but in Virginia, the Carolinas, Georgia, and eastern Florida, crisp pork skins, Brunswick stew (or "hash" in much of South Carolina), and hush puppies are obligatory sides at most places. Elsewhere, pickles, applesauce, onion slices, biscuits, cornbread, or slices of ordinary white loaf bread are preferred. Everywhere, barbecue is washed down with iced tea, Coke, and (except in the Bible Belt) beer or hard liquor.

Fifth, in the South, barbecue is prepared and eaten either at large, communal social, political, holiday, or religious gatherings or at one of the thousands of barbecue houses that dot the downtown streets, back roads, and highways of every region. Any outdoor barbecue celebration can be called a pig pickin', whereby meat is chopped or shredded ("pulled"), while a portion is left intact to be picked at with the fingers. Barbecue houses are the most socially democratic institutions on the globe, and nothing indicates a great one like the presence of pickup trucks parked out front next to expensive Cadillacs and Mercedes. Other reassuring signs are the distinct aroma of hickory in the air, Formica tables and booths inside, cheap silverware and plastic glasses, piles of paper napkins, a variety of bottled sauces, perhaps a few framed family or religious portraits on the walls, and a bottle of toothpicks next to the cash register.

Sixth, there are established and sacred ways to eat pork barbecue in the South, and anybody who veers from tradition is considered to be either a snob or a Yankee. Barbecued ribs may be disjointed with a knife, but they're consumed only with the fingers. The meat on a chopped or pulled-pork barbecue plate is expected to be tasted before any sauce is added. Chopped barbecue sandwiches are always served only on plain, unadorned, unflavored hamburger buns with a spoonful of coleslaw on top of the meat, and a cardinal sin is to sog up the bottom half of the bun by layering the slaw before the barbecue. Anybody who requests a bottle of ketchup for barbecue should be eating a hamburger somewhere else.

Southern Bulk Pork Sausage

Whereas elsewhere the term *sausage* usually describes any meat, poultry, or even seafood that is ground or chopped, mixed with a variety of other ingredients, and stuffed into link casings, in the South the word refers almost exclusively to bulk pork forcemeat seasoned with no more than salt and pepper, powdered sage, and either red pepper flakes or cayenne. Sausage meat (or "country sausage") is indispensable to Southern cookery, and while it is used to make all sorts of cocktail balls, stuffings, meat loaves, casseroles and stratas, savory pies, and breads, Southerners most often simply fry it in patties for breakfast or supper to accompany eggs, grits, biscuits, and the like.

Originally a major fresh by-product of winter hog killings, sausage today is available in huge quantities of rolls in all markets throughout the South, and virtually every region prides itself on individual brands with different proportions of lean meat and fat and different levels of seasoning. While not all Southern bulk sausage is necessarily reputable, most is certainly superior to the overly lean or fatty, tough, tasteless, frozen, commercial products found elsewhere in the country. (Jimmy Dean roll sausage is the only widely available brand I've found that approximates the Southern standard in texture and flavor.) As for the coarse, highly seasoned, Italian-style bulk and link sausage that is so popular today in other regions of the country, Southerners still consider it to be a mere novelty, not to be taken too seriously.

Southern sausage fanatics (like myself), of course, try to make their own sausage as often as possible, the main advantage being the freedom to use the right cuts of pork, the right ratio of lean meat to fat, and just the right seasoning. Generally, the cheaper, fattier cuts of pork (picnic shoulder, country-style ribs, blade or arm steaks, and rib chops) make the best sausage, and pure-white, soft fat cut from the pig's back is preferred for ideal moistness. The classic ratio is two parts of lean meat to one part of fat for tender, moist, perfectly balanced sausage. Any less lean meat and the sausage risks being greasy and burnt when fried; any less fat and it tends to be dry and tough. As for seasoning, freshly ground black pepper, powdered dried sage, and red pepper flakes or cayenne with dates that have not expired on cans and bottles are obligatory.

Sausage making, which can be fun and easy, requires either a manual or electric meat grinder or an electric mixer with grinder and sausage horn attachments. Food processors should not be used for sausage, since they make a mush of most meats and cannot produce the right texture.

APPETIZERS and SALADS

Virginia Smithfield Ham Spread

Kentucky Potted Country Ham

Salt Pork and Chicken Liver Spread

Pork Liver Cocktail Paste

Jellied Country Ham Mold

Souse (Hog's Head Cheese)

Sherried Ham Mousse

Deep-Fried Marinated Pork Nuggets

Cocktail Bacon Piggies

Spicy Sausage Balls

Birmingham Porcupine Balls

Country Ham, Cream Cheese,
and Pecan Rounds

Pork and Bell Pepper Kabobs

Deviled Pork and Bacon Kabobs

Crisp Potato Skins with Cheese
and Bacon

Bacon-Stuffed Mushrooms

Candied Pecan Bacon

Party Country Ham Deviled Eggs

Charleston Hobotee

Pork Cracklin', Black-Eyed Pea,
and Shrimp Salad

Pig Knuckle Salad with
Mustard Vinaigrette

Pork and Apple Salad with
Mustard-Mayonnaise Dressing

Missy's Ham and Macaroni Salad

Potato, Ham, and Olive Salad

Congealed Ham and Orange Salad

Spinach, Country Ham, and Egg Salad
with Warm Red-Eye Dressing

Butter Bean and Bacon Salad

Tennis Ball Salad with
Salt Pork-Buttermilk Dressing

Red Cabbage, Tangerine, and Bacon Salad
with Bacon Vinaigrette

Wilted Sallet with
Hot Bacon Dressing

VIRGINIA SMITHFIELD HAM SPREAD

**MAKES AT LEAST
12 COCKTAIL SERVINGS**

1 pound Smithfield or other cured
country ham

2½ cups half-and-half

2 tablespoons Madeira

½ teaspoon dry mustard

½ teaspoon powdered sage

Various pork spreads have been around Virginia since Jeffersonian days, and none is more distinctive than those made with the state's legendary Smithfield ham. Typically, a crock of this spread is served with toast triangles or beaten biscuits and tiny dill pickles at receptions and cocktail parties, but it's also not unusual to see on fancy buffets a ring mold of something like creamed mushrooms with a mound of spicy spread in the center. Do note that no salt or other seasoning should be added to those in the recipe, and remember that if you insist on soaking the ham to reduce the salt, you also leach out much of the sublime flavor.

1 Preheat the oven to 325°F. Grease a 6-cup ovenproof crock or mold and set aside.

2 With a sharp knife, finely chop the ham and place in a bowl. Add the remaining ingredients and stir till blended thoroughly. Scrape the mixture into the prepared crock or mold, cover tightly with foil, and bake till firm, about 30 minutes. Serve the spread hot or at room temperature with toast, crackers, or small beaten biscuits.

Kentucky Potted Country Ham

Makes about 2 cups

1½ cups cooked chopped country ham

8 tablespoons (1 stick) butter, at room temperature

½ teaspoon dry mustard

½ teaspoon ground cloves

2 tablespoons bourbon

Freshly ground black pepper to taste

No doubt the tradition of potting numerous meats and seafood with butter in the South can be traced back to our English heritage, and since Kentucky has been producing some of the region's finest country hams for well over two centuries, it's little wonder that cooks chop, grind, mince, and puree the salty delicacy for all sorts of savory cocktail spreads, pastes, and molds—many, of course, spiked with a good Kentucky bourbon. Tightly covered, this spread keeps for up to a week in the refrigerator, but be warned that if it's not brought back to room temperature before serving, it's almost impossible to spread.

In a blender or food processor, grind the ham finely, add the butter, and grind till well blended. Add the remaining ingredients and grind almost to a paste. Scrape the mixture into a crock, cover with plastic wrap, and store in the refrigerator. Allow the spread to return to room temperature about 1 hour before serving with tiny biscuit halves or crackers.

Salt Pork and Chicken Liver Spread

Makes about 3 cups

1 pound salt pork, rind removed, cut into small pieces

1 quart water

4 tablespoons bacon grease

4 tablespoons (½ stick) butter

1 medium onion, minced

1 celery rib, minced

2 garlic cloves, minced

1 pound chicken livers, trimmed of fat and patted dry

2 teaspoons ground allspice

½ cup brandy

Salt and freshly ground black pepper to taste

1 large hard-boiled egg, finely chopped

Southerners are often teased about the salt pork (or streak-o'-lean) and coffee cans of bacon grease that we always keep on hand and treasure, and this cocktail spread is but one of many ways we put these valuable staples to good use. The salt pork must be simmered for about half an hour, not only to leach out most of the salt but also to tenderize it for easy processing. Although the bacon fat is what gives this spread much of its distinctive Southern flavor, if you haven't reserved any and don't feel like frying up a few bacon strips, all butter can be used to sauté the vegetables. For the spread to have ideal texture, don't overcook the livers—cook just till they lose their pink color. Serve the spread with either toast triangles or unflavored crackers.

1 In a saucepan, combine the salt pork and water, bring to a boil, reduce the heat to moderate, and cook for about 30 minutes. Drain the pork, rinse under running water, pat dry with paper towels, and finely chop.

2 In a large skillet, combine the bacon grease and butter over low heat, add the onion, celery, and garlic, and stir for about 10 minutes. Add the salt pork, livers, allspice, brandy, and salt and pepper, return the heat to a simmer, and cook till the livers are no longer pink, about 12 minutes.

3 Transfer the mixture to a food processor, reduce to a puree, and scrape into a crock. Add the egg, mix till well blended, cover, and chill the spread for at least 2 hours before serving.

Pork Liver Cocktail Paste

1 pound pork liver, trimmed of fat and cut into pieces

1 small onion, minced

1 teaspoon dry mustard

1 teaspoon salt

½ teaspoon ground nutmeg

¼ teaspoon ground cloves

Cayenne pepper to taste

8 tablespoons (1 stick) butter, cut into pieces and softened

Although pork liver is more pungent than calf's or lamb's liver, when it is absolutely fresh, slowly simmered, and then ground with plenty of seasonings and sweet butter into a paste such as this one, nothing is more savory and succulent. When shopping, look for liver that is reddish brown and fairly firm, and reject any that is very dark and mushy. Remember that all liver is highly perishable and should be cooked within 24 hours of purchase.

1 Place the liver in a saucepan with enough water to cover, bring to a simmer, cover, and cook till very tender, about 30 minutes.

2 Drain the liver, transfer to a blender or food processor, add the remaining ingredients, and blend till very smooth. Scrape into a crock and refrigerate for at least 1 hour before serving with crackers or toast rounds.

Jellied Country Ham Mold

Makes 6 to 8 servings

3 cups chicken broth

1 cup dry white wine

One 2-pound chunk of cured country ham, trimmed of all fat and cut in half

1 medium onion, chopped

2 celery ribs, broken into thirds

1 carrot, scraped and sliced

6 black peppercorns

¼ teaspoon dried thyme

1 bay leaf

1 cup finely chopped fresh parsley leaves

2 tablespoons unflavored powdered gelatin

¼ cup warm water

2 tablespoons tarragon vinegar

Considering the Southern passion for both country ham and congealed dishes, it's hardly unusual for cooks to utilize part of a baked Smithfield or other cured ham to make a jellied mold to be proudly displayed on a buffet table or sliced as a first course for an elaborate meal. Do note that the ham must be devoid of all fat, and if it is too salty for your taste (Southerners love salty ham), simply soak it in cold water for a couple of hours before simmering it with the vegetables and aromatics. For the mold to turn out right and look attractive, the cubes of ham must be stirred and distributed evenly after the first couple of hours of congealing.

1 Pour the broth and wine into a large saucepan or small casserole and add the ham, onion, celery, carrot, peppercorns, thyme, and bay leaf. Bring the liquid to a boil, reduce the heat to low, and simmer gently for about 30 minutes. Lift out the ham, transfer to a chopping board, and cut into ½-inch cubes. Strain the broth into a clean saucepan.

2 Rinse the inside of a medium glass bowl with cold water and dust the sides thickly with one-half of the chopped parsley. Add the ham cubes to the bowl.

3 In a small bowl, soften the gelatin in the water for 5 minutes, and then stir into the strained broth. Add the remaining parsley and the vinegar to the broth and allow to cool till syrupy. Pour over the ham, distributing the cubes as evenly as possible with a fork, and, if necessary, adding a little more wine to cover.

4 Cover the bowl with plastic wrap and chill for about 12 hours, stirring once after the first 2 hours to distribute the ham evenly throughout. Unmold on a large, attractive round serving dish and serve in thick slices.

PIG PICKIN'S

"Went in to Alexandria [Virginia] to a Barbecue and stayed all Night." —George Washington, 1769

SOUSE (HOG'S HEAD CHEESE)

3 pigs' knuckles (about 2 pounds)

2 pigs' feet (about 1 pound)

2 medium onions, chopped

1 celery rib, chopped

1 carrot, scraped and chopped

2 garlic cloves, peeled and chopped

6 black peppercorns

½ teaspoon dried allspice

½ teaspoon dried thyme

1 bay leaf

Salt and freshly ground black pepper to taste

Tabasco sauce to taste

1 pound cooked ham, cut into small cubes

¼ cup dry red wine

2 tablespoons white vinegar

¼ teaspoon ground nutmeg

¼ cup chopped fresh parsley leaves

Souse (or head cheese) is a delectable jelled meat loaf traditionally made in the South from a hog's head and served chilled as an appetizer, often with chopped onion, olive oil, and vinegar. Given the impracticality of acquiring a hog's head these days (not to mention dealing with the critter), a very credible version of souse can be made with pigs' knuckles (hocks) and feet (trotters), both of which have sufficient meat and natural gelatin to produce the right texture and can be obtained from butchers and in some grocery stores. It still takes time and effort to make a good souse, but once you've tasted it, you'll understand why generations of Southerners have always considered the loaf to be a true delicacy both at the table and on the buffet. Serve the souse with a variety of pickles.

1 In a large kettle or casserole, combine the pigs' knuckles and feet and add enough water to cover. Bring to a boil, reduce the heat to low, simmer for about 5 minutes, and drain. Add the onions, celery, carrot, garlic, peppercorns, allspice, thyme, bay leaf, salt and pepper, Tabasco, and enough fresh water to cover. Bring to a boil, reduce the heat to low, cover, and simmer for about 3 hours, skimming the surface from time to time. Remove from the heat and let cool.

2 Transfer the knuckles and feet to a work surface, remove and reserve all meat and skin, and discard the bones. Strain the cooking liquid into another pot and add the reserved meat and skin, the ham, wine, vinegar, and nutmeg. Bring to a boil, cook down till the liquid is very thickened, about 30 minutes, remove from the heat, and stir in the parsley. Pour the mixture into a 9½ by 5½ by 2-inch loaf pan and let cool. Cover with plastic wrap and chill overnight.

3 To serve, unmold onto a platter and cut into slices.

 PIG PICKIN'S

"All animals interest those who raise them, but of those that are eaten, the one that stirs the most emotion in the farmer is the pig. Like himself, his pig is curious, stubborn, and independent." —John Thorne, *Serious Pig*

Sherried Ham Mousse

4 tablespoons (½ stick) butter

¼ cup all-purpose flour

1 cup milk

1 tablespoon Dijon mustard

¼ teaspoon powdered sage

Cayenne pepper to taste

¼ cup semisweet sherry

2 large egg yolks

½ cup heavy cream

2 tablespoons unflavored powdered gelatin

½ cup chicken broth

1 pound cooked ham, trimmed of fat and cut into chunks

¼ cup chopped sweet pickles

Watercress for garnish

Southerners love any molded dish (savory or sweet), and none is more elegant than this mousse made with either ordinary smoked ham or leftover baked country ham. Madeira, port, or even bourbon can be substituted for the sherry, and more or fewer pickles can be used, depending on how sweet you like cocktail spreads. I've seen ham mousse served with sliced baguettes of French bread, but I prefer crisp toast rectangles for textural contrast.

1 In a heavy saucepan, melt the butter over moderate heat, add the flour, and whisk the roux for 1 minute. Gradually add the milk, reduce the heat to low, and whisk the mixture till very thick. Add the mustard, sage, cayenne, and sherry and stir till very well blended.

2 In a small bowl, combine the egg yolks and heavy cream, whisk till well blended, and stir in a little of the hot sauce. Return the mixture to the hot sauce and continue cooking over low heat, whisking, till thickened.

3 In another small bowl, soften the gelatin in the chicken broth for 5 minutes, and then stir it into the hot sauce. Place the ham into a meat grinder or food processor, grind finely, and stir into the sauce, along with the pickles.

4 Pour the mixture into a 1-quart mold, cover with plastic wrap, and chill for at least 6 hours. Unmold the mousse on a large serving dish, garnish the edges with watercress, and serve with rectangles of toast.

Deep-Fried Marinated Pork Nuggets

Makes about 20 cocktail servings or 4 main-course servings

1 cup soy sauce

1 cup dry sherry

1 garlic clove, minced

½ teaspoon freshly ground black pepper

¼ teaspoon dry mustard

One 1½-pound pork tenderloin, trimmed of fat and cut into 1-inch cubes

1 cup all-purpose flour

Salt to taste

3 cups peanut oil

Since pork plays such an important role in Chinese cookery, for decades nothing has been deemed more exotic in many traditional Southern restaurants than a couple of "oriental" dishes adapted to regional culinary principles. One example is my adaptation of the deep-fried nuggets served with a tangy barbecue sauce at Mary Mac's Tea Room in Atlanta. While the venerable restaurant features the dish as a main course, I've discovered that the nuggets are just as good as a cocktail appetizer. Here you'll want to experiment with any number of homemade or commercial barbecue sauces that you might have on hand.

1 In a large bowl, combine the soy sauce, sherry, garlic, pepper, and mustard and whisk till well blended. Add the pork, stir well, cover with plastic wrap, and refrigerate overnight.

2 In another small bowl, whisk together the flour and salt. Dredge the pork nuggets in the flour, shaking off the excess, and place on a large plate.

3 In a deep fryer or deep cast-iron skillet, heat the oil to 350°F. Deep-fry the nuggets in batches till golden, about 10 minutes, and drain on paper towels. Serve hot on toothpicks with a favorite barbecue sauce as a cocktail appetizer or with a favorite barbecue sauce as a main course.

COCKTAIL BACON PIGGIES

MAKES 24 TO 32 PIGGIES

12 to 16 small-link pork sausages (1 to 1¼ pounds), cut in half widthwise

Powdered sage

6 to 8 slices lean bacon (about ½ pound), cut in half lengthwise

If ever the Southern passion for pork were more evident than in these simple, delightful, and utterly addictive cocktail appetizers, I don't know where it would be. What's nice is that the piggies can be made and chilled a day in advance, or they can be frozen and baked about 45 minutes before serving. Do try to use thick-sliced bacon that is not too salty.

1 Preheat the oven to 375°F.

2 Sprinkle each sausage half very lightly with sage and wrap each snugly with half a slice of bacon. Arrange the piggies on the slotted rack of a large broiling pan and bake till the bacon is almost crisp, about 30 minutes. Serve the piggies hot with toothpicks.

Spicy Sausage Balls

1 pound bulk pork sausage

1 large egg, beaten

¼ cup ketchup

2 tablespoons minced chives

1 tablespoon red pepper flakes

1 tablespoon Worcestershire
sauce

½ cup dry bread crumbs

I think sausage balls must have been a beloved staple of Southern cocktail parties and receptions ever since the first bourbon whiskey was distilled, so much so that hosts and hostesses bestow upon them the honor of being served in silver chafing dishes—plain or with some type of tomato sauce. The balls in this recipe are pretty basic, but if you care to experiment, add a little curry or chili powder, soy sauce, grated cheddar cheese, or even finely chopped mushrooms. What's really convenient is that the balls can be made well in advance and frozen till you're ready to pop them into the oven at the last minute for unexpected guests.

1 In a bowl, combine all the ingredients and mix with your hands till well blended. Form the mixture into balls about 1 inch in diameter, place on a large baking sheet, and either cover and refrigerate overnight or cover, freeze, and store in plastic bags till ready to use.

2 Preheat the oven to 400°F.

3 Arrange the balls on the slotted rack of a large broiling pan and bake till golden, about 12 minutes if chilled, 15 minutes if frozen. Serve hot with cocktails.

BIRMINGHAM PORCUPINE BALLS

MAKES ABOUT 25 BALLS

2 pounds ground cooked ham

1 pound lean pork

1 medium onion, finely chopped

1½ cups long-grain rice

½ teaspoon salt

¼ teaspoon freshly ground black pepper

¼ cup peanut oil

3 cups tomato juice

"How 'bout a porcupine ball?" the black-tied waiter uttered without cracking a smile during a formal reception at one of Birmingham's most exclusive country clubs. I was hesitant to ram a toothpick into one of the strange-looking pork-and-rice balls, but I had only to pop it in my mouth and chew before finding the hostess and asking if she could get me the recipe. Shaped into six or eight patties instead of small cocktail balls, the mixture also produces a delectable first course—with a little of the baking juice spooned over the patties. In either case, be sure to serve them piping hot.

1 In a large bowl, combine the ham, pork, onion, rice, salt, and pepper, mix with your hands till well blended, and shape the mixture into small balls.

2 Preheat the oven to 350°F.

3 In a medium casserole, heat the oil over moderate heat, add the balls, and brown for about 10 minutes, turning several times. Add the tomato juice, cover, and bake for about 30 minutes, turning the balls once. Serve hot.

Country Ham, Cream Cheese, and Pecan Rounds

Makes 24 rounds

6 ounces cream cheese, at room temperature

2 teaspoons Dijon mustard

½ cup finely chopped pecans

Cayenne pepper to taste

1½ tablespoons heavy cream

Eight 6- by 4-inch thin slices cooked country ham, trimmed of fat

Southerners love to combine cream cheese with any form of ham to make all types of canapés, and none disappears more quickly at receptions and cocktail parties than these rich, salty rounds made with well-aged country ham. If you can chill the stuffed balls overnight before cutting, so much the better, and since the texture of the rounds changes adversely at room temperature, don't let them sit around too long before serving.

1 In a bowl, beat the cream cheese and mustard with a heavy fork till smooth. Add the pecans, cayenne, and cream, and beat till well blended. Finely chop 2 slices of the ham, add to the cheese mixture, and beat till well blended.

2 On a work surface, spread each of the 6 remaining slices of ham with about 1 tablespoon of the cheese mixture, and roll up each slice snugly. Place the rolls on a plate, cover with plastic wrap, and chill for at least 1 hour.

3 Cut each roll into four 1-inch rounds, secure each round with a toothpick, and serve chilled.

Pork and Bell Pepper Kabobs

Makes 6 servings

1 loaf day-old country bread, cut into 1½-inch cubes

12 link pork sausages, cut in half

2 green bell peppers, seeded and cut into chunks

18 fresh sage leaves

1 pound lean boneless pork loin, cut into 1½-inch cubes

12 thick slices lean bacon, cut in half widthwise and folded

¼ cup peanut oil

Salt and freshly ground black pepper to taste

As any Southerner will confirm, if one form of pig is good, two or three forms can only be better, and what more sensible way to manifest this porcine passion than to make kabobs of bacon, sausage, and cubes of pork loin and serve them before maybe a simple soup and corn sticks or as a main course? Trimmed of fat, less expensive pork shoulder or butt can be substituted for the loin, but do try to use a fine, smoky artisanal bacon that won't shrink too much during the baking. I've also made these kabobs with bulk sausage tightened with a few bread crumbs and rolled into firm balls. In the South, kabobs are almost always served over beds of fluffy rice—buttered or not.

1 Preheat the oven to 375°F.

2 On each of 6 metal skewers about 12 inches long, thread a cube of bread, a sausage half, a chunk of bell pepper, a sage leaf, a cube of pork, and a piece of bacon. Repeat 2 more times, ending with a cube of bread.

3 In a baking dish or pan large enough to hold the skewers with a little space in between, pour the oil, turn the skewers in the oil to coat lightly, and season with salt and pepper. Place in the oven and bake for 15 minutes. Turn the skewers and continue baking till the meats are cooked through, 15 to 20 minutes longer. Serve hot.

Deviled Pork and Bacon Kabobs

One 1-pound pork tenderloin, trimmed of fat and cut into 1-inch cubes

Salt and freshly ground black pepper to taste

½ pound thick slices bacon, cut into 1-inch pieces

¼ cup Dijon mustard

1½ cups fresh bread crumbs

4 tablespoons (½ stick) butter, melted

What could be simpler and more appealing than threading small cubes of pork tenderloin and smoky bacon pieces on skewers, enhancing the meats with tangy mustard, rolling them in bread crumbs, and either broiling or grilling them to a crusty finish? All that's needed after a zesty appetizer such as this is a simple soup, green salad, and hot corn sticks. For these kabobs, I do strongly suggest you use a premium, artisanal, thickly sliced bacon with an equal ratio of fat to lean meat. Served over a bed of rice with a congealed salad, the kabobs also make a nice luncheon dish.

1 Preheat the oven broiler.

2 Sprinkle the pork cubes with salt and pepper. Thread the pork and bacon alternately on 4 medium skewers, brush each with mustard, roll each in bread crumbs, and arrange the skewers on a broiler pan. Baste with butter and broil the kabobs till crusty, about 15 minutes, turning the skewers several times and basting with butter. Serve hot.

CRISP POTATO SKINS WITH CHEESE AND BACON

MAKES 4 DINNER APPETIZERS OR 12 COCKTAIL CANAPÉS

12 small mealy white potatoes, scrubbed and patted dry

4 slices lean bacon

2 tablespoons butter, melted

½ cup grated extra-sharp cheddar cheese

Freshly ground black pepper to taste

Exactly why the distinctive flavors of potato skins and bacon are so complementary is a gustatory mystery, but all you have to do to prove the theory is take a bite of a crisply baked skin, then one of bacon. Stuff the buttered skins with a little cheese, top with crumbled bacon, bake till the skins are almost hard, and you have an appetizer or cocktail canapé that Southerners are absolutely crazy about. Although mealy white potatoes have the best skins for this dish, small red potatoes can be substituted in a pinch (though the skins will never bake as crisp as the sturdier white ones). Also think about preparing whole Idaho potatoes in this manner and serving them as a main course with an elaborate composed salad.

1 Preheat the oven to 400°F.

2 Pierce the potatoes with a fork, arrange on a shallow roasting pan or broiler pan, and bake till very tender when pierced with the fork, about 35 minutes.

3 Meanwhile, fry the bacon in a medium skillet over moderate heat till crisp. Drain on paper towels and crumble finely.

4 Cut the baked potatoes in half, scoop out enough pulp to leave a 1/8-inch shell, and save the pulp for another use. Brush the insides of the skins with the butter, sprinkle equal amounts of cheese into the skins, season with pepper, and top each with crumbled bacon.

5 Return the potato halves to the oven and bake till the tops are golden and the skins are very crisp, about 20 minutes. Serve hot.

 PIG PICKIN'S

"Went in to Alexandria [Virginia]
to a Barbecue and stayed all Night."

—George Washington, 1769

Bacon-Stuffed Mushrooms

Makes 30 stuffed mushrooms

30 medium fresh mushrooms

8 slices lean bacon

1 tablespoon butter

3 scallions (part of green tops included), minced

1 garlic clove, minced

1 cup sour cream

¼ teaspoon Worcestershire sauce

¼ teaspoon salt

Tabasco sauce to taste

Banal as they might sound to some, stuffed mushrooms are still as popular at Southern cocktail receptions as they were fifty years ago, and topping the many styles are those with a bacon stuffing. Today, of course, exotic mushrooms like cremini and small chanterelles might well be substituted for the more common agarics, and in Virginia, Kentucky, and the Carolinas, country-ham fanatics would most likely opt for minced ham over crumbled bacon for their stuffings. The truth is that virtually any leftover cooked part of the pig can be used to make unusual and delectable stuffings for mushrooms, so, depending on what you have on hand, let your imagination run wild. Southern cooks always make these mushrooms in large quantities, since people love them so much.

1 Rinse and dry the mushrooms, remove the stems and chop them finely, and arrange the caps in a large, shallow baking dish.

2 In a large skillet, fry the bacon over moderate heat till crisp. Drain on paper towels and crumble finely. Pour all but 2 tablespoons of grease from the skillet, add the butter, and let melt. Add the chopped mushroom stems, scallions, and garlic, cook over low heat for about 5 minutes while stirring, and transfer to a bowl. Add the crumbled bacon, sour cream, Worcestershire, salt, and Tabasco and mix till well blended.

3 Preheat the oven to 350°F.

4 Spoon equal amounts of the mixture into the mushroom caps and bake till the tops are golden, about 20 minutes. Serve the mushrooms with heavy toothpicks.

Candied Pecan Bacon

MAKES AT LEAST 8 SERVINGS

½ cup packed dark brown sugar

1 tablespoon all-purpose flour

½ cup finely chopped pecans

1 pound lean sliced bacon

These sumptuous, addictive bacon strips disappear faster than toasted pecans at cocktail parties and attest to Southerners' unique penchant for sweet goodies to nibble with their liquor. I think it's pointless to make these appetizers unless you use either a premium artisanal bacon or a reputable commercial one with at least enough lean meat to equal the amount of fat. Furthermore, the pieces should be baked till they're crisp but still slightly chewy. And if you want to add a little zing to the bacon, shake a few drops of Tabasco sauce into the sugar mixture.

1 Preheat the oven to 350°F.

2 On a plate, combine the sugar, flour, and pecans and mix till well blended.

3 Lightly dredge the bacon slices in the mixture, arrange the slices close together on a broiler pan, and bake till browned and almost but not quite crisp, about 30 minutes. Drain on paper towels, break each slice in half, and serve at room temperature with cocktails.

Party Country Ham Deviled Eggs

Makes 16 deviled eggs

- 2 ounces cooked lean country ham, minced
- 8 large hard-boiled eggs, cut in half lengthwise
- 2 tablespoons minced fresh chives
- Freshly ground black pepper to taste
- ¼ cup mayonnaise
- 2 tablespoons Dijon mustard
- ½ teaspoon Worcestershire sauce
- Paprika to taste
- Sprigs of fresh parsley leaves

Southerners are so crazy about deviled eggs that no proper host or hostess would be caught dead without a special deviled egg serving dish with shallow indentations (and I rarely see these dishes outside the South). Deviled eggs can be enhanced with everything from curry powder to minced shrimp to chopped pimentos or capers, but if you really want to see the eggs disappear at cocktail receptions (as well as from buffets and at picnics), just add minced country ham to the stuffing. Do note that because of the salty ham, mayonnaise, and mustard, no salt should be added to the stuffing mixture. When I serve these eggs on buffets, I allow two to three halves per person—so plan accordingly.

In a bowl, combine the ham, egg yolks, chives, and pepper and mash with a fork till well blended. Add the mayonnaise, mustard, and Worcestershire and stir till the mixture is very smooth. Either use a fork to stuff equal amounts of the mixture into the egg white hollows or pipe it into the hollows using a pastry bag with a star tip. Sprinkle paprika over the top of each deviled egg, arrange the eggs on a platter, and chill till ready to serve garnished with sprigs of parsley.

CHARLESTON HOBOTEE

MAKES 6 SERVINGS

3 tablespoons butter

1 medium onion, finely chopped

1 tablespoon curry powder

1½ cups finely chopped lean pork

1 slice white bread, soaked in
   milk and squeezed dry

2 tablespoons chopped almonds

2 tablespoons fresh lemon juice

3 large eggs

½ teaspoon sugar

Salt to taste

1 cup half-and-half

Dash of white pepper

6 small bay leaves

Of all the unusual dishes that constitute much of the cooking of the Carolina and Georgia Lowcountry, this curried meat custard I remember from my childhood remained a real mystery till my colleague and friend Damon Lee Fowler of Savannah recently traced its origins back to bobotee, a traditional dish of South Africa's Cape Malays that evolved from Charleston's slave culture. Today, it's rare to find hobotee in the area's homes and on restaurant menus, but served with glasses of sherry as an appetizer to any seafood meal, these small ramekins are worthy of the most sophisticated table. While virtually any form of lean pork can be used, I prefer well-trimmed, full-flavored meat left over from a shoulder or butt roast.

1 Preheat the oven to 300°F.

2 In a skillet, melt the butter over moderate heat, add the onion, and cook, stirring, till softened, 2 to 3 minutes. Add the curry powder and cook, stirring, for 2 minutes longer. Transfer the onions to a bowl, add the pork, bread, almonds, lemon juice, 1 of the eggs, the sugar, and salt and blend thoroughly.

3 Butter six ½-cup ramekins and divide the meat mixture among them. In another bowl, combine the remaining 2 eggs, the half-and-half, and white pepper and whisk till well blended. Pour equal amounts of the cream mixture into the ramekins, garnish the tops with a bay leaf, and bake till golden, about 25 minutes. Serve hot.

Pork Cracklin', Black-Eyed Pea, and Shrimp Salad

½ pound fatty corncob- or applewood-smoked bacon, diced

2 pounds medium fresh shrimp

½ lemon

2½ cups canned black-eyed peas

2 small dill pickles, diced

1 cup mayonnaise

3 tablespoons fresh lemon juice

2 tablespoons heavy cream

1 teaspoon prepared horseradish

Salt and freshly ground black pepper to taste

Leaves of chicory (curly endive)

2 medium ripe tomatoes, quartered

3 large hard-boiled eggs, quartered

I've been tampering with and revising this sumptuous salad ever since I concocted the first one years ago at a beach house on the South Carolina coast. Whether you use streaky or slab bacon, just be sure it is fatty enough to make the cracklin's, and by no means leave out the dill pickles—the "secret ingredient" that adds real mystery to the salad and never fails to baffle guests. Don't even think about making this salad without shrimp that are utterly fresh (i.e., flash frozen and thawed), and while frozen green peas (not overcooked) can be used in place of the black-eyed ones, fresh peas boiled till just barely tender do make a difference. I used to serve either hot biscuits or bread sticks with the salad, but lately I've opted for cheddar or Parmesan toast.

1 In a large, heavy skillet, render the diced bacon over low heat for 20 to 30 minutes or till crisp and golden brown, watching carefully to prevent burning. Drain the cracklin's on paper towels and set aside.

2 Place the shrimp in a large saucepan. Squeeze the lemon half over the shrimp and drop it in the pot. Add enough water to cover, bring to a boil, remove from the heat, let stand for 1 minute, and drain. When cool enough to handle, shell, devein, and place the shrimp in a large bowl. Add the peas and diced pickles, toss well, cover with plastic wrap, and chill for 1 hour.

3 In a small bowl, whisk together the mayonnaise, lemon juice, cream, horseradish, and salt and pepper. Add the dressing to the shrimp and pea mixture and toss well. Line a large salad bowl with chicory leaves, mound the salad in the center, sprinkle the cracklin's over the top, and garnish the edges with the tomatoes and eggs. Serve the salad slightly chilled on wide salad plates.

PIG KNUCKLE SALAD WITH MUSTARD VINAIGRETTE

MAKES 4 SERVINGS

For the Salad:

2 large pig knuckles
(about 2½ pounds)

1 large onion, sliced

1 carrot, scraped and sliced

1 celery rib, sliced

1 garlic clove, smashed

1 dried red chile pepper

1 teaspoon coriander seeds

½ teaspoon dried thyme

½ teaspoon black peppercorns

2 whole cloves

2 cups white wine

2 tablespoons chopped fresh
thyme, sage, or marjoram
(or a combination of all three)

Bibb lettuce leaves

Pork knuckles (or hocks) are one of the most succulent parts of the pig, and when you simmer them slowly with various aromatics and combine the tender meat with a tangy vinaigrette dressing, you have a substantial luncheon salad worthy of the most noteworthy occasion. Typically, a Southern cook would serve this salad on a large platter garnished with wedges of hard-boiled eggs and tomatoes, pimento-stuffed olives, and maybe tender green peas or broccoli florets. If preferred, the knuckles can be boiled a day in advance, boned, and the meat refrigerated, but the salad is best served at room temperature.

1 Place the pig knuckles in a large kettle or casserole, and add the onion, carrot, celery, garlic, chile pepper, coriander, thyme, peppercorns, cloves, wine, and enough water to cover. Bring to a simmer, skimming scum from the surface, cover, and simmer till the meat begins to fall off the bones, about 3 hours, skimming from time to time and adding more water if necessary. Transfer the knuckles to a plate to cool and discard the contents of the pot.

For the Vinaigrette:

¼ cup red wine vinegar

1 tablespoon Dijon mustard

Salt and freshly ground black
   pepper to taste

½ cup olive oil

2 To make the vinaigrette, whisk together the vinegar, mustard, and salt and pepper in a small bowl till well blended, then gradually add the oil, whisking till well blended. Set aside.

3 Bone the knuckles, discarding the skin and fat, cut the meat into medium dice, and place in a bowl. Sprinkle the herb over the top, add the vinaigrette, and toss till well blended.

4 To serve, spread lettuce leaves to cover a platter, mound the pork in the center, and arrange any garnishes of your choice around the edges.

 PIG PICKIN'S

"I grew up eating well—cheese grits, homemade biscuits smothered in butter, home-cured ham with red-eye gravy—and that was just breakfast."

—Oprah Winfrey

Pork and Apple Salad with Mustard-Mayonnaise Dressing

MAKES 4 SERVINGS

1 cup mayonnaise

1 tablespoon Dijon mustard

2 cups diced cold cooked
   pork loin

1 cup diced celery

½ apple, cored and diced

2 scallions (part of green tops
   included), chopped

Salt and freshly ground black
   pepper to taste

Red-tipped leaf lettuce leaves

2 sliced large hard-boiled eggs,
   cherry tomatoes, and capers
   for garnish

I knew a lady in Chattanooga, Tennessee, who always insisted that her butcher cut at least a five-pound pork loin just so she'd have enough leftover meat to make this simple salad for members of her bridge club. Since I personally like more zip to my dressing, I use two or more tablespoons of zesty mustard, and if I serve the salad at lunch during the summertime, I might also add a couple of minced fresh sage leaves to the dressing. Capers, in my opinion, enhance virtually any pork dish, so be sure to include a couple of tablespoons in the garnish.

1 In a small bowl, combine the mayonnaise and mustard and stir till well blended. Set the dressing aside.

2 In a bowl, combine the pork, celery, apple, scallions, and salt and pepper and toss. Add the dressing, toss till the ingredients are well coated, cover with plastic wrap, and chill for 1 hour.

3 To serve, line a platter with lettuce leaves, mound the salad in the center, and garnish the edges with the eggs, tomatoes, and capers. Serve either chilled or at room temperature.

Missy's Ham and Macaroni Salad

Makes 6 to 8 servings

For the Salad:

4 cups cooked elbow macaroni

1¼ pounds lean cooked ham,
    cut into ½-inch cubes

½ pound Swiss cheese, cut into
    ½-inch cubes

3 large hard-boiled eggs, chopped

1 medium onion, chopped

2 large celery ribs, chopped

¼ cup chopped sweet pickles

½ cup chopped fresh parsley
    leaves

Romaine lettuce leaves

For the Dressing:

¾ cup mayonnaise

½ cup buttermilk

1 tablespoon Dijon mustard

¼ teaspoon Worcestershire sauce

Freshly ground black pepper
    to taste

Years ago, my North Carolina mother came up with the idea of throwing what she calls a "salad party" for family and friends during the summertime, and the event involves not only three or four different composed salads but also a homemade bread, a churn of fresh peach ice cream with various cookies, and, of course, plenty of iced tea and chilled white wine. The salads might include soused shrimp and avocado, tomatoes stuffed with crabmeat, and a congealed fruit salad, but by far the most popular item on the buffet is always this ham and macaroni salad studded with Swiss cheese, hard-boiled eggs, and sweet pickle and tossed with a tangy buttermilk dressing. Frankly, I don't know a better way to use up a pound or so of leftover baked ham.

1 In a large bowl, combine the macaroni, ham, cheese, eggs, onion, celery, pickles, and parsley leaves and toss to mix well.

2 In a small bowl, whisk together the dressing ingredients till well blended, and pour over the salad. Toss well, cover with plastic wrap, and chill for at least 1 hour before serving in a large lettuce leaf–lined salad bowl.

Potato, Ham, and Olive Salad

Makes 4 to 6 servings

- 1 pound small new potatoes, scrubbed
- 1 pound (about 2 cups) diced baked ham
- 1 medium onion, chopped
- 2 celery ribs, chopped
- 1 cup sliced pimento-stuffed olives
- Salt and freshly ground black pepper to taste
- ½ cup mayonnaise
- ½ cup sour cream
- 1 tablespoon Dijon mustard

Potatoes, ham, and pimento-stuffed olives are a classic combination for salad throughout the South, and I know one cook in Baltimore who even adds either crumbled fried slab bacon or a few pork cracklin's to enhance both the flavor and texture. There's nothing like small, unpeeled, new red potatoes for this salad, but if these are not available, use regular red ones (peeled). Although the salad is also good with a mustardy vinaigrette, I think the mayonnaise–sour cream dressing gives it an elegant silkiness. In the South (especially in Virginia and Maryland), this style of composed salad would be served with lots of crisp beaten biscuits or a savory shortbread.

1 Cut the potatoes into 1-inch cubes, place in a saucepan with enough water to cover, and bring to a boil. Reduce the heat to moderate, cover, and cook till just tender, about 10 minutes. Drain in a colander and let cool.

2 In a large bowl, combine the potatoes, ham, onion, celery, olives, and salt and pepper and toss lightly. In a small bowl, combine the mayonnaise, sour cream, and mustard, and stir till well blended. Add to the salad and toss gently till the ingredients are well coated with the dressing. Cover the salad with plastic wrap and chill till ready to serve.

Congealed Ham and Orange Salad

Two 6-ounce packages lemon-flavored Jell-O

2 cups orange juice

One 16-ounce carton sour cream

1½ cups chopped cooked ham

1½ cups orange sections, seeded and pith removed

Bibb or Boston lettuce leaves

Mayonnaise for garnish

This is the type of Southern congealed salad commonly made with leftover baked ham and either featured at a social luncheon with small pimento cheese sandwiches or included on a brunch buffet. Depending on the season, tangerines, clementines, or fresh pineapple can be substituted for the oranges. Serving this style of salad with dollops of mayonnaise is a long-standing Southern tradition.

1 Place the Jell-O in a large bowl. In a saucepan, heat the orange juice to the boiling point, then add to the Jell-O and stir till Jell-O dissolves completely. Place the bowl in the refrigerator and chill till slightly thick, about 20 minutes. Fold in the sour cream, add the ham and orange sections, and stir till well distributed. Scrape the mixture into a 9 by 3 by 2-inch flat dish and return to the refrigerator to set completely, about 2 hours.

2 To serve, cut the salad into squares, place each square on a lettuce leaf arranged on a plate, and garnish with a dollop of mayonnaise on top.

Spinach, Country Ham, and Egg Salad with Warm Red-Eye Dressing

Makes 4 servings

¼ cup cider vinegar

1 teaspoon Dijon mustard

1 teaspoon sugar

1 garlic clove, minced

½ pound fresh spinach, stemmed, rinsed, and patted dry

½ red onion, thinly sliced

½ pound sliced country ham (about ⅛ inch thick; fat untrimmed)

½ cup olive oil

2 large hard-boiled eggs, coarsely chopped

To be sure, Southerners love classic American wilted spinach and bacon salad (not necessarily with avocado, by the way) as much as anybody else, but when tangy country ham is substituted for bacon and the warm dressing is made partly with red-eye gravy, then you know you're really whistling "Dixie." Just remember that the ham must have enough fat to render about two tablespoons for the dressing. Also, no seasoning is needed for this salad. Serve the salad with hot buttered corn sticks.

1 In a small bowl, combine the vinegar and mustard and whisk till well blended. Add the sugar and garlic, stir well, and set aside.

2 In a large salad bowl, combine the spinach and onion and set aside.

3 Trim all the fat from the ham slices, place the pieces of fat in a large skillet, and render them over low heat till crisp. Discard the pieces and fry the ham in the fat on both sides till lightly browned, about 8 minutes in all; transfer to a cutting surface. Add the oil plus the vinegar-mustard mixture to the fat in the skillet and stir till the dressing is hot. Pour the dressing over the spinach and toss well. Chop the ham coarsely, add to the salad along with the eggs, toss well again, and serve immediately on wide salad plates.

Butter Bean and Bacon Salad

2 pounds fresh butter beans or lima beans (or three 10-ounce packages frozen baby lima beans)

Salt to taste

4 thick slices lean bacon

3 scallions (part of green tops included), chopped

¼ cup chopped fresh parsley leaves

2 tablespoons cider vinegar

1 teaspoon Dijon mustard

Olive oil

Freshly ground black pepper to taste

Creamy-white butter beans speckled with red and purple ("specs") were once common in all Southern markets and considered ideal for various types of composed salads because of their dense richness. Today, I'm lucky to find "specs" even at summer farm stands, but when I do, I always buy enough to make this smoky luncheon salad that my South Carolina aunt loved to serve at her beach cottage with a big platter of crusted cheese toast and a pitcher of iced tea. If absolutely fresh, small lima beans can be almost as good as genuine butter beans, and so long as you use good meaty bacon, frozen limas will also suffice. Serve this salad warm or at room temperature.

1 Place the beans in a large saucepan and add enough salted water to cover. Bring to a boil, reduce the heat to low, cover, and simmer till just tender, about 20 minutes for butter beans, 10 minutes for limas. Drain the beans and place in a large salad bowl.

2 In a large skillet, fry the bacon over moderate heat till almost crisp. Drain on paper towels, reserving about 2 tablespoons of the fat. Chop the bacon, add to the beans, add the scallions and parsley, and toss.

3 In a small bowl, combine the reserved bacon fat, the vinegar, and mustard and whisk till well blended. Add enough olive oil to make ½ cup of dressing, add the pepper, and whisk till well blended. Pour the dressing over the beans and toss till the ingredients are well coated. Serve at room temperature.

Tennis Ball Salad with Salt Pork-Buttermilk Dressing

MAKES 4 SERVINGS

½ pound chunk of lean salt pork (streak-o'-lean), cut into 1-inch pieces

1¼ cups mayonnaise

¼ cup buttermilk

1 tablespoon red wine vinegar

Tabasco sauce to taste

1 cup crumbled blue cheese

1 large, firm head iceberg lettuce, wilted leaves discarded, partly cored, and cut into 4 wedges

1 small red onion, thinly sliced

There is good evidence that the "tennis ball lettuce" grown by Thomas Jefferson in Virginia, at Monticello, was the ancestor of our iceberg lettuce, and even when classic wedges of iceberg with blue cheese dressing were being disparaged by food snobs, Southerners were still enriching the salad not only with the mellow cheese but also with some form of porky buttermilk dressing. Do make sure that the salt pork has a good quota of lean meat, and remember that since the pork, blue cheese, and mayonnaise are all fairly salty, no seasoning is necessary. When shopping for iceberg lettuce, look for heads that are firm, with a stem that is not discolored ("rusty"). The salad is served as a first course before something like Brunswick stew, as a side dish to roasted meats and fowl, or for lunch with plenty of ham biscuits.

1 Place the salt pork in a small saucepan with enough water to cover, bring to a boil, reduce the heat to moderate, and cook for about 20 minutes. Drain the pork, rinse under running water, and pat dry with paper towels. In a medium skillet, fry the salt pork over moderately low heat till nicely browned and crisp. Drain on paper towels.

2 In a bowl, combine the mayonnaise, buttermilk, vinegar, and Tabasco and stir till well blended. Add the salt pork and blue cheese and gently stir till well blended. Chill the dressing for about 30 minutes.

3 Arrange the lettuce wedges on salad plates, spoon equal amounts of dressing over the tops, and garnish with the onion slices.

PIG PICKIN'S

"The pig, if I am not mistaken,
Gives us ham, pork, and bacon.
Let others think his heart is big,
I think it's stupid of the pig."

—Ogden Nash

Red Cabbage, Tangerine, and Bacon Salad with Bacon Vinaigrette

1 small head red cabbage
(about 1½ pounds)

2 tangerines

6 slices lean bacon

¼ cup red wine vinegar

2 teaspoons Dijon mustard

Salt and freshly ground black
pepper to taste

3 tablespoons peanut oil

2 scallions (part of green tops
included), thinly sliced

In the South, red cabbage shows up as much as green in our ubiquitous coleslaws, but when a host or hostess wants to serve a cool-weather buffet salad that is both flavorful and colorful, combining shredded red cabbage leaves, some form of citrus, smoky bacon, and a bacon-flavored vinaigrette is almost as natural as adding cracklin's to the accompanying cornbread. Some like to chill a salad such as this, but I think the flavors and textures are much more pronounced when it's kept at room temperature. Also delicious is about a cup of diced cooked country ham or smoked ham hock substituted for the bacon—in which case no salt is needed.

1 Quarter the cabbage, remove the core, shred the leaves, and place in a large salad bowl. Peel, section, and seed the tangerines, removing as much white pith as possible. Add the sections to the cabbage, toss, and set aside.

2 In a large skillet, fry the bacon over moderate heat till crisp. Drain on paper towels and crumble coarsely. Pour off all but about 2 tablespoons of fat from the skillet, add the vinegar, and boil down till reduced by half. Add the mustard and stir till well incorporated. Remove from the heat, add the salt and pepper, and then gradually add the oil, stirring briskly to form a smooth dressing.

3 Pour the vinaigrette over the salad in the bowl, add the crumbled bacon and the scallions, and toss till the ingredients are well coated with the dressing. Chill briefly or serve at room temperature.

Wilted Sallet with Hot Bacon Dressing

10 ounces fresh spinach,
  dandelion greens, or watercress

2 large hard-boiled eggs,
  cut into wedges

6 slices bacon

2 scallions (part of green tops
  included), coarsely chopped

1 garlic clove, minced

½ cup red wine vinegar

2 tablespoons ketchup

Salt and freshly ground black
  pepper to taste

In Southern parlance, the word *sallet* derives from the old English word for greens and refers to every leaf from spinach to kale to chicory to dandelions to collards to turnip greens. The most common way of dealing with the tougher vegetables is to boil them slowly with a piece of side meat (salt pork, streak-o'-lean, or chunk of country ham) for flavor, but almost as popular is the tearing of more-tender leaves into pieces; combining them with crumbled bacon, some form of onion, and hard-boiled eggs; anointing everything with a hot, vinegary dressing; and serving the sallet with buttered biscuits or cornbread. Remember that it's important not to toss the sallet with dressing till just ready to serve.

1 Wash the greens well, remove any coarse stems, and pat dry with paper towels. Tear into bite-size pieces, place in a large salad bowl, add the eggs, and set aside.

2 In a medium skillet, fry the bacon over moderate heat till crisp. Drain on paper towels and crumble. Add the scallions and garlic to the skillet and stir for about 5 minutes. Add the vinegar, ketchup, and salt and pepper, stir till well blended, and simmer for about 5 minutes. Pour the hot dressing over the greens and eggs, add the crumbled bacon, toss well, and serve immediately.

Soups, Chowders, and Gumbos

Great Smokies Pork, Leek, and Wild Mushroom Soup

Spiced Pork Meatball Soup

Plantation Pork and Rice Soup

Pork Rib, Turnip, and Two-Potato Soup

Kentucky Potato, Country Ham, and Sour Grass Soup

Pot Likker Soup

Memphis Country Ham and Corn Chowder with Bourbon

Creamed Country Ham and Rutabaga Soup

Birmingham Red Bean and Ham Bone Soup

Old-Fashioned Ham Bone Vegetable Soup

Appalachian Ham Hock and Cabbage Soup

Ham Hock, Bacon, and Black-Eyed Pea Soup

Commander's Split Pea, Carrot, and Ham Hock Soup

Georgia Ham Hock, Bacon, and Chicken Chowder

Miami Black Bean and Pig Knuckle Soup

Tennessee Pigs' Feet and Field Pea Snert

Lentil and Bacon Soup

Canadian Bacon, Vegetable, and White Bean Soup

Outer Banks Muddle

Farmhouse Sausage and Kidney Bean Soup

Sausage-Ball, Spinach, and Rice Soup

Arkansas Sausage and Red Bean Chowder

Creole Seafood, Sausage, and Okra Gumbo

Cajun Chicken and Sausage Gumbo

Gumbo z'Herbes

Eula Mae's Sausage, Shrimp, and Okra Gumbo

GREAT SMOKIES PORK, LEEK, AND WILD MUSHROOM SOUP

MAKES 4 TO 6 SERVINGS

1 pound pork shoulder, trimmed of excess surface fat and diced

3 tablespoons peanut oil

1 medium leek (white part only), chopped

1 celery rib (leaves included), chopped

¼ pound wild mushrooms (cep, oyster, or chanterelle), rinsed and chopped

2 garlic cloves, minced

6 medium ripe tomatoes, peeled and diced

½ teaspoon minced fresh tarragon leaves

Salt and freshly ground black pepper to taste

4 cups chicken broth

Cep, chanterelle, morel, oyster, shiitake, and other wild mushrooms are all native to the Appalachian Mountains of Tennessee, North Carolina, and Virginia, and folks like the man who produces my exceptional country hams in Glendale Springs, North Carolina (near Boone), are as adept at foraging for mushrooms as at breeding and raising superior hogs. Fat from the pork shoulder is what gives this soup much of its smooth texture and savor, so if the meat is not too fatty, there's really no need to subject it to an initial simmering to release fat. Do make the effort to find fresh tarragon, which has a much subtler flavor than the dried.

1 Place the pork in a saucepan with enough water to cover, bring to a boil, reduce the heat to low, and simmer for 15 minutes. Drain the pork and set aside.

2 In another large saucepan, heat the oil over moderate heat, add the leek, celery, mushrooms, and garlic, and stir for 5 minutes. Add the reserved pork, tomatoes, tarragon, and salt and pepper and stir for 5 minutes longer. Add the broth, bring to a boil, reduce the heat to low, cover, and simmer till the pork is fork-tender, about 30 minutes.

3 Serve the soup hot in wide soup bowls.

SPICED PORK MEATBALL SOUP

MAKES 6 SERVINGS

2 tablespoons peanut oil

1 medium onion, finely chopped

1 garlic clove, minced

2 quarts beef broth

½ cup tomato puree

1 teaspoon ground allspice

½ teaspoon ground cinnamon

1½ pounds lean ground pork

½ cup halfway-cooked long-grain rice

1 large egg, beaten

Salt and freshly ground black pepper to taste

Bound with rice instead of bread or cracker crumbs, the pork meatballs in this sturdy soup might well also be turned into a casserole or simply broiled and served on their own with something like bowls of spicy succotash and red cabbage coleslaw. What makes this soup so distinctive, however, is the way the relatively bland meatballs are enhanced by the spiced broth, making it qualify as much as an unusual appetizer soup (in smaller portions) as it does as a main course. Ground pork can be found packaged in most grocery stores, but if I suspect by the color that it's too fatty, I buy a pork loin or lean shoulder and grind it myself.

1 In a large saucepan or pot, heat the oil over moderate heat. Add the onion and garlic and stir till softened, about 5 minutes. Add the broth, tomato puree, allspice, and cinnamon, bring to a boil, reduce the heat to low, cover, and simmer for about 20 minutes.

2 Meanwhile, combine the pork, rice, egg, and salt and pepper in a large bowl, mix thoroughly with your hands till well blended, and beat vigorously with a wooden spoon till the mixture is fluffy. To shape the meatballs, roll the mixture into balls about ½ inch in diameter.

3 Drop the meatballs into the simmering broth and stir gently to keep them from sticking to one another. Cover the pan and simmer the soup for about 30 minutes longer.

4 Serve piping hot in wide soup bowls.

PLANTATION PORK AND RICE SOUP

2 tablespoons peanut oil

1 pound pork shoulder or butt, trimmed of excess fat and cut into 1-inch cubes

1 medium onion, chopped

1 medium celery rib, chopped

½ cup chopped fresh parsley leaves

10 fresh sage leaves, chopped

Salt and freshly ground black pepper to taste

6 cups beef broth

½ cup regular long-grain rice

During the era of the great rice plantations in the Carolina and Georgia Lowcountry, records indicate that this standard soup would most likely have been made with salt pork (or "white pork"), slab bacon, jowl, or any other cured secondary pig parts kept in the sacred pork barrel. Today, on the other hand, such a midday staple is best prepared with a full-flavored chunk of shoulder or butt, and unlike our ancestors, cooks enrich the soup by using beef broth instead of water as the liquid base. Be sure to collect all the tasty debris possible from the pan after the pork has been browned.

1 In a large saucepan, heat the oil over moderate heat, add the pork, and brown on all sides. Add the onion, celery, parsley, sage, and salt and pepper and stir till the onion is golden, about 5 minutes. Add about 1 cup of the broth and scrape the bottom of the pan to collect any browned bits. Add the rice and stir for about 5 minutes. Add the remaining broth, bring to a boil, reduce the heat to low, cover, and simmer for about 40 minutes.

2 Serve the soup hot in heavy soup bowls.

Pork Rib, Turnip, and Two-Potato Soup

2 pounds country-style pork ribs, cut into serving pieces

3½ quarts water

Salt and freshly ground black pepper to taste

2 medium onions, coarsely chopped

2 celery ribs, coarsely chopped

2 carrots, scraped and coarsely chopped

2 medium ripe tomatoes, coarsely chopped

2 medium turnips, carefully peeled and diced

2 medium red potatoes, peeled and diced

2 medium sweet potatoes, peeled and diced

Tabasco sauce to taste

Cut from the shoulder end of a pork loin, lean, meaty country-style ribs are not only delicious slowly baked with a tangy barbecue sauce but also ideal for a robust soup like this one with turnips and both regular and sweet potatoes. Southerners like their ribs so tender that they almost fall apart, so if the ribs are the least bit tough after an hour of initial simmering, cook them for an additional 20 to 30 minutes. The turnips and potatoes, on the other hand, should not be overcooked and should be just barely fork-tender, so test them carefully after they've simmered for 12 to 15 minutes. All you need to serve with this soup is hot corn sticks or biscuits.

1 In a large pot or kettle, combine the ribs, water, and salt and pepper, bring to a boil, and skim scum off the top for about 3 minutes. Reduce the heat to low, cover, and simmer till the ribs are tender, about 1 hour. Add the onions, celery, carrots, and tomatoes, stir well, return to a simmer, and cook for about 20 minutes. Add the turnips and all the potatoes, return to a simmer, cover, and cook till the turnips and potatoes are just tender, 15 to 20 minutes.

2 Add the Tabasco, stir well, and serve the soup piping hot in wide soup bowls.

Kentucky Potato, Country Ham, and Sour Grass Soup

5 starchy potatoes (about 2½ pounds), peeled and cubed

5 quarts water

6 tablespoons (¾ stick) butter

2 large Spanish onions, chopped

½ cup finely chopped lean country ham

3 cups chopped sour grass (sorrel) leaves, torn

1½ cups milk

Freshly ground black pepper to taste

6 finely chopped sour grass (sorrel) leaves for garnish

Sour grass (sorrel), which flourishes throughout much of Kentucky during the spring, is a key ingredient in any number of tangy soups, stews, and salads and one that has an amazing affinity with the region's famous country hams. Now widely available at fine markets in spring and early summer, fresh sorrel should have bright, crisp, light-green leaves with no trace of yellow; be sure to remove the tough stems before using the leaves. Genuine Kentucky country ham can be intensely salty, but, as the friend in Louisville who makes this soup his specialty is constantly reminding, if you soak the ham in water for even 30 minutes, you're removing not only part of the salt but also part of the distinctive flavor. You can make this soup in a food processor so long as you're extra careful to reduce it only to a coarse puree.

1 In a large saucepan, combine the potatoes and water, bring to a boil, reduce the heat to moderately low, and simmer till tender, about 15 minutes.

2 Meanwhile, in a large, heavy skillet, melt the butter over moderate heat, add the onions and ham, and cook, stirring, for 5 minutes. Add the sour grass and cook, stirring, till it wilts, 1 to 2 minutes. Add this mixture to the potatoes in the pan, add the milk, stir, and simmer for about 5 minutes. Transfer the mixture to a blender, add the pepper, and reduce just to a rough puree. Return to the saucepan and heat gently till piping hot.

3 Serve in soup plates and sprinkle a little chopped sour grass over the top.

Pot Likker Soup

MAKES 6 SERVINGS

1 pound fresh turnip greens, rinsed and stems removed

2 tablespoons peanut oil

2 cups diced cooked ham

1 large onion, chopped

1 garlic clove, minced

3 medium red potatoes, scrubbed and diced

2½ cups chicken broth

One 16-ounce can black-eyed peas, drained

One 16-ounce can crowder peas, drained

1 cup water

1½ teaspoons white vinegar

½ teaspoon salt

Freshly ground black pepper to taste

Tabasco sauce to taste

Pot likker is the delicious broth left over in a pot of greens and/or field peas simmered with smoked ham or a meaty ham bone, salt pork, or slab bacon, and throughout the Deep South and much of Appalachia, debate never stops over whether turnip greens, collards, mustard greens, kale, or beet greens produce the most flavorful likker. Nobody, however, disagrees that pot likker is simply meaningless without cornbread—either crumbled into the soup or used for constant dunking. This hearty concoction was created by my Georgia grandmother and is obviously intended to be a meal in itself. Feel free to use whichever greens look freshest in the market, by all means substitute diced lean slab bacon or the chopped leftover meat from boiled ham hocks for the regular ham, and if you can't find canned crowder peas, just double the quantity of black-eyes.

1 Tear the turnip greens into small pieces and place in a large pot with enough water to cover. Bring to a boil, reduce the heat to moderately low, cover, and cook for 15 minutes. Drain the greens, set aside, and drain the water from the pot.

2 Heat the oil in the same pot over moderate heat, add the ham, onion, and garlic, and stir for about 5 minutes. Add the turnip greens and all of the remaining ingredients and stir till well blended. Bring to a boil, reduce the heat to low, and let simmer for about 1 hour, stirring from time to time.

3 Serve hot in wide soup bowls.

MEMPHIS COUNTRY HAM AND CORN CHOWDER WITH BOURBON

¼ pound country ham, fat trimmed and reserved and lean meat diced

1 small onion, diced

¼ cup bourbon

5 medium red potatoes, peeled and diced

3½ cups milk

6 large ears fresh corn, shucked and kernels cut from the cobs (about 3 cups)

2 tablespoons butter

¼ teaspoon grated nutmeg

Freshly ground black pepper to taste

¼ cup chopped fresh parsley leaves for garnish

Frankly, this Southern-style chowder is just as good with leftover regular smoked ham or three to four thick slices of premium bacon, and if fresh corn is out of season, you can substitute a 10-ounce package of frozen corn kernels (but not canned corn). The gentleman in Memphis who concocted this chowder one late-summer evening used the hock of a whole baked country ham, but if your only option is packaged raw ham and you don't care for a salty chowder, you might want to soak the ham in water for about 30 minutes before cooking it. (Also, if the ham doesn't have much fat to render, brown it in about a tablespoon of butter or oil.)

1 In a small skillet, render the ham fat over moderate heat till crisp and discard the pieces of fat. Add the lean meat to the skillet and brown lightly, about 5 minutes. Add the onion to the skillet, stir till golden, about 5 minutes, and set the ham and onion aside.

2 In a small saucepan, heat the bourbon over low heat, ignite it, and let it flame for 1 minute, and then set aside.

3 In a large, heavy saucepan, combine the potatoes with enough water to cover, bring to a low boil, and cook till tender and most of the water has boiled away, about 15 minutes. Add the ham and onion, the bourbon, milk, corn, butter, nutmeg, and pepper and stir till well blended. Bring to a simmer, stirring, and cook till the corn is tender, about 10 minutes.

4 Serve the chowder piping hot in wide soup bowls with parsley sprinkled over the top.

PIG PICKIN'S

After the Civil War in the South, a "community sinker" was a ham bone or large piece of pork fatback that was tied on a string and passed from house to house, hanging for a while in each family's pot of beans or cabbage.

CREAMED COUNTRY HAM AND RUTABAGA SOUP

MAKES 8 SERVINGS

3 tablespoons bacon grease

¼ pound lean country ham, diced

5 to 6 rutabagas (about 2½ pounds), peeled and cubed

1 medium onion, finely chopped

3 cups chicken broth

½ cup heavy cream

Freshly ground black pepper to taste

Grated nutmeg to taste

Resembling large turnips (four to five inches in diameter), rutabagas are a member of the cabbage family; have thin, yellow skins and sweet, pale flesh; and grow widely in the South from about July through April. Loved by most Southerners, rutabagas can be delicious simply boiled with side meat or butter and mashed, or simmered slowly in casseroles, but never is their distinctive flavor more obvious than in an elegant, pureed, creamy soup such as this one highlighted by complementary smoky country ham. Ordinary turnips can be substituted for the rutabagas if necessary, so long as they're carefully peeled with a knife to remove the tough skins. This soup freezes very well in airtight plastic containers.

1 Pour the bacon grease into a large pot over moderate heat, add the country ham, and stir till browned on all sides, about 8 minutes. Transfer half of the ham to a plate and reserve.

2 Add the rutabagas and onion to the pot and stir for about 8 minutes. Add the broth, bring to a simmer, cover, and cook till the rutabagas are soft, about 20 minutes. Transfer the mixture to a blender or food processor and reduce to a puree. Scrape the mixture back into the pot, add the cream, reserved ham, pepper, and nutmeg, stir well, and bring to a simmer.

3 Serve the soup hot in soup plates.

Birmingham Red Bean and Ham Bone Soup

MAKES 4 SERVINGS

2 pounds dried red kidney beans, rinsed and picked over

1½ pounds cooked lean ham, cut into chunks

2 large onions, chopped

2 celery ribs, chopped

1 green bell pepper, seeded and chopped

2 garlic cloves, chopped

1 or 2 smoked ham bones

4 quarts water

¼ teaspoon dried thyme

3 bay leaves

1 teaspoon salt

¼ teaspoon cayenne pepper

Red beans are popular throughout the South, and since most soups made with beans are pretty earthy concoctions, this smooth, rich version with subtle smoky and spicy flavor, which I encountered at a country club in Birmingham, Alabama, came as a pleasant surprise. The soup is really intended as a sophisticated first course, but I don't hesitate a minute to scoop up the leftover pulpy beans and ham, maybe add a little more water or any stock I might have on hand, and come up with a tasty stew for Sunday-night supper. Do remember that this soup must simmer initially for about five hours to develop the right texture and flavor.

1 Place the beans in a large bowl with enough water to cover, and soak overnight.

2 Drain the beans and place in a large, heavy pot or kettle. Add all the other ingredients, bring to a boil, reduce the heat to low, cover, and simmer for about 5 hours.

3 With a slotted spoon, remove and discard the ham bone(s). Scoop out the chunks of ham and save for another use. Strain the soup through a heavy sieve into another bowl, mashing the beans with a heavy spoon to extract as much liquid as possible. Transfer the soup to a large saucepan and heat it over low heat for about 5 minutes, stirring to keep it smooth.

4 Serve piping hot in crystal soup bowls.

Old-Fashioned Ham Bone Vegetable Soup

Makes 10 to 12 servings

3 quarts water

1 meaty ham bone, trimmed of excess fat

Two 28-ounce cans whole tomatoes with juice

6 medium onions, coarsely chopped

6 celery ribs, coarsely chopped

4 carrots, scraped and cut into ½-inch rounds

2 cups fresh or frozen lima beans

2 cups fresh or frozen corn kernels

1 cup fresh or frozen green beans, snapped into thirds

1 pound fresh or frozen okra, cut into thirds

1 tablespoon salt

Freshly ground black pepper to taste

1 cup regular long-grain rice

Tomato paste as needed

Handed down on my mother's Georgia side of the family through at least four generations, this quintessential Southern vegetable soup can be made with either a chunk of beef shoulder and a couple of marrow bones or, preferably, with a large, meaty ham bone from a baked butt or shank. I'm prejudiced, of course, but I've never eaten a more sumptuous vegetable soup and wouldn't dream of preparing it without the intention of freezing at least half in plastic containers for cold winter nights. Nor can I imagine serving the soup without a big basket of buttered cornbread. I know that keeping a big ham bone takes up lots of room in the freezer, so when I bake a ham and notice that I'm out of soup, I try to plan accordingly.

1 Pour the water into a large, heavy pot, add the ham bone, and bring to a boil. Add the tomatoes, cutting each into halves or quarters depending on size. Add the onions, celery, carrots, lima beans, corn, green beans, okra, salt, and pepper, reduce the heat to low, cover, and simmer gently for about 2½ hours. Remove the ham bone from the soup and, when cool enough to handle, cut the meat from the bone, cut it into small dice, return it to the soup, and discard the bone. Add the rice plus more water if needed, return the soup to a simmer, and cook till the rice is tender, about 30 minutes longer. If the soup is too thin, stir in tomato paste by the spoonful till it reaches the desired consistency.

2 Serve hot in deep soup bowls.

Appalachian Ham Hock and Cabbage Soup

Makes 6 to 8 servings

3 tablespoons bacon grease

1 large onion, chopped

2 celery ribs, chopped

2 carrots, scraped and chopped

2 garlic cloves, minced

1 small head green cabbage, shredded

1 medium smoked ham hock

1 teaspoon dried rosemary, crumbled

2 bay leaves

Salt and freshly ground black pepper to taste

Tabasco sauce to taste

Vast cabbage fields flourish all along the Appalachian borders of Virginia, North Carolina, and Tennessee (many possibly dating back to those started by the region's original Scotch-Irish settlers), and nothing is more common for home cooks than to combine the vegetable with various cuts of pork to make all sorts of savory soups, stews, casseroles, and puddings. This soup makes a hearty Sunday supper with nothing more than hot buttered cornbread, ham biscuits, or crusty country bread, and to round out the flavor, one lady I know in Gatlinburg, Tennessee, always stirs in a tablespoon or so of cider vinegar and serves a bowl of grated Swiss cheese to be sprinkled over the top.

1 In a large saucepan or pot, heat the bacon grease over moderate heat, add the onion, celery, carrots, and garlic, and stir for 5 minutes. Add the cabbage and stir till it begins to wilt, 5 to 10 minutes. Nestle the ham hock in the cabbage, add the remaining ingredients plus enough water to just cover, and stir. Bring to a boil, skimming any scum off the top, reduce the heat to low, cover, and simmer till the ham hock is very tender, about 2 hours.

2 With a slotted spoon, remove the hock, discard any skin and fat, and chop the meat coarsely. Return the meat to the soup, stir well, and simmer till piping hot.

3 Serve in deep soup bowls.

Ham Hock, Bacon, and Black-Eyed Pea Soup

¼ pound lean slab bacon (rind removed), cut into cubes

One 10-ounce package frozen black-eyed peas, thawed

1 smoked ham hock

2 medium leeks (white parts only), chopped

1 celery rib, chopped

1 carrot, scraped and diced

1 garlic clove, minced

¼ teaspoon dried thyme, crumbled

Salt and freshly ground black pepper to taste

4 cups water

1 cup dry white wine

Contrary to what the name might imply, this is actually a very elegant soup worthy of the most sophisticated Southern table. I like to serve it as a first course with miniature cornbreads, but for a more substantial winter lunch or Sunday supper, you can just as easily not strain the soup, chop the meat from the hock more coarsely, add even more fried bacon, and serve a tart spinach or dandelion salad on the side. In either case, the soup does need to simmer for at least two hours to develop the right flavors and texture.

1 In a small skillet, fry the bacon over moderate heat till almost crisp, stirring, and drain on paper towels. Set aside.

2 In a large pot, combine all the remaining ingredients, bring to a boil, reduce the heat to low, cover, and simmer for about 2½ hours, stirring from time to time. Remove the ham hock, cut away and discard the bone, fat, and gristle, and chop the meat finely.

3 Strain the soup into a large saucepan, add the bacon and chopped ham, and stir well. Bring the soup almost to a boil, reduce the heat to low, and simmer for about 15 minutes, adding a little more water if it seems too thick.

4 Serve piping hot in glass or china soup bowls.

Commander's Split Pea, Carrot, and Ham Hock Soup

Makes 6 to 8 servings

3 tablespoons butter

3 large leeks (white parts only), rinsed thoroughly and sliced widthwise ¼ inch thick

6 medium carrots, scraped and cut into large dice

4 celery ribs, cut into large dice

8 garlic cloves, thinly sliced

2 lean smoked ham hocks

2 pounds dried split peas, rinsed and picked over

3 quarts chicken broth

2 bay leaves

Salt and freshly ground black pepper to taste

Tabasco sauce to taste (optional)

This is my adaptation of one of the many great soups served at the legendary Commander's Palace restaurant in New Orleans. As I was taught by the chef, the reason for cooking the soup uncovered for the first 30 minutes is not only to reduce the broth slightly but also to release the initial flavor of the ham hocks. At Commander's, fresh ham hocks are used, but these are becoming increasingly difficult to find today, and I actually prefer the intense flavor of smoked hocks. Personally, I cannot imagine eating this delectable soup without at least a few dashes of Tabasco.

1 In a large pot or kettle, melt the butter over moderate heat, add the leeks, carrots, celery, and garlic, and stir till softened, about 8 minutes. Add the hocks and stir till the aroma of ham becomes evident, about 3 minutes. Add the peas, stirring constantly, and cook till they turn bright green, about 3 minutes.

2 Add the broth, bay leaves, and salt and pepper, bring to a boil, reduce the heat slightly, and cook, uncovered, for 30 minutes. Reduce the heat to low, cover, and continue cooking till the liquid is creamy and the peas start to break down, about 30 minutes, stirring from time to time and adding a little water if the soup seems too thick.

3 Remove the hocks and, when cool enough to handle, remove and dice the meat, add it to the soup, and stir well. Add the Tabasco if desired, stir well, and serve the soup piping hot in wide soup bowls.

Georgia Ham Hock, Bacon, and Chicken Chowder

6 slices bacon, cut into 1-inch pieces

One 3½-pound chicken, disjointed

1 small meaty ham hock

1 large onion, studded with 3 cloves

3 celery ribs (leaves included), broken in half

½ teaspoon dried tarragon

½ teaspoon dried thyme, crumbled

Salt and freshly ground black pepper to taste

3 quarts water

2 medium red potatoes

1 medium red bell pepper, seeded and finely diced

Like most Southerners, my North Carolina mother (like her Georgia father before her) has never paid any heed to the notion that a chowder should contain seafood. If the soup involves diced or cubed potatoes, it's a chowder. Period. And never will you encounter a more succulent example than this elaborate concoction that's been in the family repertory for over a century. I remember that my granddaddy Paw Paw used the entire chicken to make his chowder; Mother prefers only the white meat, saving the dark for hash or salads. In either case, nothing more is needed with the chowder than a beautiful salad, some sesame sticks or crackers, and beer or iced tea.

1 In a large, heavy skillet, fry the bacon over moderate heat till cooked but not crisp, and drain on paper towels. Add the chicken pieces to the fat and brown on all sides, turning once. Meanwhile, in a large, heavy pot, combine the ham hock, onion, celery, tarragon, thyme, salt and pepper, and water and bring to a boil. When the chicken has browned, add it to the pot along with the bacon, return the mixture to a boil, reduce the heat to low, cover, and simmer for 1 hour. With a slotted spoon, remove the chicken to a plate and continue simmering the stock for about 45 minutes.

2 When they are cool enough to handle, skin the chicken breasts and wings, remove the meat from the bones, cut into small dice, and reserve the dark meat for hash or salads. Peel the potatoes and cut into dice. Transfer the ham hock to a cutting board, strain the stock through a fine sieve into another large pot, and discard all the solids. Shred the ham finely and add to the stock. Add the potatoes, bell pepper, and, if the mixture is too thick, more water. Bring to a simmer over moderate heat and cook till the potatoes are just tender, about 15 minutes. Add the chicken, stir well, taste for salt and pepper, and ladle the hot chowder into wide soup bowls.

Miami Black Bean and Pig Knuckle Soup

Makes 6 to 8 servings

1 pound dried black beans, rinsed and picked over

3 quarts water

½ pound lean salt pork (rind removed), cut into small cubes

2 medium onions, finely chopped

1 celery rib, finely chopped

1 large carrot, scraped and finely chopped

2 garlic cloves, minced

1 fresh long green chile pepper, seeded and finely chopped

½ teaspoon dried oregano, crumbled

½ teaspoon dried thyme, crumbled

½ teaspoon ground coriander

Salt and freshly ground black pepper to taste

2 medium ripe tomatoes, peeled, seeded, and chopped

½ cup Madeira or dry sherry

2 smoked pigs' knuckles (hocks)

Miami black bean (or "turtle bean") soup simply would not be genuine if it didn't include at least two types of pork, and it's not unusual for cooks to simmer this hearty but elegant soup for up to 10 or 12 hours to intensify flavors and attain just the right consistency. In truth, the soup can be made with any leftover pork, ham, or sausage, but what gives it real character (and succulent flavor) are smoked pigs' knuckles (hocks). For a more velvety soup, you might want to simmer the beans even longer than the time indicated here, and then puree everything through a fine sieve with a teaspoon or so of fresh lemon juice. In either case, the soup is best when allowed to stand overnight, and some cooks like to garnish the top of each serving with finely chopped hard-boiled eggs.

1 Place the beans and water in a large, heavy pot or casserole, bring to a boil, reduce the heat the low, cover, and simmer till the beans are almost tender, about 1½ hours.

2 Meanwhile, render the salt pork in a large skillet over moderate heat till lightly browned and crisp, add the onions, celery, carrot, garlic, and chile pepper, and stir for about 8 minutes. Add the seasonings, tomatoes, and Madeira and stir for about 5 minutes longer.

3 When the beans are almost tender, add the contents of the skillet to the pot and nestle the knuckles in the liquid. Bring to a boil, skimming scum from the top, reduce the heat to low, cover, and simmer till the beans and knuckles are very tender, 2 to 3 hours.

4 Remove the knuckles, discard any fat, chop the meat finely, and return the meat to the beans. Heat till piping hot and serve in wide soup bowls.

PIG PICKIN'S

The pig is man's second oldest domesticated animal, after the dog.

Tennessee Pigs' Feet and Field Pea Snert

2 pigs' feet, singed and partially split between the toes

½ pound lean salt pork (rind removed), diced

2 medium onions, chopped

2 celery ribs (leaves included), chopped

1 carrot, scraped and chopped

¼ cup chopped fresh parsley leaves

½ teaspoon dried thyme, crumbled

2 whole cloves

Salt and freshly ground black pepper to taste

Two 12-ounce packages dried black-eyed or crowder peas

2 large potatoes, peeled and diced

Don't ask me why the mountain folks of Tennessee refer to any pig and pea soup as *snert*—or how the colorful term came about. Snert can be made with pig knuckles, ears, or jowl, but nothing produces the rugged soup's gelatinous quality so beloved by locals better than a couple of bony pigs' feet. Any good butcher should be able to dress the feet for cooking (and I've seen them frozen in some grocery stores), but, if necessary, simply scrub the feet with a wire brush, singe or shave off any hair, and split the toes partially with a cleaver. Since tiny bones can fall off the feet during the long simmering, be sure to wrap the feet carefully in cheesecloth, and don't fail to skim as much scum as possible off the top at the beginning of the cooking process.

1 Tie each pig's foot in cheesecloth, place in a large pot, and add the salt pork plus enough water to cover. Bring to a boil, reduce the heat to low, and simmer for about 30 minutes, skimming scum from the top. Drain the water from the pot.

2 Add the onions, celery, carrot, parsley, thyme, cloves, salt and pepper, and peas to the pot and add enough fresh water to cover. Bring to a boil, reduce the heat to low, cover, and simmer for 2½ hours, stirring from time to time.

3 Remove the pigs' feet, discard the cheesecloth and all bones, chop any meat, and return the meat to the soup. Add the potatoes, return the soup to a simmer, and cook till the potatoes are tender, 15 to 20 minutes.

4 Serve the soup hot in wide soup bowls.

LENTIL AND BACON SOUP

½ pound lean slab bacon (rind removed), cut into small cubes

2 medium onions, chopped

1 pound dried lentils

⅛ teaspoon dried rosemary, crumbled

1 small bay leaf

Salt and freshly ground black pepper to taste

Tabasco sauce to taste

3 quarts water

Dried brown lentils were virtually unknown in the South till about fifty years ago, but once they were introduced to markets, it didn't take Southern cooks long to realize that, simmered slowly with some form of pork, they could be just as tasty as black-eyed, crowder, cow, or split peas. As is true with any type of field peas, lentils should be watched carefully while cooking to make sure they are tender but not mushy. On the other hand, if you're careless and do overcook the lentils (as I've done on occasion), the best solution is to pick out the bay leaf, puree the soup in a blender or food processor, reheat it gently, and serve with a dollop of sour cream on top of each portion. Pureed, the soup freezes well.

1 In a large saucepan, fry the bacon over moderate heat till almost crisp, drain on paper towels, and pour off all but about 2 tablespoons of fat from the pan. Add the onions to the pan and stir till golden, about 8 minutes. Add the drained bacon, the lentils, rosemary, bay leaf, salt and pepper, and Tabasco and stir till well blended. Add the water, bring to a low boil, reduce the heat to low, cover, and simmer till the lentils are tender but not mushy, about 45 minutes.

2 Serve the soup piping hot in heavy soup bowls.

Canadian Bacon, Vegetable, and White Bean Soup

5 cups beef broth

¼ pound Canadian bacon, diced

1 medium onion, diced

3 celery ribs, diced

6 carrots, scraped and diced

2 garlic cloves, minced

One 15-ounce can diced tomatoes

One 19-ounce can Great Northern beans, drained

Salt and freshly ground black pepper to taste

Smoky Canadian bacon (or "back bacon") is as popular in the South as it was half a century ago, not only fried for breakfast but also used in layered casseroles and, since it is already virtually cooked, in numerous quick and easy soups. This soup is delicious as is, but nobody says that a little grated sharp cheddar cheese sprinkled over the top does any harm.

1 In a large saucepan, combine the broth, Canadian bacon, onion, celery, carrots, and garlic. Bring to a low boil, reduce the heat to low, cover, and simmer for about 20 minutes. Add the tomatoes, beans, and salt and pepper, stir well, return to a simmer, and cook for about 10 minutes longer.

2 Serve the soup piping hot in heavy soup bowls.

Outer Banks Muddle

½ pound lean salt pork
    (rind removed), cut into
    small cubes

3 medium onions, diced

2 celery ribs, diced

1 small red bell pepper, seeded
    and diced

2 garlic cloves, minced

3 medium ripe tomatoes, diced

2 cups bottled clam juice

2 cups water

2 teaspoons fresh lemon juice

2 teaspoons Worcestershire sauce

Tabasco sauce to taste

Salt and freshly ground black
    pepper to taste

1 teaspoon dried thyme, crumbled

1 bay leaf

½ pound fresh shrimp, shelled
    and deveined

½ pound sea scallops, quartered

From Manteo down to Okracoke on North Carolina's Outer Banks, nothing is more popular than the variety of muddles ("mess of fish"), mulls, and other thick, robust soups served in homes and at seafood houses and shacks. And what's most interesting is that what gives these concoctions at least part of their distinction is the traditional addition of bacon, salt pork, or other form of pig used to heighten flavor (the same pedigreed pigs, by the way, raised on huge inland farms just west of Pamlico Sound). This particular muddle is made with small, rendered cubes of lean salt pork (streak-o'-lean), but using four or five strips of thick, lean, diced bacon is just as good. All you need with this soup is plenty of fresh coleslaw and some form of cornbread.

1 In a large, heavy pot, fry the salt pork over moderate heat till crisp, drain on paper towels, crumble, and reserve. Add the onions, celery, bell pepper, and garlic to the pot and cook, stirring till very soft, about 7 minutes. Add the tomatoes, clam juice, water, lemon juice, Worcestershire, Tabasco, salt and pepper, thyme, and bay leaf, bring to a low simmer, cover, and cook for 1 hour.

2 Add the shrimp and scallops, return to a simmer, and cook till the shrimp turn fully pink, about 8 minutes.

3 Serve the muddle in deep soup bowls with crumbled bacon sprinkled over the top of each portion.

Farmhouse Sausage and Kidney Bean Soup

½ pound bulk pork sausage

1 medium onion, chopped

½ medium green bell pepper, seeded and chopped

1 garlic clove, minced

One 15½-ounce can kidney beans, undrained

One 15-ounce can diced tomatoes with juice

¼ teaspoon powdered sage

1 bay leaf

Salt and freshly ground black pepper to taste

Tabasco sauce to taste

2 cups water

It was while visiting a hog farm in eastern North Carolina that I was first exposed to this absurdly simple but incredibly satisfying soup that our hostess whipped up in little more than an hour and served with a congealed vegetable salad and piping-hot onion hush puppies. Of course, she used her own whole-hog sausage made right on the farm, but given the virtual impossibility of finding such a glorious and rare product outside the region, your best bet is to use a respectable and widely available bulk sausage that has the right proportions of fat and lean meat, such as Jimmy Dean.

1 In a large saucepan, break up the sausage and cook, stirring, over moderate heat till no trace of pink color is left. Pour off all but about 2 tablespoons of grease, add the onion, bell pepper, and garlic to the pan, and stir till the vegetables soften, about 5 minutes. Add the remaining ingredients and stir well. Bring to a boil, reduce the heat to low, cover, and simmer for about 1 hour, stirring from time to time.

2 Discard the bay leaf and serve the soup hot in deep soup bowls.

Sausage-Ball, Spinach, and Rice Soup

Makes 6 to 8 servings

½ pound bulk pork sausage

¼ teaspoon red pepper flakes

⅛ teaspoon powdered sage

6 cups chicken broth

Two 10-ounce packages frozen spinach, thawed

½ cup instant rice

Whether it's along the coastal South Carolina and Georgia Lowcountry or in rice-producing Louisiana, sausage-ball soup is not only a specialty of roadside diners and humble country restaurants but is also almost always made with a leafy green and thickened with rice. Since the sausage must be full flavored and spicy, most cooks mix their own with any number of seasonings (as I do), and while I've yet to fully understand why sausage-ball soup must stand for at least an hour before being reheated and served, I would never dream of defying the tradition. Needless to say, a soup such as this is always served with some form of cornbread (I prefer oniony corn sticks).

1 In a bowl, combine the sausage, red pepper flakes, and sage and mix thoroughly with your hands. Form the sausage into 1-inch balls and place on a plate.

2 In a large skillet, brown the sausage balls on all sides over moderate heat till cooked through, and drain on paper towels.

3 In a large saucepan, bring the broth to a boil, add the spinach, and when the broth returns to a boil, reduce the heat to moderate and cook the spinach for 4 minutes, stirring. Add the rice, stir well, remove from the heat, and let stand for 5 minutes. Add the sausage balls, cover, and let stand for about 1 hour.

4 When ready to serve, reheat the soup and serve hot in wide soup bowls.

Arkansas Sausage and Red Bean Chowder

Makes 6 to 8 servings

1 pound bulk pork sausage

Two 16-ounce cans kidney beans, drained

One 28-ounce can crushed tomatoes with juice included

1 large onion, chopped

1 garlic clove, minced

½ teaspoon dried thyme, crumbled

1 bay leaf

Salt and freshly ground black pepper to taste

1 quart water

2 medium red potatoes, rinsed and diced

½ green bell pepper, seeded and diced

All legitimate chowders should involve seafood, but don't try telling that to Southerners, who freely apply the term to any thick soup that contains diced or cubed potatoes. This particular sausage and bean chowder hails from a friend's small ranch on the Arkansas-Mississippi border, and he and his wife wouldn't dream of serving it without hoecakes fresh from the griddle and a bottle of Tabasco sauce to give the chowder "personality." What's nice about this easy chowder is that the base can be prepared well in advance and the potatoes and bell pepper added shortly before serving.

1 In a large skillet, break up the sausage, fry over moderate heat till browned, stirring, and drain on paper towels.

2 In a large pot or kettle, combine the sausage, beans, tomatoes, onion, garlic, thyme, bay leaf, salt and pepper, and water. Bring to a boil, reduce the heat to low, cover, and simmer for 1 hour.

3 Add the potatoes and bell pepper, return the chowder to a simmer, cover, and cook till the potatoes are tender, about 20 minutes.

4 Remove the bay leaf and serve the chowder hot in wide soup bowls.

CREOLE SEAFOOD, SAUSAGE, AND OKRA GUMBO

MAKES 6 TO 8 SERVINGS

½ cup vegetable oil

½ cup all-purpose flour

2 medium onions, diced

2 celery ribs, diced

1 green bell pepper, seeded and diced

2 garlic cloves, minced

Pinch of dried thyme

Pinch of dried oregano

2 bay leaves

Salt and freshly ground black pepper to taste

2 quarts water

3 live blue crabs, top shells and gills removed and claws cracked

½ pound andouille (or kielbasa) sausage, cut into ¼-inch rounds

¼ pound fresh okra, cut into thin rounds (or ¼ pound frozen and thawed cut okra)

1 pound medium fresh shrimp, peeled and deveined

½ quart shucked oysters, liquor included

Tabasco sauce to taste

Boiled rice

Of all the glorious Creole gumbos found in New Orleans, this seafood one enhanced by thin rounds of smoky andouille sausage is and always has been my favorite. For a full-flavored stock, it is important to use live crabs, and for this particular gumbo, okra (fresh or frozen) is a much better thickening agent than filé powder. The same serious attention must be paid to this roux as to any other to prevent burning, meaning the heat should not be too hot, the whisking should be constant, and the timing carefully monitored. If, by chance, the roux displays black spots, your only alternative is to toss it out and start again. Remember also not to overcook the shrimp and oysters—they should be simmered just long enough to impart their savor to the gumbo.

1 In a large cast-iron pot, heat the oil over moderate heat and gradually add the flour, whisking constantly till the roux is dark brown, 12 to 15 minutes. (Do not allow to burn.) Stirring, add the onions, celery, bell pepper, garlic, thyme, oregano, bay leaves, and salt and pepper, and stir for 3 minutes. Stirring constantly, add the water, crabs, and sausage, bring to a boil, reduce the heat to low, and simmer for about 45 minutes, skimming any scum off the top and stirring from time to time.

2 Add the okra, stir, and simmer for 15 minutes longer. Add the shrimp and oysters, return to a boil, reduce the heat to low, and simmer for about 10 minutes longer.

3 Add the Tabasco, stir well, and serve the gumbo over mounds of rice in deep soup bowls.

Cajun Chicken and Sausage Gumbo

Makes 6 to 8 servings

²/₃ cup vegetable oil

One 3-pound chicken, cut into
    serving pieces

½ cup all-purpose flour

1½ pounds andouille
    (or kielbasa) sausage,
    cut into ½-inch cubes

1 medium onion, chopped

1 celery rib, chopped

½ green bell pepper, seeded
    and chopped

1 garlic clove, minced

1 bay leaf

2 quarts water

2 tablespoons filé powder

Boiled rice

In the Louisiana Bayou, it would be almost inconceivable to prepare this gumbo in anything but a large, black, cast-iron pot that maintains an even and steady heat, and unlike most seafood gumbos that include okra, this one is thickened with ground sassafras, known as filé powder (now available in bottles at most markets). Do be warned that filé powder must always be stirred into a gumbo at the end, after it's removed from the heat; otherwise, it will be tough and stringy. The ideal sausage for this gumbo is Cajun andouille, but if it's not available in your market, substitute kielbasa or any other smoky sausage. And, as always, be extra careful not to burn the roux, which must be whisked constantly over moderate or moderately low heat. (If the roux does develop black spots, toss it out and start again.)

1 In a large cast-iron pot, heat the oil over moderate heat, add the chicken pieces, brown them on all sides, and transfer to a plate. Gradually add the flour to the oil in the pot, whisking constantly till a medium-brown roux forms, about 8 minutes. (Be careful not to burn.) Add the sausage, onion, celery, bell pepper, garlic, and bay leaf and stir for about 8 minutes. Add ¼ cup of the water plus the chicken pieces and stir well. Add the remaining water, bring to a boil, reduce the heat to low, and simmer the gumbo till the chicken is tender, about 1 hour, stirring from time to time.

2 Remove the pot from the heat, let stand for about 10 minutes, stir in the filé powder, and let the gumbo stand for about 5 minutes.

3 Serve the gumbo over mounds of rice in deep soup bowls.

PIG PICKIN'S

The main purpose of Louisiana's official state dog, the Catahoula, is to chase wild hogs out of the bayous so that hunters can shoot them.

Gumbo z'Herbes

Makes 6 to 8 servings

²/₃ cup vegetable oil

²/₃ cup all-purpose flour

3 large onions, chopped

3 celery ribs, chopped

1 medium green bell pepper,
   seeded and chopped

2 garlic cloves, minced

1 pound tasso ham, cut into
   ½-inch dice (see page xix)

2 quarts chicken broth

1 bunch each collard greens,
   turnip greens, spinach,
   watercress, and beet greens
   (or other greens), rinsed,
   stems removed, and coarsely
   chopped

1 teaspoon dried thyme, crumbled

⅛ teaspoon allspice

2 whole cloves

2 bay leaves

Salt and freshly ground black
   pepper to taste

½ cup Herbsaint (or Pernod)
   liqueur

Boiled rice

A mainstay of New Orleans Creole cookery, gumbo z'herbes ("with herbs") is traditionally served on Good Friday and is thought to bring good luck. In the old days, the gumbo was prepared with no less than seven greens and no meat, but today it's rare to find a version that's not enriched with andouille sausage, tasso ham, a ham hock, or some other form of pork. What makes the gumbo so distinctive is the flavor of licorice, so if you're unable to find a bottle of local Herbsaint (a liqueur created when absinthe was banned in the early twentieth century), use the more readily available Pernod. As for the greens, any variety will do—and the more, the better. As always, every precaution should be made not to burn the roux while whisking; if black spots appear in the mixture, you must start again.

1 In a large, heavy skillet, heat the oil over moderate heat and gradually add the flour, whisking constantly till the roux is light brown, 8 to 10 minutes. (Be careful not to burn.) Add the onions, celery, bell pepper, garlic, and tasso, stir till the vegetables are soft, about 8 minutes, and remove from the heat.

2 In a large pot or kettle, bring the broth to a boil, add the roux mixture, and whisk till well blended. Add the greens, thyme, allspice, cloves, bay leaves, salt and pepper, and Herbsaint and stir well. Bring back to a boil, reduce the heat to low, and simmer for about 1 hour.

3 Remove about 2 cups of solids from the pot, puree in a food processor, return the puree to the pot, and stir till the gumbo is piping hot.

4 Serve the gumbo over mounds of rice in deep soup bowls.

 ## PIG PICKIN'S

Well into the nineteenth century, the smokehouse, larder, and pork barrel were useful measures of a family's fortune.

Eula Mae's Sausage, Shrimp, and Okra Gumbo

Makes 6 to 8 servings

3 tablespoons vegetable oil

1 pound andouille (or kielbasa) sausage, cut crosswise into ¼-inch slices

2 tablespoons all-purpose flour

1 medium onion, chopped

1 medium green bell pepper, seeded and chopped

1 garlic clove, minced

2 cups chicken broth

¾ pound fresh okra, sliced (or one 10-ounce package frozen sliced okra, thawed)

Salt and freshly ground black pepper to taste

½ teaspoon Tabasco sauce

2 bay leaves

1 pound medium fresh shrimp, peeled and deveined

2 scallions (green tops only), chopped

Boiled rice

On Avery Island, Louisiana, where the McIlhenny family has been making Tabasco sauce since the mid-nineteenth century, Eula Mae Doré cooked for special McIlhenny events and entertained friends and out-of-town visitors for over fifty years. Cooking strictly from instinct and memory, Eula Mae was known for numerous Cajun specialties, but what chefs, restaurateurs, and food writers really flocked here to watch her make and sample were her inimitable gumbos, like this hearty one prepared with local andouille sausage, fat Gulf shrimp, and okra. When, not long ago, her recipes were finally gathered together in *Eula Mae's Cajun Kitchen*, she had only two pieces of advice about the dish: Never try to rush the gumbo, and do not overcook the shrimp. I would also advise making every effort to find genuine andouille sausage, now available in finer markets all over the country.

1 In a large skillet, heat 1 tablespoon of the oil over moderate heat, add the sausage, stir till slightly browned, about 8 minutes, and transfer to a plate.

2 Add the remaining oil to the skillet, increase the heat slightly, and, whisking constantly, add the flour till a light brown roux forms, 3 to 4 minutes. (Make sure the roux does not burn. If it does, discard it and start again with equal parts of oil and flour.) Add the onion, bell pepper, and garlic and stir till soft, about 5 minutes. Gradually stir in the broth, bring to a boil, and add the sausage, okra, salt and pepper, Tabasco, and bay leaves. Reduce the heat to low, cover, and simmer the mixture for 20 minutes.

3 Stir in the shrimp and scallions and simmer till the shrimp turn pink, about 5 minutes. Remove the bay leaves and serve the gumbo over mounds of rice in wide soup bowls.

Above: **COUNTRY HAM, CREAM CHEESE, AND PECAN ROUNDS (PAGE 15)**

Opposite: **MEMPHIS COUNTRY HAM AND CORN CHOWDER WITH BOURBON (PAGE 46)**

Carolina Pork, Sweet Potato, and Apple Stew (page 80)

Opposite: **Florida Rock Shrimp and Bacon Casserole (page 96)**

Above: **Slab Bacon and Mushroom Strata (page 108)**

Above: **Baked Pork Chops with Hominy and Orange (page 116)**

Opposite: **Mississippi Smothered Pork Cutlets (page 136)**

Carolina Pork and Sweet Potato Pie with Biscuit Batter Crust (page 150)

HAM CROQUETTES WITH PARSLEY SAUCE (PAGE 174)

JEANNE'S ROAST PORK WITH SAUSAGE-
CORNBREAD STUFFING (PAGE 188)

Opposite: ROAST PORK TENDERLOIN STUFFED WITH HONEYED APPLES AND PECANS (PAGE 205)

Above: SLOW-ROASTED PORK SHOULDER WITH ORANGE-RAISIN SAUCE (PAGE 208)

Baked Smithfield Ham with Bourbon, Honey, and Pecan Glaze (page 234)

Stews, Casseroles, and Stratas

Virginia Brunswick Stew

Cajun Ham, Sausage, and Red Bean Stew

Pork and Eggplant Stew

Pork Sparerib and Oxtail Stew

Carolina Pork, Sweet Potato, and Apple Stew

Kentucky Country Ham and Black-Eyed Pea Stew

West Virginia Pork, Wild Mushroom, and Walnut Stew

Frogmore Stew

Stewed Ham Hocks and Lima Beans

Ray's Stewed Pork Chops and Dried Apricots

Braised Pork, Onion, Bell Pepper, and Pecans

Braised Pork, Apples, and Collard Greens

Cherokee Pork Chili

Leah's Pork Chops and Cornbread Casserole

Sausage and Leek Buffet Casserole

Sherried Ham and Squash Casserole

Florida Rock Shrimp and Bacon Casserole

Pork, Prune, and Orange Casserole

Links and Hominy Casserole

Chicken, Sausage, and Mushroom Supreme

Company Ham and Turkey Bake

Creamed Fresh Ham and Turnip Hotpot

Spicy Breakfast Sausage and Cheese Bake

Country Sausage, Apple, and Bean Strata

Sausage and Mixed Vegetable Strata

Slab Bacon and Mushroom Strata

Pork, Pea, and Noodle Strata

Bacon and Lima Bean Scallop

Virginia Brunswick Stew

Makes 6 servings as a main course, 10 to 12 servings as a side dish

½ cup vegetable oil

One 4-pound chicken (preferably a hen), quartered

1 cup chopped onions

1 cup chopped celery (leaves included)

1 medium ham hock, trimmed of skin

3 large ripe tomatoes, chopped

1 small fresh red chile pepper, seeded and minced

Salt and freshly ground black pepper to taste

1½ quarts water

1½ cups fresh or frozen corn kernels

1½ cups fresh or frozen sliced okra

1½ cups fresh or frozen lima beans

1½ cups mashed cooked potatoes

Probably the South's most famous stew, Brunswick stew would be inconceivable without at least one form of pig to enhance the rather neutral flavors of chicken (or, in rare incidences, squirrel) and vegetables. Of course, arguments can flare over whether the stew was originally concocted in Brunswick County, Virginia; Brunswick, Georgia; or Brunswick County, North Carolina—each of these states still hold very serious annual Brunswick-stew cook-offs—and debates on whether the stew is best eaten by itself or served as a side dish with pork barbecue are endless. Overwhelming evidence points to Virginia as the true home of the glorious dish, and this is basically the style of my own stew that I serve at special Brunswick-stew parties maybe three times a year. The main thing to remember about any Brunswick stew is that it will quickly and easily scorch if not stirred repeatedly, so keep a close eye on the pot at all times—or be prepared to deal with utter disaster.

1 In a large, heavy skillet, heat ¼ cup of the vegetable oil over moderate heat, add the chicken, brown on all sides, and transfer to a large plate. In a large stew pot, heat the remaining ¼ cup oil over moderate heat, add the onions and celery, and stir for about 5 minutes. Add the browned chicken, ham hock, tomatoes, chile pepper, salt and pepper, and water, stir, bring to a boil, reduce the heat to low, cover, and simmer for 1 hour.

2 Remove the chicken with a slotted spoon and simmer the mixture for 1 hour longer. When the chicken has cooled, skin, bone, and shred the meat and set aside.

3 Bring the mixture in the pot to a boil, add the corn, okra, and lima beans, reduce the heat to low, and simmer for 30 minutes, stirring from time to time. Remove the ham hock with a slotted spoon and, when cool enough to handle, bone and shred the meat, and return the meat to the casserole along with the reserved chicken. Add the mashed potatoes, stir well, and continue to cook till nicely thickened, about 20 minutes, stirring often.

4 Serve the stew in wide soup bowls as a main course or in small bowls as a side dish with pork barbecue.

Cajun Ham, Sausage, and Red Bean Stew

Makes 4 servings

1½ cups dried red kidney beans, rinsed and picked over

½ cup peanut oil

½ cup all-purpose flour

1 medium onion, chopped

2 celery ribs, chopped

1 small green bell pepper, seeded and chopped

1 garlic clove, minced

½ teaspoon dried thyme, crumbled

Salt and freshly ground black pepper to taste

Tabasco sauce to taste

½ pound smoked ham, diced

½ pound andouille, chaurice, or kielbasa sausage, diced

1 quart chicken broth

In and around Lafayette, Louisiana, reddish-brown kidney beans are known exclusively as "red beans" to Cajun cooks, and the ways they prepare them with local sausages and hams are limitless. For this hearty stew, andouille sausage is now available in better markets all over the country, or you can make your own chaurice (page 252). Otherwise, use kielbasa. Ideally, the highly spiced, smoked regional ham called tasso should be used, but given the virtual impossibility of finding this product outside Louisiana, the appropriate substitute is any ordinary smoked ham.

1 Place the beans in a bowl with enough water to cover and let soak overnight (or, preferably, for 24 hours).

2 In a large, heavy pot, heat the oil over moderate heat, add the flour, and whisk steadily till the roux turns dark brown, 15 to 20 minutes. (Take special care not to burn the roux.) Add the onion, celery, bell pepper, garlic, thyme, salt and pepper, and Tabasco and stir till the vegetables soften, about 5 minutes. Add the beans, ham, and sausage and stir for 5 minutes longer. Add the broth, bring to a boil, reduce the heat to low, and simmer, uncovered, till the beans are tender and the stew nicely thickened, about 1½ hours, stirring from time to time.

3 Serve hot.

Pork and Eggplant Stew

2 thick slices bacon, cut into pieces

1½ pounds pork shoulder butt, trimmed of excess fat and cut into 1-inch cubes

¼ pound smoked ham, cut into small cubes

2 medium onions, chopped

1 large green bell pepper, seeded and chopped

2 medium ripe tomatoes, peeled, seeded, and chopped

2 medium eggplants, rinsed and cut into 1-inch cubes

Salt and freshly ground black pepper to taste

Tabasco sauce to taste

¼ cup water

Contrary to popular opinion, Southerners do like eggplant, so long, that is, as its bland flavor is enhanced by either plenty of butter and sharp cheese or at least two forms of fatty and/or smoked pig. No dish could be simpler or quicker in preparation than this toothy stew, and served with a bowl of coleslaw and plenty of cornbread, the stew makes an ideal Sunday supper.

1 In a large, heavy saucepan or pot, fry the bacon over moderate heat till half cooked, add the pork and ham, and stir till they are lightly browned. Add the onions and bell pepper and stir till softened, about 5 minutes. Add the tomatoes and eggplants, salt and pepper, and Tabasco and stir for about 5 minutes. Add the water, bring to a simmer, cover the pan, and cook over low heat till the pork is tender, about 1 hour.

2 Serve hot.

PORK SPARERIB AND OXTAIL STEW

MAKES 6 TO 8 SERVINGS

¼ cup peanut oil

2 pounds oxtails, cut into 2-inch sections

2 cups beef broth

2 cups red wine

One 8-ounce can tomato sauce

½ teaspoon dried thyme, crumbled

¼ teaspoon dried rosemary, crumbled

4 whole cloves

2 bay leaves

Salt and freshly ground black pepper to taste

2 pounds meaty pork spareribs, separated

4 medium onions, quartered

4 celery ribs, cut into 2-inch pieces

4 carrots, scraped and cut into thick rounds

4 medium red potatoes, peeled and quartered

Gone are the days, even in the South, when both pork spareribs and oxtails were deemed "poor man's meat" and could be snapped up for next to nothing even in fancy butcher shops. Today, pricey ribs in various guises are often featured in the finest restaurants, and innovative Southern chefs have come up with ways to prepare oxtails (which are actually beef or veal tails) that turn the bony but succulent meat almost into a luxury food. Of course, the key to cooking fatty spareribs (cut from the lower portion of the hog's ribs) and oxtails is long, slow braising to break down tough connective tissues, and when the two are combined in a substantial stew such as this one, the complementary gelatinous textures and intense flavors of the meats are memorable. And this is one stew that needs to be served with knives, forks, and soup spoons.

1 In a large, heavy casserole or kettle, heat the oil over moderate heat, add the oxtails, and brown on all sides. Pour off the oil and fat, add the broth and wine plus enough water to cover, the tomato sauce, thyme, rosemary, cloves, bay leaves, and salt and pepper, and stir well. Bring to a boil, reduce the heat to low, and skim scum from the top. Cover and simmer the oxtails for 2 hours, skimming fat from the surface from time to time.

2 Add the pork ribs plus more water to cover, return to a boil, reduce the heat to low, cover, and simmer for 1 hour, skimming any fat from the surface.

3 Add the onions, celery, carrots, and potatoes plus more water to cover, return to a boil, reduce the heat to low, and simmer for 1 hour.

4 Pick out and discard the bay leaves, taste for salt and pepper, and serve the stew hot in wide soup bowls.

PIG PICKIN'S

"On our parents' and grandparents' farms we saw hogs grow fat and meaty, and we understood why a child eating a huge meal or taking the largest piece of pie was called a pig."

—Jeanne Voltz and Elaine J. Harvell,

The Country Ham Book

Carolina Pork, Sweet Potato, and Apple Stew

MAKES 6 SERVINGS

2 pounds boneless pork shoulder, trimmed of excess fat and cut into 1-inch cubes

¼ cup all-purpose flour

3 tablespoons butter

1 large onion, chopped

1 celery rib, chopped

1 Granny Smith apple, cored and thinly sliced

¼ teaspoon dried sage, crumbled

1 cup dry red wine

Salt and freshly ground black pepper to taste

Beef broth as needed

2 sweet potatoes, peeled and cut into large cubes

North Carolina is the South's leading producer of sweet potatoes (though even Carolina Tarheels have to admit that Louisiana's sumptuous Beauregard potatoes are in a class by themselves), as well as being the country's second largest hog-breeding state. Little wonder, therefore, that pork and sweet potatoes are often combined to make all sorts of stews, casseroles, savory pies, and even rustic breads. In this particular stew, the acid in the apple serves to balance not only the sweetness of the potatoes but also the unctuousness of the pork shoulder. And if you really love pork and apples the way most people do, by all means add another Granny Smith.

1 On a plate, dredge the pork cubes in the flour, tapping off any excess. In a large, heavy pot, heat 2 tablespoons of the butter over moderate heat, brown the pork on all sides, and transfer to a bowl. Heat the remaining 1 tablespoon of butter in the pot, add the onion and celery, and stir till softened, about 5 minutes. Return the pork to the pot, add the apple, sage, wine, salt and pepper, and enough broth to just cover the ingredients. Bring the liquid to a gentle simmer, cover, and cook till the pork is almost tender, about 1 hour. Add the potatoes, stir, return to a simmer, and cook till the pork and potatoes are very tender, about 30 minutes.

2 Serve hot.

Kentucky Country Ham and Black-Eyed Pea Stew

Makes 6 servings

¾ pound shelled fresh black-eyed peas (1½ pounds unshelled peas), rinsed and picked over

1 pound country ham, trimmed of excess fat and cut into small cubes

1 large onion, chopped

1 celery rib, chopped

½ green bell pepper, seeded and chopped

1 bay leaf

¼ teaspoon dried sage, crumbled

Freshly ground black pepper to taste

3 cups water

2 tablespoons tomato ketchup

Worcestershire and Tabasco sauces to taste

1 tablespoon all-purpose flour mixed with 1 tablespoon water

While ordinary ham and field pea stew has been a country staple for centuries in homes throughout the South, when Kentuckians fix it with their superlative cured and aged ham and fresh black-eyed peas, the stew takes on real pedigree. If you're forced to use dried peas, boil them for two minutes, let them soak off the heat for about an hour, and substitute the soaking liquid for part of the fresh water in the stew. Allowing the stew to stand overnight in the refrigerator only enhances its flavor, and the traditional way of serving it is over rice.

1 In a large, heavy pot, combine the peas, ham, onion, celery, bell pepper, bay leaf, sage, and pepper, add the water, and stir. Bring to a boil, reduce the heat to a gentle simmer, cover, and cook for 1 hour. Add the ketchup, Worcestershire, and Tabasco and cook till the peas are tender, about another 30 minutes. Add the flour-and-water mixture and stir till the stew is thickened.

2 Serve immediately.

West Virginia Pork, Wild Mushroom, and Walnut Stew

Makes 6 to 8 servings

3 tablespoons butter

One 3-pound boneless pork loin, trimmed of fat and cut into 1-inch cubes

1 large onion, chopped

1 garlic clove, minced

1 pig's foot, dressed

½ teaspoon dried thyme, crumbled

½ teaspoon powdered sage

Salt and freshly ground black pepper to taste

1 quart chicken broth

3 tablespoons all-purpose flour

1 pound fresh chanterelle or oyster mushrooms, stems removed and caps cut in halves or quarters

1 pound shelled walnuts

If West Virginia cannot boast a distinctive regional cuisine equal to those of Creole and Cajun Louisiana and the Carolina and Georgia Lowcountry, the state can at least pride itself on an abundance of exotic wild mushrooms, as well as sweet, oily, and relatively rare black walnuts, which are used to make any number of succulent stews. Pork is by far the most popular meat in this mainly rural state, and a pig's foot added to a stew such as this one creates not only a richer flavor but also a gelatinous texture that is nothing less than beguiling. Although black walnuts do retain more flavor than English walnuts when cooked, if you're unable to find them, the more ordinary variety is almost as good.

1 Preheat the oven to 325°F.

2 In a large ovenproof casserole or pot, melt the butter over moderate heat, add the pork, and brown on all sides. Add the onion and garlic and stir till softened, about 5 minutes, scraping up any bits off the bottom of the casserole. Add the pig's foot, thyme, sage, salt and pepper, and broth, stir, and bring to a boil, skimming any scum off the top. Cover the casserole, place in the oven, and bake for 1 hour.

3 Remove from the oven and spoon off as much fat as possible. In a small bowl, blend about 2 tablespoons of the fat with the flour and whisk the paste into the stew. Add the mushrooms and walnuts, stir, cover, and bake for 30 minutes longer.

4 Remove and discard the pig's foot, return the stew to the oven, and bake till the pork is very tender and the sauce slightly thickened, about 30 minutes.

5 Serve hot.

PIG PICKIN'S

William Byrd, an eighteenth-century planter, diarist, and the founder of Richmond, Virginia, wrote that Virginians ate so much pork that they were "hoggish in their temper and prone to grunt rather than speak."

FROGMORE STEW

MAKES 8 TO 10 SERVINGS

2 gallons water

¼ cup Old Bay seasoning

4 pounds small, whole, new red
   potatoes, rinsed

2 pounds hot smoked link
   sausages (such as kielbasa),
   cut into 1½-inch slices

6 to 8 ears fresh corn on the cob,
   broken into 2 or 3 pieces

4 pounds large fresh shrimp,
   unpeeled

A specialty of St. Helena Island near Hilton Head, South
Carolina, frogmore stew (named after the island's town center)
is one of the oldest and most popular dishes of the Carolina
Lowcountry. Composed basically of shrimp, sausage, new
potatoes, and corn on the cob simmered in a highly seasoned
stock, the stew is traditionally cooked and served outdoors
on picnic tables with plenty of crackers, coleslaw, and beer.
Naturally, it's more fun to heat up a big stockpot outside over
an open fire when the weather's nice and summer corn and new
potatoes are at their best, but I must say I've had just as much
success cooking the stew in a large kettle on top of the stove.
In either case, just make sure you don't overcook either the
corn or the shrimp, and that you spread out lots of newspapers
on the table to catch all the mess.

1 In a large, heavy stockpot or kettle, combine the water and
Old Bay seasoning and bring to a rolling boil. Add the potatoes,
reduce the heat slightly, and cook till almost tender, about
15 minutes. Add the sausage and cook for 5 minutes longer.
Add the corn and cook for about 1 minute. Add the shrimp and
cook till they turn fully pink, about 2 minutes.

2 To serve, remove all the ingredients with a slotted spoon
onto a large serving platter or simply onto a newspaper-lined
picnic table set with paper plates.

Stewed Ham Hocks and Lima Beans

Makes 6 servings

4 slices bacon

1 large onion, chopped

1 celery rib, chopped

½ green bell pepper, seeded and chopped

2 garlic cloves, minced

2 large ripe tomatoes, chopped, juice reserved

1 tablespoon chopped fresh thyme leaves

1 tablespoon chopped fresh sage leaves

1 tablespoon Dijon mustard

Salt and freshly ground black pepper to taste

6 meaty smoked ham hocks, trimmed of all traces of skin

5 cups water

1 pound fresh or frozen lima beans

When shopping for a smoked ham to bake, Southerners will select a shank over a butt any day, just so they can use the hock to make all sorts of soups and stews. (Although any good butcher should be willing to saw off a hock, I keep a hacksaw on hand just for that purpose.) I remember when I literally had to collect hocks in a deep freezer to make a stew such as this one, but today most markets package plenty of hocks, most of which are fully dressed and ready to cook. This stew is also delicious made with black-eyed, crowder, or any variety of field peas (fresh, dried, or frozen); and yes, the fresh herbs do make all the difference.

1 In a large, heavy pot, fry the bacon over moderate heat till crisp. Drain on paper towels and crumble. Add the onion, celery, bell pepper, and garlic to the pot and stir till softened, about 5 minutes. Add the tomatoes and their juice, the thyme, sage, mustard, and salt and pepper, and stir well. Add the ham hocks and water, bring to a boil, and skim any scum from the top. Reduce the heat to low, cover, and simmer for about 2 hours. Add the reserved bacon and the beans, return to a simmer, and cook for about 30 minutes longer.

2 With a slotted spoon, transfer the hocks to a large platter and arrange the beans around them. Serve hot.

Ray's Stewed Pork Chops and Dried Apricots

Makes 4 to 6 servings

3 tablespoons butter

6 thick boned pork loin chops

4 scallions (white parts only), chopped

3 cups dried apricots

1 cup chicken broth

2 tablespoons bourbon

1 cup heavy cream

1 tablespoon fresh lemon juice

The feller in Chattanooga, Tennessee, who gave me this unusual recipe always used pork chops on the bone, insisting (correctly) that the bones add flavor while the chops are baking. If you have a very large casserole, by all means use the whole chops as Ray did. If, on the other hand, you prefer a more manageable (and sophisticated) stew in which the apricots almost disappear as they blend sensuously with the pork cutlets and cream, try my method. For a variation on the dish, dried pears, pitted prunes, apples, and even chunks of fresh pineapple also complement the pork—though you may want to substitute more chicken broth for the cream and cook the dish a little longer to reduce the sauce.

1 Preheat the oven to 325°F.

2 In a heavy, ovenproof 2-quart casserole, melt the butter over moderate heat, add the pork chops, and brown on both sides. Add the scallions and stir till softened, about 2 minutes. Add the apricots and broth, place the casserole in the oven, and bake till the chops are almost tender, 35 to 40 minutes.

3 Remove the casserole from the oven and place over moderate heat. Add the bourbon, ignite, and, when the flames disappear, add the cream and lemon juice and stir well. Reduce the heat to low and stew till the sauce is thickened, 15 to 20 minutes.

4 Serve the chops hot with the apricots and sauce spooned over the top.

Braised Pork, Onion, Bell Pepper, and Pecans

Makes 6 servings

3 tablespoons lard

2 pounds boneless pork loin, trimmed of excess fat and cut into 1-inch cubes

1 medium onion, thinly sliced

1 medium green bell pepper, seeded and thinly sliced

1 garlic clove, minced

2 tablespoons all-purpose flour

1 cup dry white wine

Beef broth as needed

Salt and freshly ground black pepper to taste

1 pound shelled pecans

Were it not for the slight crunch of pecans to contrast with the mellow texture of pork in this simple braise, the recipe would be like a dozen other conventional Southern pork stews that require minimum time and effort. Lard does lend its own special flavor, but if you want to add even more character to the dish, fry two thick slices of applewood- or hickory-smoked bacon, brown the pork cubes in the fat, and add the crumbled bacon to the other ingredients.

1 In a large, heavy saucepan or pot, melt the lard over moderate heat, add the pork, and brown on all sides, stirring. Add the onion, bell pepper, and garlic and stir till the vegetables soften, about 5 minutes. Sprinkle the flour over the top and stir about 1 minute. Add the wine plus enough broth to cover the ingredients and season with salt and pepper. Bring to a low boil, reduce the heat to low, cover, and braise for about 45 minutes. Add the pecans, stir, and braise till the pork is fork-tender and the sauce is thickened, about 30 minutes.

2 Serve hot.

Braised Pork, Apples, and Collard Greens

MAKES 6 SERVINGS

3 pounds collard greens

2 thick slices bacon, cut into pieces

1½ pounds pork shoulder, trimmed of excess fat and cut into 1-inch cubes

1 large onion, thinly sliced

2 Granny Smith apples, peeled, cored, and thinly sliced

2 tablespoons light brown sugar

1 teaspoon ground cinnamon

3 whole cloves

½ cup dry white wine

3 tablespoons cider vinegar

In the South, collard greens (as well as turnip and mustard greens) are usually simply boiled with some form of pork and served as a side dish, but when they're included in a spicy pork and apple stew such as this one, the greens take on a subtlety that even the most finicky Yankee is bound to appreciate. In truth, virtually any form of pork (fresh ham, boneless country-style ribs, loin, lean belly) can be used for this braise, but since shoulder has just the right proportion of fat to lean meat, this is the cut I prefer. Do test the pork after it has simmered for about an hour; if it's not fork-tender, cook it till it is (the apples provide adequate liquid for additional braising).

1 Remove and discard the stems and ribs of the greens, place the leaves in a sink or large pot of cold water, and swish around to remove all dirt and grit, repeating the procedure with more fresh water if necessary. Tear the leaves into small pieces and set aside.

2 In a large, heavy casserole or pot, fry the bacon over moderate heat till almost crisp; transfer to a plate. Add the pork to the fat and brown on all sides. Add the onion and stir till softened, about 5 minutes. Add the bacon, the apples, and the collard greens and stir till the apples are softened and the greens have wilted, about 10 minutes. Add the remaining ingredients and stir till well blended. Bring the liquid to a low simmer, cover, and braise till the pork is tender and the greens are very soft, about 1 hour, stirring once.

3 Serve hot.

CHEROKEE PORK CHILI

¼ cup corn oil

2 pounds pork butt, trimmed
   of excess fat and cut into
   large dice

2 medium onions, finely chopped

1 small green bell pepper, seeded
   and finely chopped

3 garlic cloves, minced

2 tablespoons chili powder

1 teaspoon ground cumin

1 teaspoon dried oregano,
   crumbled

Salt and freshly ground black
   pepper to taste

Tabasco sauce to taste

3 large ripe tomatoes, peeled
   and chopped

1 cup beef broth

1 cup water

One 12-ounce can corn kernels,
   drained (optional)

Just like American Indians in the Southwest, the Cherokees in North Carolina's Blue Ridge Mountains are much more likely to make their stews, casseroles, and chilis with pork rather than beef—often enhanced by the addition of corn. Although pork butt is ideal for this particular style of chili, you can also use either part of a large fresh ham or about eight meaty country-style spareribs cut from the bones. Up on the Cherokee reservation, this chili would be served with maybe a large salad of dandelion greens or shredded cabbage and either hoecakes or skillet cornbread.

1 In a large, heavy pot, heat the oil over moderate heat, add the pork, and brown on all sides. Add the onions, bell pepper, and garlic and stir till lightly browned, about 8 minutes. Sprinkle the chili powder, cumin, and oregano over the pork and vegetables and stir well. Add the salt and pepper and Tabasco, and continue stirring for 2 minutes. Add the tomatoes, broth, and water and stir well. Bring the liquid to a boil, reduce the heat to a gentle simmer, cover, and cook for 1 hour. Add the corn if desired, stir well, return the chili to a simmer, and cook till the chili has the desired consistency, about 30 minutes, adding a little more broth or water if necessary.

2 Serve hot in soup bowls.

LEAH'S PORK CHOPS
AND CORNBREAD CASSEROLE

MAKES 6 TO 8 SERVINGS

6 tablespoons (¾ stick) butter

8 loin pork chops, about ½ inch thick, trimmed of excess fat

1 medium onion, chopped

1 celery rib, chopped

1 small green bell pepper, seeded and chopped

1 garlic clove, minced

2 cups crumbled leftover cornbread

1 large egg, beaten

One 16-ounce can whole tomatoes with juice, cut up

One 8-ounce can tomato sauce

1 teaspoon light brown sugar

¼ teaspoon chili powder

Salt and freshly ground black pepper to taste

Tabasco sauce to taste

At Dooky Chase restaurant in New Orleans, Leah Chase has made an art of transforming ordinary soul food into creative masterpieces, and never is she more adept than when dealing with various forms of pork. If you've had the impression, for example, that Southern pork chops are always either fried or baked with one barbecue sauce after another, wait till you try this layered casserole that includes cornbread mixed with egg and vegetables.

1 In a large, heavy skillet, melt 3 tablespoons of the butter over moderate heat, brown half the pork chops on both sides, and transfer to a plate. Brown the remaining chops and transfer to the plate. Melt the remaining 3 tablespoons of butter in the skillet, add the onion, celery, bell pepper, and garlic, stir for about 5 minutes, and remove from the heat.

2 Preheat the oven to 350°F. Butter a 3- to 3½-quart casserole and set aside.

3 In a large bowl, combine the cornbread, egg, and half the sautéed vegetable mixture till well blended; set aside.

4 Add the tomatoes, tomato sauce, brown sugar, and chili powder to the remaining vegetables in the skillet, season with salt and pepper and Tabasco, mix well, and simmer over moderate heat till the sauce is nicely thickened, about 10 minutes. Remove from the heat.

5 Arrange 4 of the pork chops in the prepared casserole and spread the cornbread mixture evenly over the top. Arrange the remaining chops over the top, scrape the sauce evenly over the chops, cover, and bake till the chops are very tender, about 1 hour.

6 Serve hot.

PIG PICKIN'S

"Side meat" refers to pork fatback, salt pork, sowbell, middlings, white meat, streak-o'-lean, white bacon, and other seasoning meats used to enhance boiled greens, peas, beans, and cabbage.

Sausage and Leek Buffet Casserole

Makes 8 servings as
a buffet dish, 4 to 6
servings as a main course

1 pound bulk pork sausage

10 large leeks (3 to 3½ pounds)

3 tablespoons butter

2 garlic cloves, minced

2 cups heavy cream

Large pinch of ground nutmeg

Salt and freshly ground black
pepper to taste

⅓ cup dry bread crumbs

4 tablespoons (½ stick) butter,
melted

Elaborate buffet casseroles (for wedding, birthday, graduation, and funeral receptions) have long been a legacy of the Southern kitchen, and with more than a smidgeon of filial prejudice, I often proclaim this masterpiece created by my enterprising mother to be at least one of the queens of casseroles. Not that it's at all difficult to assemble and bake; it's simply one of the most mouthwatering dishes you'll ever serve—on buffets or at the table. And, best of all, the basic casserole can be made well in advance and, without the bread crumbs and melted butter, frozen for future needs. Also, if you want a more dramatic presentation, you can substitute about a pound of small, browned link sausages for the bulk style. No wonder Mother calls this her "Casserole Supreme."

1 In a large, heavy skillet, break up the sausage, fry over moderate heat till browned, and drain on paper towels.

2 While the sausage is frying, trim the leeks of all but about 2 inches of green tops, slice the whites down the middle almost to the root ends, and rinse the layers thoroughly under cold running water to remove all grit. Slice the leeks crosswise into 2-inch pieces.

3 Preheat the oven to 425°F. Butter a large, shallow baking dish and set aside.

4 In a large, heavy saucepan, heat the 3 tablespoons of butter over moderate heat, add the garlic, and stir for 1 minute. Add the leeks and cook, stirring till they have wilted, about 5 minutes. Add the cream and nutmeg, season with salt and pepper, and cook till the leeks are tender, 12 to 15 minutes.

5 Scrape the mixture into the prepared baking dish and spoon the sausage over the top. Sprinkle the bread crumbs on top, drizzle the melted butter evenly over the crumbs, and bake till golden, about 20 minutes.

6 Serve hot.

SHERRIED HAM AND SQUASH CASSEROLE

2 tablespoons butter

2 medium onions, chopped

2 garlic cloves, minced

2 teaspoons minced fresh sage leaves, or ½ teaspoon dried, crumbled

2½ pounds smoked ham, cut into 1½-inch pieces

1½ pounds (about 4 medium) yellow squash, ends trimmed and cut into ½-inch-thick rounds

Salt and freshly ground black pepper to taste

2 tablespoons dry sherry

1½ to 2 cups chicken broth, as needed

1 cup dry bread crumbs

2 tablespoons butter, melted

Many Southern hotels and country clubs are known for the elegant casseroles featured in their dining rooms or at special social receptions, and none is more memorable for me than this one that was served in individual earthenware dishes at the old Fort Sumpter Hotel in Charleston, South Carolina. While you can indeed layer the ingredients in small, separate casseroles intended as an unusual first course, I prefer to prepare and serve the dish as a main course with a colorful congealed salad and tiny beaten biscuits. Do note that this casserole should not be at all soupy, so add the extra broth at the end only if the casserole seems too dry.

1 Preheat the oven to 325°F. Butter a 2- to 2½-quart casserole and set aside.

2 In a skillet, melt the 2 tablespoons butter over moderate heat, add the onions, garlic, and sage, and stir till softened, about 5 minutes.

3 Arrange half the ham and half the onion mixture on the bottom of the prepared casserole, layer half the squash evenly over the top, season with salt and pepper, and drizzle half the sherry over the top. Repeat with the remaining ham and onion mixture, squash, salt and pepper, and sherry. Pour 1½ cups of the broth over the top, cover the casserole, and bake for 1 hour, adding a little more broth if the casserole seems too dry.

4 Sprinkle the bread crumbs over the top, drizzle the melted butter evenly over the crumbs, and bake till golden, about 15 minutes.

5 Serve hot.

PIG PICKIN'S

In Greenville, South Carolina, members of the Short Snout Society gather every year for their Swine Ball and dress up in pig costumes.

Florida Rock Shrimp and Bacon Casserole

MAKES 4 SERVINGS

6 to 8 slices lean applewood-
smoked bacon

1½ cups half-and-half

½ cup bottled clam juice

2 tablespoons dry sherry

2½ cups crumbled soda crackers

12 tablespoons (1½ sticks)
butter, melted

Salt and freshly ground black
pepper to taste

Tabasco sauce to taste

1½ pounds fresh rock shrimp,
shelled and deveined

Tasting like a cross between shrimp and lobster, the rock shrimp harvested off Florida's Atlantic and Gulf coasts are now processed with special equipment to remove the hard shells and sand veins and are available not only throughout Florida but in the finest seafood markets elsewhere. Of course, the rich, delectable shrimp are relished locally in chowders, omelettes, salads, and pies, but never did I appreciate them more than when they were combined with premium bacon and sherry in this creamy casserole served one day in Tampa. Remember that rock shrimp are very perishable and should be used within a day of purchase. The casserole is also delicious made with ordinary white or brown fresh shrimp. Note: four individual ramekins or crocks could be used in place of a casserole for this recipe.

1 Preheat the oven to 350°F. Butter a 1½-quart casserole and set aside.

2 In a skillet, fry the bacon over moderate heat till almost crisp. Drain on paper towels and chop coarsely.

3 In a bowl, combine the half-and-half, clam juice, and sherry, stir well, and set aside. In another bowl, combine the cracker crumbs and butter, season with salt and pepper and Tabasco, and set aside.

4 Sprinkle about a third of the crumbs over the bottom of the prepared casserole, arrange half the shrimp on top, sprinkle half the bacon over the shrimp, and pour half the half-and-half mixture over the top. Add another third of the crumbs, arrange the remaining shrimp on top, sprinkle on the remaining bacon, pour on the remaining half-and-half mixture, and top with the remaining crumbs. Bake till bubbly and lightly browned, about 35 minutes.

5 Serve piping hot.

Pork, Prune, and Orange Casserole

¼ pound pitted dried prunes

1 lemon, peel removed and cut into strips, juice strained

¼ cup all-purpose flour

Salt and freshly ground black pepper to taste

1 pound boneless pork loin, trimmed of excess fat and cut into 1-inch cubes

1 tablespoon lard

1 large orange, peeled, white pith removed and sections separated

Prunes and oranges are married with pork in cuisines around the world, but only in the American South have I ever seen the three components commonly used together in a casserole. I learned the technique of substituting the prune soaking liquid for beef or chicken broth from a lady in Roanoke, Virginia, who knows a thing or two about cooking, and, believe me, it makes all the difference in the overall flavor of the dish. Be sure to stew the prunes initially till they're just tender and not in the least mushy.

1 Place the prunes and lemon peel in a small saucepan with just enough water to cover, bring to a simmer, and stew them till tender, about 20 minutes. Strain and reserve the cooking liquid and discard the lemon peel.

2 On a plate, combine the flour and salt and pepper and mix till well blended. Coat the pork cubes with the flour mixture, tapping off and reserving the excess flour.

3 Preheat the oven to 350°F. Grease a 1½-quart casserole or baking dish and set aside.

4 In a medium skillet, melt the lard over moderate heat, add the pork, brown on all sides, and arrange the cubes in the prepared casserole. Layer the prunes over the pork, then layer the orange sections over the prunes. Add the reserved flour to the skillet over moderate heat and stir briefly. Add about 1¼ cups of the reserved prune cooking liquid to the skillet, bring to a boil, stirring, and pour over the orange sections in the casserole. Drizzle the lemon juice over the top, cover the casserole, and bake for 1 hour.

5 Serve hot directly from the casserole.

PIG PICKIN'S

Pork contains less cholesterol than beef, veal, lamb, and the dark meat of chicken and turkey.

LINKS AND HOMINY CASSEROLE

MAKES 6 SERVINGS

1 tablespoon bacon grease

½ pound small link sausages, pricked with a fork

1 medium onion, finely chopped

1 small fresh green chile pepper, seeded and minced

½ pound extra-sharp cheddar cheese, grated

One 1-pound can hominy, drained

1½ cups milk

2 large eggs, beaten

¼ cup chopped fresh parsley leaves

Salt and freshly ground black pepper to taste

1½ cups fresh bread crumbs

2 tablespoons butter, melted

Hominy, which is dried corn kernels from which the hull and germ have been removed, is either ground for grits or cornmeal in the South or used whole in any number of beloved casseroles. One of the most popular rural Southern dishes is "hogs and hominy," a simple mixture of whole hominy and any form of fried pork, but when a more sophisticated preparation is needed for a breakfast or brunch buffet, the corn is paired with sausage, bacon, or ham for a stylish casserole such as this one. For a less dramatic presentation, you can also use about ¾ pound of bulk sausage that is crumbled, fried, and incorporated into the hominy mixture.

1 In a medium skillet, heat the bacon grease over moderate heat, add the sausages, and brown lightly on all sides. Drain on paper towels and reserve. Add the onion and chile pepper to the skillet and stir till softened, about 5 minutes.

2 Preheat the oven to 350°F. Grease a 2-quart casserole and set aside.

3 In a large bowl, combine half the cheese, the hominy, milk, eggs, parsley, salt and pepper, and 1 cup of the bread crumbs and stir till well blended. Scrape the mixture into the prepared casserole and arrange the sausages over the top. In a small bowl, combine the remaining cheese and bread crumbs, toss, and scatter over the sausages. Drizzle the butter over the top and bake till golden, about 45 minutes.

4 Serve hot directly from the casserole.

Chicken, Sausage, and Mushroom Supreme

Makes 6 to 8 servings

One 3-pound chicken, cooked and meat diced

1 pound bulk pork sausage, cooked

One 6-ounce package Uncle Ben's long grain and wild rice, cooked

One 10¾-ounce can cream of mushroom soup

One 6-ounce jar sliced mushrooms with juice

If casseroles are one of the major foundations of Southern cookery, it's only fair to include a typical, unedited recipe (verbatim) given me by an elegant lady in Macon, Georgia, known for the casseroles she serves routinely at fancy bridge parties, wedding receptions, weekend brunches, and, of course, bereavement buffets. Patsy is way too busy to fool with recipe details, but if you must have the particulars, she's talking about a three-pound chicken that is cut up, simmered in water for about one hour, skinned and boned, and then diced; bulk sausage (preferably "whole-hog") broken up and fried till nicely browned; six ounces of long-grain and wild rice cooked according to package directions; and, yes, bottled mushrooms and a 10¾-ounce can of condensed soup. Naturally, salt and pepper would be added, the mixture would be baked in a very handsome porcelain two-quart casserole, and it should feed about six hungry guests. And how does the "supreme" taste? Be assured there won't be a morsel left in the casserole.

1 Preheat the oven to 350°F.

2 Mix together the chicken meat, cooked sausage, cooked rice, cream of mushroom soup, and mushrooms and their juice in a 2-quart baking dish or casserole and bake for 45 minutes.

3 Serve hot directly from the casserole.

COMPANY HAM AND TURKEY BAKE

**MAKES AT LEAST
12 SERVINGS**

6 tablespoons (¾ stick) butter

2 medium onions, chopped

6 tablespoons all-purpose flour

1 teaspoon salt

½ teaspoon freshly ground
black pepper

1½ cups milk

½ pound fresh mushrooms, sliced

5 tablespoons dry sherry

4 cups chopped cooked turkey

3 cups chopped cooked ham

Two 5-ounce cans water
chestnuts, drained and sliced

1 cup shredded Swiss cheese

2 cups fresh bread crumbs

4 tablespoons (½ stick) butter,
melted

There's hardly a meat or bird that Southerners can't turn into one casserole or another, and what better way to deal with leftover holiday ham and turkey than to combine the two in an elaborate buffet dish intended to serve a sizeable crowd. Of course, baked or roasted fresh ham, pork loin or shoulder, chicken, or even goose could also be used, and sharp cheddar cheese or grated Parmesan would be just as appropriate as the Swiss. For a more intimate gathering of family or friends, simply halve this recipe, choose a smaller baking dish, and serve the casserole with a tart green salad and maybe some yeast rolls. Or, better yet, make the entire recipe, scrape part of the mixture into another small casserole or baking dish (without the buttered bread crumbs), and freeze it for another occasion.

1 Preheat the oven to 400°F. Butter a large, shallow baking dish or casserole and set aside.

2 In a large, heavy skillet, melt 4 tablespoons of the butter over moderate heat, add the onions, and stir till softened, about 5 minutes. Sprinkle the flour, salt, and pepper over the onions and stir for 2 minutes. Reduce the heat to low and gradually add the milk, stirring constantly till the mixture is thickened and smooth. Remove the pan from the heat.

3 In a small skillet, melt the remaining 2 tablespoons of butter over moderate heat, add the mushrooms, and stir till golden, 5 to 7 minutes. Add the mushrooms to the milk mixture, add the sherry, turkey, ham, and water chestnuts, and stir till well blended. Spoon the mixture into the prepared baking dish and sprinkle the cheese evenly over the top. In a small bowl, combine the bread crumbs and melted butter, toss well, spoon the mixture over the cheese, and bake till the casserole is lightly browned, about 35 minutes.

4 Serve hot.

CREAMED FRESH HAM AND TURNIP HOTPOT

MAKES 4 SERVINGS

4 thick slices bacon, coarsely chopped

1 pound fresh ham, cut into 1-inch cubes

2 pounds white turnips (about 6), peeled and cut into 1-inch pieces

1 medium onion, chopped

¼ teaspoon powdered sage

Salt and freshly ground black pepper to taste

1 cup half-and-half

1 cup sour cream

2 teaspoons Dijon mustard

In the South, a hotpot is something between a stew and a casserole; the ingredients always include at least two forms of pork (in some regions, pigs' ears and feet are favored); and the dish may well be topped with buttered bread crumbs. As for the tangy sauce in this creamy version, a true Southern touch would be to add a tablespoon or so of mayonnaise to the half-and-half and sour cream. Simple and relatively quick to make, the hotpot is ideal for a fall Sunday supper, maybe served with spiced baked apples and hot corn sticks.

1 Preheat the oven to 350°F.

2 In a large, ovenproof casserole, fry the bacon over moderate heat till almost crisp, add the ham, turnips, and onion, and stir for about 8 minutes. Add the sage and salt and pepper, stir, cover the casserole, and bake till the turnips are almost tender, about 45 minutes.

3 In a bowl, whisk together the half-and-half, sour cream, and mustard till well blended, scrape the mixture over the ham and turnips, stir well, and continue baking till the ham is very tender, 15 to 20 minutes.

4 Serve hot.

Spicy Breakfast Sausage and Cheese Bake

Makes 4 servings

1 pound bulk pork sausage

12 large eggs

¾ cup milk

Salt and freshly ground black pepper to taste

One 4-ounce can green chile peppers, drained and chopped

¼ pound sharp cheddar cheese, grated

Southerners love a good breakfast casserole as a change from ordinary eggs with fried bacon, sausage, or country ham, and nothing fits the bill better than this simple sausage bake spiked with a few green chile peppers (or, in the Georgia Lowcountry, local bird's-eye hot red peppers). Double the recipe and use a larger baking dish or casserole, and you'll have a perfect addition to a breakfast or brunch buffet. Do be sure that the sausage is top quality and relatively lean, and that the cheddar is sharp—if not extra sharp.

1 Preheat the oven to 325°F. Grease a 1½-quart baking dish or casserole and set aside.

2 In a large skillet, break up the sausage, fry over moderate heat till fully cooked, and drain on paper towels.

3 In a bowl, whisk together the eggs, milk, and salt and pepper till well blended.

4 Scatter the sausage over the bottom of the prepared baking dish, pour the egg mixture over the sausage, sprinkle the chiles and cheese evenly over the top, and bake till golden, 20 to 25 minutes.

5 Serve piping hot.

COUNTRY SAUSAGE, APPLE, AND BEAN STRATA

¼ cup molasses

3 tablespoons Dijon mustard

2 tablespoon fresh lemon juice

2 teaspoons Worcestershire sauce

Salt and freshly ground black
    pepper to taste

1 pound small pork link sausages

Two 1-pound cans high-grade
    baked beans

2 medium Granny Smith apples,
    peeled, cored, and thinly sliced

Once served for brunch at a friend's lakeside retreat north of Montgomery, Alabama, this has to be one of the most memorable stratas I've ever eaten. Some might call it just doctored baked beans, but when those beans are layered with tart apples, top-quality pork sausages, and a beguiling molasses and mustard mixture, I can almost promise there won't be a bean left in the casserole. Serve the strata with no more than a big bowl of fresh fruit and maybe a basket of plain soda crackers.

1 Preheat the oven to 350°F. Grease a 2-quart casserole or baking dish and set aside.

2 In a bowl, combine the molasses, mustard, lemon juice, Worcestershire, and salt and pepper, whip with a fork till well blended, and set aside.

3 Prick the sausages with a fork or small knife, place in a large skillet over moderate heat, brown on all sides, and drain on paper towels.

4 Spoon half the beans into the prepared casserole, spread half the apple slices over the top, and spoon half the molasses mixture over the apples. Repeat with the remaining beans and apples, arrange the sausages over the top, spoon the remaining molasses mixture over the sausages, and bake till the top is nicely glazed, 30 to 40 minutes.

5 Serve piping hot.

Sausage and Mixed Vegetable Strata

Makes 6 servings

1 pound fresh country sausage (page 248) or top-quality commercial bulk pork sausage

4 medium potatoes, peeled and boiled in water to cover till tender

1 cup fresh shelled green peas

1 cup fresh corn kernels (plus any milk scraped from the cobs)

2 medium carrots, scraped and cut into ¼-inch rounds

Salt and freshly ground black pepper to taste

1 cup half-and-half

1 cup fine dry bread crumbs

2 tablespoons butter, melted

This is the style of Southern strata that would be served for lunch in someone's home following Sunday church. Typically, the strata would be layered and chilled in advance, and then, while everybody sips a midday toddy (especially in the case of Episcopalians and Catholics), the dish would be topped with buttered bread crumbs, stuck in the oven, and served directly from the casserole with maybe a congealed salad and sesame crackers. And this is one time when every effort would be made to use fresh country sausage (page 248) and whatever fresh vegetables might be in season.

1 In a skillet, break up the sausage, fry over moderate heat till browned, and drain on paper towels.

2 Preheat the oven to 350°F. Grease a 2-quart casserole and set aside.

3 Cut the potatoes into thin slices, and then arrange alternate layers of potatoes, sausage, peas, corn, and carrots, seasoning each layer with salt and pepper. Pour the half-and-half over all, sprinkle the bread crumbs over the top, drizzle the butter evenly over the crumbs, and bake till golden brown, 30 to 40 minutes.

4 Serve hot.

Slab Bacon and Mushroom Strata

4 to 5 slices white bread, crusts trimmed

1 pound lean slab bacon, cut into small dice

½ pound mushrooms, finely chopped

1 medium onion, finely chopped

2 teaspoons Dijon mustard

1 cup finely shredded Swiss cheese

2 cups half-and-half

3 large eggs, beaten

1 teaspoon Worcestershire sauce

Salt and freshly ground black pepper to taste

Tabasco sauce to taste

Although nobody knows when, how, or why the term *strata* (referring to a layered casserole) became part of the Southern culinary vernacular, it's for sure that hosts and hostesses would be at a loss without these tasty, substantial dishes prepared traditionally for special breakfasts and casual brunches. Although a strata can be made with virtually any ingredients, by far the vast majority always feature some form of bacon, sausage, or ham. For a more exotic version of this particular strata, I might well substitute earthy morels, chanterelles, or other wild mushrooms for the button variety, just as I might use a full-flavored English Cheshire or French Comté in place of the Swiss cheese.

1 Grease a 2- to 2½-quart casserole, arrange the bread slices across the bottom in a single layer, and set aside.

2 In a large skillet, fry the bacon over moderate heat till almost crisp. Drain on paper towels, and pour off all but about 2 tablespoons of the grease. Add the mushrooms and onion to the skillet and stir till almost golden, about 8 minutes. Return the bacon to the skillet, add the mustard, and stir till well blended.

3 Spoon the bacon mixture evenly over the bread in the casserole and sprinkle the cheese over the top. In a bowl, combine the half-and-half, eggs, and Worcestershire, season with salt and pepper and Tabasco, whisk till well blended, and pour over the cheese. Cover the strata with plastic wrap and refrigerate for at least 2 hours.

4 Preheat the oven to 350°F, then bake the strata 45 to 50 minutes and serve piping hot.

PIG PICKIN'S

The first pigs to enter the United States were 13 animals landed in 1539 near Tampa, Florida, by Hernando de Soto.

PORK, PEA, AND NOODLE STRATA

MAKES 4 SERVINGS

2 thick slices bacon, cut into small cubes

¾ pound pork shoulder, trimmed of excess fat and cut into 1-inch cubes

6 ounces Swiss cheese, shredded

1 cup half-and-half

½ cup mayonnaise

½ pound dried egg noodles

1 cup fresh or thawed frozen green peas

½ cup grated Parmesan cheese

Salt and freshly ground black pepper to taste

1 cup dry bread crumbs

2 tablespoons butter, melted

Confirmed Southerners really don't cook that much bland pasta (still known in most circles as "noodles"), but when they do, the result is likely to be a casserole or strata containing meats, vegetables, cheeses, nuts, and any other ingredients that guarantee plenty of flavor. And, of course, since pig always tops the list of flavorful meats, you can expect a little streaky or Canadian bacon, plus anything from browned cubes of pork butt to boiled country-style ribs cut from the bone to country ham. No Southerner can really explain why, but, much as it might make others cringe, mayonnaise added to the half-and-half in a strata such as this does contribute lots to the sumptuous texture.

1 In a large skillet, fry the bacon till almost crisp. Drain on paper towels. Add the pork to the skillet, brown on all sides, add to the bacon, and set aside.

2 In a bowl, combine the Swiss cheese, half-and-half, and mayonnaise, stir till well blended, and set aside.

3 Preheat the oven to 350°F. Butter a 2-quart casserole or baking dish and set aside.

4 Bring a large pot of salted water to a rolling boil, add the noodles, reduce the heat slightly, and cook till just tender, 8 to 9 minutes. Drain the noodles, transfer to a large bowl, add the peas, half the bacon and pork, and the cheese mixture, and toss till well blended.

5 Arrange the noodles in the prepared casserole, sprinkle the Parmesan over the top, season with salt and pepper, and distribute the remaining bacon and pork over the top. Sprinkle the bread crumbs over the meats, drizzle the butter evenly over the crumbs, and bake till golden, 30 to 35 minutes.

6 Serve hot.

Bacon and Lima Bean Scallop

MAKES 4 SERVINGS

1 pound fresh lima beans
(or one-and-a-half 10-ounce
packages frozen limas, thawed)

6 thick slices bacon, diced

2 medium onions, chopped

2 medium red bell peppers,
seeded and chopped

1 teaspoon dried oregano,
crumbled

Salt and freshly ground black
pepper to taste

Tabasco sauce to taste

1 cup half-and-half

1 cup fine cracker crumbs

3 tablespoons butter, melted

In Southern parlance, a scallop is not only a bivalve mollusk but also any casserole that is topped with bread or cracker crumbs before being baked. While this particular scallop might well be served as a side vegetable with a large pork roast, it is also delicious at lunch or a late supper when featured with a big platter of country ham biscuits and small pimento cheese sandwiches. Try to use fresh limas for the scallop, as well as an applewood- or corncob-smoked artisanal bacon—both of which do make a difference in the dish's overall flavor.

1 Preheat the oven to 350°F. Butter a 1½-quart baking dish and set aside.

2 Place the limas in a saucepan with enough water to cover, bring to a boil, reduce the heat to low, cover, and cook till barely tender, about 8 minutes (5 minutes for frozen beans). Drain and set aside.

3 In a large skillet, fry the bacon over moderate heat till almost crisp. Drain on paper towels and pour off all but about 2 tablespoons of the grease. Add the onions and bell peppers to the skillet and stir till slightly golden, about 8 minutes.

4 Arrange half the limas over the bottom of the prepared baking dish, arrange half the onions, bell peppers, and bacon over the top, and season with half the oregano plus salt and pepper and Tabasco. Repeat with the remaining limas, onions, bell peppers, bacon, and seasonings, then pour the half-and-half over the top. Sprinkle the cracker crumbs evenly over the top, drizzle the butter over the crumbs, and bake till golden, 30 to 35 minutes.

5 Serve hot directly from the baking dish.

Chops, Cutlets, and Steaks

Baked Pork Chops with Hominy and Orange

Baked Pork Chops with Spiced Applesauce Glaze

Double Pork Chops Stuffed with Blue Cheese and Mushrooms

Baked Double Pork Chops Stuffed with Oysters

Baked Apple- and Corn-Stuffed Pork Chops

Curried Pork Chops with Sticky Peaches

Braised Pork Chops with Spiced Apricot Glaze

Betty Jane's Braised Pork Chops with Port Gravy

Bill Neal's Braised Pork Chops with Limas and Whole Garlic

Smoked Pork Chops and Lentils

Creamed Pork Chops Stuffed with Wild Mushrooms

Maw Maw's Mustard Pork Chops and Dumplings in Cider

Broiled Pork Chops with Peachy Cheese Crust

Broiled Marinated Center-Cut Pork Chops

Creamed Pork Cutlets with Vidalia Onions and Potatoes

Breaded Pork Cutlets with Lemon and Capers

Mississippi Smothered Pork Cutlets

Glazed Pork Cutlets with Peach-Mango Chutney

Deep-Fried Stuffed Pork Cutlets

Herbed Pork Steaks with Honey-Mustard Sauce

Pork Steaks with Vermouth, Corn, and Raisins

Creole Pork Steaks

Baked Pork Chops with Hominy and Orange

4 thick pork loin or rib chops

½ cup all-purpose flour

1 large onion, sliced

1 garlic clove, minced

2 cups canned hominy, drained

2 oranges, peeled, sectioned, seeded, and white pith removed

1 teaspoon ground cinnamon

Salt and freshly ground black pepper to taste

½ cup orange juice

Hominy, which is dried corn kernels from which the hull and germ have been removed, is a Southern staple that has been paired with all types of pig ever since American Indians introduced it to the first colonists. Nothing is more popular in rural areas of the Deep South than fried pork chops or belly with a side dish of boiled and buttered hominy grits (dried hominy ground to meal), but things become more sophisticated in the Middle Atlantic states, where you're more likely to find the chops slowly baked with a spicy combination of hominy, onions, and some form of citrus. Canned hominy is now available in all major grocery stores.

1 Preheat the oven to 350°F. Grease a shallow 1½-quart baking dish and set aside.

2 Trim the fat off the pork chops and render it in a large, heavy skillet over moderate heat, discarding the rendered pieces. On a plate, dredge the chops in the flour, tapping off the excess, brown them on both sides in the fat, and transfer to a plate. Add the onion and garlic to the skillet, stir till softened, about 5 minutes, and remove from the heat.

3 Arrange the chops in the bottom of the prepared baking dish and spoon the onions evenly over the top. Pour the hominy evenly over the top, arrange the orange sections over the hominy, sprinkle the cinnamon over the top, and season with salt and pepper. Add the orange juice, cover, and bake till the chops are very tender, about 1¼ hours.

4 Serve hot directly from the baking dish.

 ## PIG PICKIN'S

Wild hogs, highly dangerous and destructive,
are hunted for barbecues throughout the
Carolinas, Louisiana, and Florida, and the
largest on record is a 565-pounder shot
near Coward, South Carolina, in 1996.

Baked Pork Chops with Spiced Applesauce Glaze

2 cups applesauce (not chunky)

¼ cup firmly packed light brown sugar

¼ teaspoon ground cinnamon

Pinch of ground cloves

3 tablespoons all-purpose flour

1 teaspoon dry mustard

Salt and freshly ground black pepper to taste

6 pork loin or rib chops, about 1 inch thick

The natural affinity between the pig and the apple is respected in kitchens all over the country, but only in the South do cooks routinely bake pork chops, cutlets, steaks, country-style ribs, and even ham glazed with spicy applesauce—homemade or bottled. You can also braise these glazed chops for about an hour in a half cup of either apple or orange juice, in which case they need basting only once or twice to retain their moistness.

1 Preheat the oven to 325°F.

2 In a bowl, combine the applesauce, brown sugar, cinnamon, and cloves, stir till well blended, and set aside.

3 On a plate, combine the flour, mustard, and salt and pepper and mix till well blended. Dust the pork chops in the flour mixture, then spread both sides of each with the applesauce glaze. Arrange the chops on the rack of a broiling pan and bake till golden brown, about 1 hour, turning once.

4 Serve hot.

Double Pork Chops Stuffed with Blue Cheese and Mushrooms

MAKES 6 SERVINGS

6 pork loin chops, about 1¼ inches thick

Salt and freshly ground black pepper to taste

2 tablespoons butter

1 small onion, finely chopped

3 ounces mushrooms, finely chopped

¼ pound blue cheese, crumbled

¾ cup fine dry bread crumbs

½ cup water

Inspired by the rich, smooth, complex Clemson Blue Cheese produced in small quantities on the campus of Clemson University in Clemson, South Carolina, these stuffed pork chops are probably the most luscious you'll ever taste. Any quality blue cheese (such as Maytag) can be substituted for the hard-to-find Clemson, but be sure to secure the pocket openings of the chops as tightly as possible so the stuffing doesn't ooze out during the baking. I like to serve these chops with crisp roasted potato wedges and minted green peas.

1 Preheat the oven to 350°F.

2 With a sharp paring knife, cut a deep pocket in the fat side of each chop, season with salt and pepper, and set aside.

3 In a small skillet, melt the butter over moderate heat, add the onion and mushrooms, and stir till softened, about 5 minutes. Remove from the heat, add the cheese and bread crumbs, and stir till the cheese begins to melt and the mixture is soft, returning the pan to the heat momentarily if necessary.

4 Stuff the chops with equal amounts of the cheese mixture and secure the openings with small metal skewers or heavy toothpicks. Arrange the chops in a shallow 2-quart baking dish, add the water around the sides, cover, and bake till golden brown, about 1 hour, turning once.

5 Serve hot.

BAKED DOUBLE PORK CHOPS STUFFED WITH OYSTERS

6 pork loin chops, about 1¼ inches thick

1 cup coarsely chopped fresh oysters, liquor reserved

1 scallion (white part only), minced

2 tablespoons bread crumbs

Salt and freshly ground black pepper to taste

Tabasco sauce to taste

2 tablespoons butter

Bottled clam juice as needed

It's never unusual in Florida and the other Southern Gulf states to find roasted game birds stuffed with various local oysters, but throughout the Carolinas, Virginia, Maryland, and other pig-breeding states, cooks are just as likely to stuff oysters into thick double pork chops or between pounded cutlets that are slowly baked just till the meat is tender and the stuffing still moist and luscious. For this dish to come out right, you need loin chops that are at least 1¼ inches thick, so if you can't find them in the supermarket case, ask the butcher to cut them special. Chops such as these are traditionally served with buttered rice.

1 Preheat the oven to 350°F.

2 Using a sharp paring knife, carefully cut a deep pocket in the fatty side of each pork chop. In a small bowl, combine the chopped oysters, scallion, bread crumbs, salt and pepper, and Tabasco and stir till well blended. Stuff equal amounts of the mixture into the pockets of the chops and secure the openings with heavy toothpicks.

3 In a large, heavy skillet, melt the butter over moderate heat, add the chops, and brown on each side. Transfer the chops to a large, shallow roasting pan, season the tops with salt and pepper, add the reserved oyster liquor plus 1 or 2 tablespoons of clam juice if necessary to cover the bottom of the pan, cover, and bake till the chops are tender, about 1 hour.

4 Serve hot.

Baked Apple- and Corn-Stuffed Pork Chops

Makes 4 servings

4 pork rib chops, about 1½ inches thick, excess fat trimmed and reserved

2 tablespoons butter

1 small onion, minced

½ cup fresh or thawed frozen corn kernels

½ cup finely chopped peeled and cored apple

1 cup dry bread crumbs

⅛ teaspoon powdered sage

Salt and freshly ground black pepper to taste

¼ cup all-purpose flour

½ cup water

The reason for using rib instead of loin chops for this impressive dish is that the extra internal fat in the meat serves to baste the stuffing and keep it as moist as possible. For added flavor, apple cider, orange juice, chicken broth, or even dry white wine can be substituted for the water, in which case a little basting during the final 15 minutes of baking won't hurt. These chops are just as delicious stuffed with corn and chopped pears, and feel free to experiment with different herbs.

1 With a sharp paring knife, cut a wide slit from the bone side of the chops almost to the fat side to form a deep pocket.

2 In a large, heavy skillet, melt the butter over low heat, add the onion, and stir for 2 minutes. Add the corn, apple, bread crumbs, sage, and salt and pepper and stir till the apple releases its juices and the mixture is moistened, about 10 minutes. With a spoon, stuff the pocket of each chop with equal amounts of the mixture and secure the openings with small metal skewers or heavy toothpicks.

3 Preheat the oven to 325°F.

4 Render the reserved pork fat in the skillet over moderate heat and discard the pieces. Dredge the stuffed chops in the flour, then brown them on both sides in the fat. Transfer the chops to a shallow baking dish or casserole, season with salt and pepper, add the water around the sides, cover, and bake for 1 hour. Uncover and bake for about 15 minutes longer or till the meat is slightly browned.

5 Serve hot.

CURRIED PORK CHOPS WITH STICKY PEACHES

1 tablespoon curry powder

1 tablespoon light brown sugar

¼ teaspoon ground allspice

Salt and freshly ground black
   pepper to taste

1 tablespoon peanut oil

4 pork loin or rib chops, about
   ¾ inch thick, trimmed of
   excess fat

½ cup red currant jelly, melted

⅔ cup orange juice

4 large, ripe peaches, peeled,
   pitted, and cut in half

The combination of pork and peaches is as Southern as that of sweet potatoes and pecans, and when you curry the meat, glaze it along with a few ripe peaches with a little jelly, and bake the two together in orange juice, the flavor sensation is unique. Chops are the most practical cut of pork for this dish, but you could also use cutlets, steaks, or country-style ribs. Of course, you might also broil or grill the glazed meat and peaches, but be warned that unless the chops are at least ¾ inch thick and cooked slowly to retain moisture inside, they risk being tough, dry, and stringy.

1 Preheat the oven to 350°F.

2 In a cup, combine the curry powder, brown sugar, allspice, salt and pepper, and oil and stir till well blended. Using your hands, rub both sides of the pork chops with the curry mixture, and brush one side of the chops with a little jelly. Arrange the chops brushed-side-up in a large baking dish, pour the orange juice around the chops, cover, and bake for 30 minutes.

3 Meanwhile, brush the cut sides of the peach halves with a little jelly and set aside.

4 Turn the chops over in the dish, brush with a little more jelly, and bake for 15 minutes longer. Arrange the peach halves brushed-side-up around the chops and bake till the chops and peaches are nicely glazed, about 15 minutes, basting once with the cooking liquid.

5 To serve, arrange the hot chops and peaches on a platter and spoon a little of the glazing liquid over the top.

BRAISED PORK CHOPS WITH SPICED APRICOT GLAZE

MAKES 6 SERVINGS

2 tablespoons butter

6 pork loin chops, trimmed of excess fat

½ cup orange juice

¼ cup firmly packed light brown sugar

2 teaspoons cornstarch

¼ teaspoon ground allspice

⅛ teaspoon ground cloves

3 teaspoons minced lemon rind

Salt and freshly ground black pepper to taste

6 ripe apricots, peeled, pitted, and finely chopped

Braising is by far the preferred way to ensure that pork chops remain moist and tender, and, in the South, orange juice is not only the most popular braising liquid but also the base for numerous fruit glazes used to enhance chops, steaks, country-style ribs, and baked hams. If fresh apricots are not available, substitute a couple of large peaches, mangoes, or eating apples. For added flavor in this dish, you can also lightly brown the glazed pork chops under the broiler, so long as you're careful not to dry them out or burn them.

1 In a large, heavy stainless-steel or enameled skillet, melt the butter over moderate heat, arrange the pork chops in the pan, and brown well on both sides. Add half the orange juice, reduce the heat to low, cover, and braise slowly till the chops are tender but still moist inside, about 45 minutes, adding a little more orange juice if necessary.

2 Meanwhile, combine the brown sugar, cornstarch, allspice, cloves, lemon rind, and salt and pepper in a small saucepan and stir till well blended. Add the remaining orange juice and stir over low heat till smooth, about 5 minutes. Add the apricots, return to a simmer, and cook till the apricots are soft and well incorporated into the glaze, about 15 minutes.

3 To serve, arrange the hot pork chops on serving plates and spoon apricot glaze over the top.

Betty Jane's Braised Pork Chops with Port Gravy

MAKES 4 SERVINGS

½ cup all-purpose flour

1 teaspoon fresh rosemary leaves, minced

Salt and freshly ground black pepper to taste

4 pork loin chops, about ¾ inch thick

3 tablespoons butter

1 cup beef broth

¼ cup port wine

Sprigs of watercress for garnish

The lady in Richmond, Virginia, who prided herself on these rather fancy pork chops believed firmly that they hark back to colonial days, when so much pork was served with either a Madeira or port wine gravy. Betty Jane flavored the chops with fresh rosemary or sage leaves, but she warned (correctly) that overdoing the herbs by as little as ½ teaspoon could virtually destroy the succulent flavor of both the meat and gravy. This is one time when a dried herb should not be substituted for the fresh. After about 45 minutes of braising, prick the chops with a small knife to see if they're already tender but still moist inside.

1 On a plate, combine and mix together the flour, rosemary, and salt and pepper; dredge the pork chops in the mixture, shaking off excess flour, and place the chops on another plate.

2 In a large, heavy skillet, melt 2 tablespoons of the butter over moderate heat, add the chops, and brown on both sides. Add the broth, reduce the heat to low, cover, and simmer till the chops are very tender, about 1 hour.

3 Transfer the chops to a serving platter, increase the heat under the skillet to moderate, add the port, and reduce the liquid till nicely thickened, 3 to 5 minutes. Add the remaining tablespoon of butter, swirl till melted and well incorporated, and spoon the gravy over the chops.

4 Serve the hot chops garnished with sprigs of watercress.

Bill Neal's Braised Pork Chops with Limas and Whole Garlic

3 tablespoons olive oil

4 pork loin chops, about 1 inch thick

1 large onion, chopped

½ cup dry vermouth

1½ cups chicken broth

24 whole garlic cloves, papery skins removed but not peeled

4 sprigs fresh thyme

4 sprigs fresh rosemary

Salt and freshly ground black pepper to taste

One 10-ounce package thawed frozen lima beans

2 tablespoons all-purpose flour dissolved in 2 tablespoons cold water

Before his untimely death, Bill Neal was producing some of the South's most innovative dishes at Crook's Corner restaurant in Chapel Hill, North Carolina, and none was more distinctive than these pork chops braised with handfuls of whole garlic cloves that almost melted as they cooked. Notice that only the outer papery skins of the garlic should be removed, thus retaining the vegetable's natural sweetness by not peeling the cloves and releasing their pungent juices. (The same cooking principle applies to roasted whole garlic cloves, which, when the thin inner skins are left unpeeled, resemble soft, golden, sweet almonds.) Bill served these chops with mounds of buttery corn mush (or polenta, if that term is more comfortable), and I can think of no more appropriate and delicious accompaniment.

1 Preheat the oven to 325°F.

2 In a large, heavy skillet, heat 2 tablespoons of the olive oil over moderate heat, add the pork chops, brown on both sides, and arrange in a 2-quart casserole or large baking pan. Add the remaining oil to the skillet, add the onion, and stir till softened, about 5 minutes. Add the vermouth and let cook till reduced by half. Add the broth, garlic cloves, thyme, rosemary, and salt and pepper and bring to a boil, stirring. Pour the sauce over the chops, cover, and bake for 1 hour.

(continued)

3 Add the lima beans to the casserole, stir to distribute evenly, and bake till the limas are tender, about 20 minutes longer.

4 To thicken the sauce slightly, place the casserole over low heat, add the flour paste, and stir for 5 to 10 minutes.

5 Serve the chops hot surrounded by limas.

SMOKED PORK CHOPS AND LENTILS

¼ cup peanut oil

2 medium onions, finely chopped

1 garlic clove, minced

2½ cups chicken broth

2½ cups dried lentils, rinsed
 and picked over

Salt and freshly ground black
 pepper to taste

6 smoked pork loin or rib chops,
 about 1 inch thick

Chopped parsley leaves for
 garnish

Lentils, of course, will most likely never play the same major role as butter beans and black-eyed peas in Southern cooking, but just in the past few decades, cooks have discovered that no legume goes better with smoked pork than creamy brown lentils cooked slowly till they are just tender (and nothing is worse than mushy lentils). No lentils are marketed fresh, and the commonly available dried ones keep well in an airtight jar for up to about six months. Note also that nothing is more delicious than a side dish of lentils that are boiled for about 45 minutes and topped with crisply browned cubes of salt pork.

1 In a medium baking pan, heat the oil over moderate heat, add the onions and garlic, and stir till softened, about 5 minutes. Add the broth and bring to a boil. Add the lentils, season with salt and pepper, and, when the liquid returns to a boil, add the pork chops and turn to moisten evenly. Reduce the heat to low, cover the pan, and simmer till the chops and lentils are tender but the lentils are not mushy, 45 to 50 minutes.

2 To serve, mound the lentils on a serving platter, arrange the chops around them, and sprinkle parsley over the top.

CREAMED PORK CHOPS STUFFED WITH WILD MUSHROOMS

½ ounce dried cep or morel mushrooms

4 tablespoons (½ stick) butter

1 medium onion, finely chopped

1 small celery rib, finely chopped

1 garlic clove, minced

¼ teaspoon dried sage, crumbled

1 cup dry bread crumbs

1 tablespoon finely chopped fresh parsley leaves

Salt and freshly ground black pepper to taste

6 pork loin chops, about 1½ inch thick

3 tablespoons vegetable oil

2 cups heavy cream

Creamed pork chops can really make a very elegant dish, and when they're stuffed with earthy wild mushrooms, the overall flavor is rich and phenomenal. With easy access now to an array of fresh woodsy mushrooms, Southern cooks are not only using the aromatic fungi like never before in soups and stews but also learning that the highly pungent dried variety of some species (ceps, morels, shiitakes) is actually preferable for stuffings (not to mention less expensive). Another major advantage to using dried wild mushrooms is that the bosky liquid in which they've been soaked makes the perfect base for braising. (Stored in an airtight jar, dried wild mushrooms keep almost indefinitely.)

1 In a small bowl, soak the mushrooms in 1 cup of warm water about 1 hour. Rinse well, pat dry with paper towels, and chop finely. Strain the soaking liquid through cheesecloth into a bowl and set aside.

2 In a large skillet, heat 2 tablespoons of the butter over low heat, add the mushrooms, and stir till very soft, about 15 minutes. Add the remaining butter to the skillet, add the onion, celery, garlic, and sage, and continue stirring for about 5 minutes. Stir in the bread crumbs, parsley, and salt and pepper, mix well, and remove from the heat.

3 With a sharp paring knife, cut a deep pocket in the fat side of each pork chop, stuff each with equal amounts of the mushroom mixture, and secure the edges with small metal skewers or heavy toothpicks.

4 In another large, heavy skillet, heat the oil over moderate heat, add the chops, and brown on both sides. Add the reserved mushroom soaking liquid, bring to a boil, reduce the heat to low, cover, and simmer till the chops are tender, about 1 hour.

5 Transfer the chops to a hot platter, skim fat from the skillet, add the cream, increase the heat to moderate, and cook down, stirring, till slightly thick. Pour the sauce over the chops and serve immediately.

Maw Maw's Mustard Pork Chops and Dumplings in Cider

MAKES 6 SERVINGS

6 boneless pork rib chops, trimmed of excess fat

3 tablespoons grainy mustard

Salt and freshly ground black pepper to taste

2 tablespoons peanut oil

1 medium onion, finely chopped

2 cups apple cider

1½ cups self-rising flour

2 tablespoons chilled vegetable shortening

¾ cup milk

Southerners love dumplings in any shape or form, and no one more so than my Georgia grandmother, who prided herself on these tangy pork chops topped with tender steamed dumplings. If Maw Maw didn't have any "hard" cider (which was rare, since she drank it diluted by the quart), she'd use plain "sweet" apple juice or even chopped boiled apples reduced almost to a liquid, and I remember she preferred to drop the sticky dumplings simply with her fingers (a technique I've never mastered). If you want more-flavorful dumplings, you can add extra mustard, caraway seeds, or a little powdered sage to the dough. And if you have no self-rising flour on hand, blend two tablespoons of baking powder into 1½ cups of all-purpose.

1 Coat one side of each pork chop with mustard and season both sides with salt and pepper. In a large, heavy skillet, heat the oil over moderate heat, add the chops uncoated-side-down, and brown for about 5 minutes. Add the onion and stir for about 2 minutes. Add ½ cup of the cider, bring to a simmer, cover, and cook over low heat till the chops are almost tender, 45 to 50 minutes. Add the remaining cider and return to a simmer.

2 In a bowl, combine the flour and shortening and cut with a pastry cutter till the mixture is mealy. Add the milk and stir till well blended and sticky. Drop the dough by tablespoons onto the pork chops (not in the liquid) and cook, uncovered, for 10 minutes. Cover the skillet, cook for 10 minutes longer, and transfer the chops and dumplings to a serving platter. Increase the heat, cook down the liquid till thickened, and spoon over the chops and dumplings.

3 Serve piping hot.

PIG PICKIN'S

Founded in 1757 in Harnett County, North Carolina, the Barbecue Presbyterian Church is still attended by communicants in and around Fort Bragg.

BROILED PORK CHOPS WITH PEACHY CHEESE CRUST

2 medium ripe peaches, peeled, pitted, and finely chopped

½ cup finely grated Parmesan cheese

1 tablespoon bourbon

Freshly ground black pepper to taste

4 pork loin chops, about 1 inch thick

1½ cups fine dry bread crumbs

Although broiling is generally not the preferred way to cook pork chops if you want them to remain moist and tender, it's the only way I know to produce this luscious crust that all Rebs love on any kind of pork. The trick is not to broil the chops too close to the heat and to check them carefully with a small knife after about 20 minutes to see if they're tender. The crust should be slightly browned but still moist.

1 Preheat the oven broiler. Grease the rack of a broiler pan and set aside.

2 In a bowl, combine the peaches, cheese, bourbon, and pepper and mash with a heavy fork till well blended and almost smooth. Spread the mixture on both sides of the pork chops, pressing it into the meat. Dredge the chops lightly on both sides in the bread crumbs, arrange on the prepared rack, and broil about 5 to 6 inches from the heat till fully cooked but still moist, about 20 minutes.

3 Serve hot.

BROILED MARINATED CENTER-CUT PORK CHOPS

MAKES 4 SERVINGS

¹/₃ cup apple juice

2 tablespoons fresh lemon juice

2 tablespoons soy sauce

1 tablespoon peanut oil

2 teaspoons minced fresh ginger

1 garlic clove, minced

1 teaspoon minced fresh sage
leaves

Freshly ground black pepper
to taste

4 pork center-cut loin chops,
about 1 inch thick

Generally, broiling and grilling are not the best ways to cook ordinary pork chops, steaks, or cutlets, since they're almost guaranteed to be tough and stringy if in the least overcooked. When, on the other hand, you marinate center-cut chops that are at least 1 inch thick and broil or grill them just till golden, the results can be delectable. Chops that are 1 to 1½ inches thick are perfect for this method, and just remember that the thinner the chops, the shorter the marinating and cooking times. This particular marinade can be used for virtually any form of pork—adjusted, of course, to accommodate the size of various cuts.

1 In a small bowl, combine the juices, soy sauce, oil, ginger, garlic, sage, and pepper and whisk till the marinade is well blended. Arrange the chops in a glass baking dish, pour the marinade over the tops, and let marinate, uncovered, at room temperature for about 1 hour, turning the chops twice and spooning the marinade over the tops.

2 Preheat the oven broiler.

3 Arrange the chops on the rack of a broiling pan and broil about 5 inches from the heat till golden, about 8 minutes. Turn the chops and broil till golden brown but still moist inside, 8 to 9 minutes.

4 Serve hot.

CREAMED PORK CUTLETS WITH VIDALIA ONIONS AND POTATOES

MAKES 4 TO 6 SERVINGS

4 to 6 boneless pork loin chops, about ½ inch thick

3 tablespoons peanut oil

3 medium russet potatoes, peeled and thinly sliced

1 large Vidalia onion, thinly sliced

½ teaspoon dried rosemary, crumbled

Salt and freshly ground black pepper to taste

1½ cups sour cream

2 tablespoons finely chopped fresh chives

While I suppose that, technically, this is a layered casserole, I view it more as a baked pork dish by virtue of the size of the cutlets. In fact, I may well leave out the potatoes altogether if another starch comes to mind; you could simply "smother" the cutlets with at least two large sliced Vidalias, and serve everything over mounds of rice. In either case, the way the ultra-sweet onions almost caramelize into the tender pork and sour cream makes the dish one of the most succulent you'll ever taste. And nothing could be easier to prepare.

1 Preheat the oven to 350°F. Grease a 1½- to 2-quart baking dish and set aside.

2 On a flat surface, pound the pork chops with a mallet or heavy skillet till about ¼ inch thick. In a large, heavy skillet, heat the oil over moderate heat, add the cutlets, brown lightly on both sides, and remove from the heat.

3 Layer half the potatoes over the bottom of the prepared baking dish, cover with half the onions, and season with half the rosemary and salt and pepper. Arrange the cutlets over the top, layer the remaining potatoes and onions over the cutlets, and season with the remaining rosemary and salt and pepper. Spoon the sour cream evenly over the top, cover, and bake till the cutlets are nicely glazed, about 40 minutes.

4 Sprinkle the chives over the top and serve hot from the baking dish.

BREADED PORK CUTLETS WITH LEMON AND CAPERS

4 boneless pork loin chops, about ½ inch thick

½ cup all-purpose flour

¼ teaspoon dried thyme, crumbled

¼ teaspoon dried oregano, crumbled

Salt and freshly ground black pepper to taste

2 large eggs, beaten

1½ cups fresh bread crumbs

2 tablespoons peanut oil

¼ cup chicken broth

2 to 3 tablespoons capers, drained

2 teaspoons minced lemon rind

In Southern cooking, imported Mediterranean capers have long been used in seafood salads and as a component of mayonnaise, tartar sauce, and various stuffings and sauces for fish, poultry, and pork; and, according to my historian friend and colleague in Savannah, Damon Lee Fowler, so popular (and expensive) were capers in the early days that cooks unable to acquire or afford the genuine item often substituted pickled nasturtium buds, since the flavors were so similar. In this recipe, capers are combined with lemon to produce a sauce for breaded herbed pork cutlets that is almost delicate, a dish that couldn't be simpler and quicker to execute and one guaranteed to impress any guests. And if you want a slightly richer sauce, swirl in about a tablespoon of butter during the final reduction.

1 On a flat surface, pound the chops with a mallet or heavy skillet till about ¼ inch thick. On a plate, combine and mix together the flour, thyme, oregano, and salt and pepper and dredge the cutlets in the mixture, tapping off excess flour. Dip each into the eggs, and then coat both sides with the bread crumbs, pressing to adhere.

2 In a large, heavy skillet, heat the oil over moderate heat, add the cutlets, and brown on each side. Add the broth, capers, and lemon rind, bring to a simmer, cover, and cook over low heat till the cutlets are tender, 15 to 20 minutes. Transfer the cutlets to a platter, increase the heat, simmer the sauce till cooked down slightly, and spoon over the cutlets.

3 Serve hot.

MISSISSIPPI SMOTHERED PORK CUTLETS

One 1½-pound pork tenderloin

2 tablespoons butter

2 tablespoons all-purpose flour

1½ cups beef broth

¼ teaspoon minced fresh sage leaves

Tabasco sauce to taste

1 cup all-purpose flour for dredging

⅛ teaspoon dry mustard

Salt and freshly ground black pepper to taste

8 tablespoons lard

3 large onions, thinly sliced

1 celery rib, finely chopped

2 garlic cloves, minced

Pork, poultry, and game dishes smothered in onions are popular all over the South, but nowhere will you find the concept more elevated almost to an art than in the state of Mississippi, where, sometimes, the "smothering" is intensified by preparing a dish in a black cast-iron skillet and covering the ingredients with a weighted plate. There, it's unheard of to serve a smothered pork dish that has no gravy, and only onions that are soft and golden (never in the least burnt) are acceptable. A delectable variation I once experienced (at a diner in Jackson) that you might want to try involved adding about half a cup of seedless golden raisins to the onions during the final baking. Pork chops, steaks, and country-style ribs are also delicious prepared in this manner, and there's no better way to tame the snappy flavor of sautéed pork liver than by smothering it with sweet onions.

1 Preheat the oven to 350°F.

2 Cut the pork tenderloin widthwise into ½-inch-thick cutlets; on a flat surface, pound the cutlets slightly with a mallet or heavy skillet and set aside.

3 In a small saucepan, melt the butter over moderate heat, add the 2 tablespoons of flour, and whisk till lightly browned, about 5 minutes. Add the broth, sage, and Tabasco, stir well, remove from the heat, and set aside.

4 On a plate, combine the 1 cup of flour, mustard, and salt and pepper, mix well, and dredge the cutlets in the mixture. In a large, heavy skillet, melt 4 tablespoons of the lard over moderate heat, add the cutlets, brown on both sides, and transfer to a large baking dish. Add the remaining lard to the skillet, add the onions, celery, and garlic, stir till the onions are just golden, about 8 minutes, and spoon the vegetables over the cutlets.

5 Pour off all fat from the skillet, add the broth from the saucepan, and stir for 1 minute, scraping bits from the bottom of the skillet. Pour the gravy over the cutlets and onions, cover the dish tightly with a lid or aluminum foil, and bake for 30 minutes.

6 Serve hot.

GLAZED PORK CUTLETS WITH PEACH-MANGO CHUTNEY

MAKES 4 SERVINGS

For the Cutlets:

¼ cup packed light brown sugar

1 teaspoon dry mustard

Salt and freshly ground black pepper to taste

1 tablespoon cider vinegar

One 1½-pound pork tenderloin

2 tablespoons butter

1 cup dry white wine

One of the major summer activities at many churches throughout the South is the ritual of women making all types of fruit preserves, conserves, and chutneys for fundraising bazaars, and Southerners have known for generations that nothing goes better with pork than a spicy tomato, nectarine, apricot, or peach chutney. I learned from putting up peach preserves that the addition of just a single ripe mango blissfully transforms the condiment, and when these two fruits are combined with other ingredients and at least one spice to make chutney, you have something truly special. I like to braise a whole pork tenderloin and slice my own cutlets in various widths for this dish, but feel free to pound a few boneless pork loin chops or one or two pork steaks and either braise them till tender or sauté them briefly in butter.

1 To prepare the cutlets, combine the brown sugar, mustard, salt and pepper, and vinegar in a small bowl, mix to form a paste, and, using your hands, rub the paste evenly over the entire pork tenderloin. In a large, heavy skillet, melt the butter over moderate heat, add the tenderloin, and brown lightly on all sides, taking care not to burn. Add the wine around the meat, bring to a simmer, cover, and simmer over low heat till the pork is tender, about 1 hour.

For the Chutney:

2 to 3 large peaches, peeled, pitted, and cut into ½-inch chunks

1 large mango, peeled, seeded, and cut into ½-inch chunks

¼ cup commercial pickled red bell peppers, drained and chopped

¼ cup seedless dark raisins

1 scallion (part of green top included), chopped

1 teaspoon light brown sugar

¼ teaspoon ground ginger

¼ teaspoon ground allspice

Salt and freshly ground black pepper to taste

2 tablespoons cider vinegar

2 Meanwhile, to prepare the chutney, combine all the ingredients in a heavy stainless-steel or enameled saucepan, bring to a simmer, cover, and cook till the peaches and mango are soft but not mushy, about 15 minutes. Remove from the heat.

3 On a flat surface, cut the tenderloin into thin cutlets, arrange on a platter, and spoon warm chutney over the top.

PIG PICKIN'S

"We North Carolinians, of course, know—we are not taught, we are born knowing—that barbecue consists of pork cooked over hickory coals and seasoned with vinegar and red pepper pods."

—Tom Wicker, New York Times

Deep-Fried Stuffed Pork Cutlets

Makes 4 servings

4 boneless pork loin chops, about ½ inch thick

Salt and freshly ground black pepper to taste

¼ pound Swiss cheese, shredded

¼ pound cooked ham, minced

½ teaspoon powdered sage

½ cup all-purpose flour

2 large eggs, beaten

1 cup dry bread crumbs

Peanut oil for deep frying

What can be more Southern than any food that is stuffed, breaded, and deep fried, and what is more delicious than thick pork chops or thin cutlets that are stuffed with ham (ordinary smoked or country cured) and some type of cheese and fried (or baked) to a golden finish? Most markets today do carry packaged pork cutlets, but since I don't relish paying a good deal extra for the convenience and prefer to control the meat's thickness, I almost always buy loin chops (with or without the bone) and pound them to the exact size I need. Do note that for this dish, the chops should weigh about eight ounces apiece—more with the bone.

1 On a flat surface, pound the pork chops with a mallet or heavy skillet till about ¼ inch thick and sprinkle with salt and pepper. In a bowl, combine the cheese, ham, and sage, mix well with your hands, divide the mixture into 4 equal portions, and shape each into an oval. Place an oval in the center of each pounded cutlet, bring up the edges of the cutlets to enclose the ovals envelope-style, and press the seams tightly to seal.

2 Dredge each cutlet in the flour, shaking off excess, dip each into the egg, and then dredge each in the bread crumbs.

3 In a large, heavy skillet, heat about 1 inch of oil over moderate heat, add the cutlets, and cook till nicely browned, 6 to 7 minutes, turning as necessary. Drain briefly on paper towels and serve immediately.

Herbed Pork Steaks with Honey-Mustard Sauce

Makes 4 servings

¼ teaspoon powdered sage

¼ teaspoon dried rosemary, crumbled

½ garlic clove, minced

Salt and freshly ground black pepper to taste

2 pork blade steaks, about ¾ inch thick

2 tablespoons peanut oil

½ cup dry white wine

1 tablespoon Dijon mustard

2 tablespoons honey

Many Southerners much prefer a fatty, full-flavored, baked pork shoulder to a lean loin or rib roast, and when I buy a large shoulder (or Boston butt) to simply bake or cook slowly on the grill for chopped barbecue, I might well first cut off a couple of steaks for another occasion, season them well, and serve them with this delectable honey-mustard sauce. Feel free to experiment with the herb rub, and check the steaks after about an hour of cooking to see if they're already fork-tender.

1 In a small bowl, combine the sage, rosemary, garlic, and salt and pepper and mix till well blended. Rub the mixture into the steaks, place the steaks on a large plate, cover with plastic wrap, and let stand for about 30 minutes.

2 In a large, heavy skillet, heat the oil over moderate heat, add the steaks, brown on both sides, and return the steaks to the plate. Add the wine and mustard to the skillet and whisk with a fork till well incorporated, scraping up any browned bits in the pan. Add the honey and stir till well blended. Return the steaks to the skillet and spoon the sauce over the tops. Reduce the heat to low, cover, and simmer till tender, 1¼ to 1½ hours, adding a little more wine if necessary.

3 Cut the steaks in half and serve hot with a little more sauce spooned over the tops.

PORK STEAKS WITH VERMOUTH, CORN, AND RAISINS

MAKES 4 SERVINGS

2 tablespoons butter

2 pork blade steaks, about ¾ inch thick

¼ cup sweet vermouth

¼ cup water

One 16-ounce can cream-style corn

1 small onion, minced

½ cup seedless dark raisins

Salt and freshly ground black pepper to taste

1 cup fresh bread crumbs

Cut from the pig shoulder (or Boston butt), a blade steak is one of the most flavorful and economical cuts of pork and is usually large enough to feed two persons. Since, on the other hand, blade steaks are relatively tough compared with loin and rib chops, it's almost imperative that they be slowly braised to guarantee tenderness and moisture—preferably in a little acidic wine or apple cider. If you can't find steaks in a market display case, either ask the butcher to cut a couple or buy a whole shoulder roast, cut your own steaks from the leanest portion, and bake the remaining roast the same way you'd bake a ham. For the most tender steaks, let them marinate for about an hour in the vermouth and water before braising them with the corn and raisin topping.

1 Preheat the oven to 350°F. Butter a 2-quart baking dish and set aside.

2 In a large, heavy skillet, melt the butter over moderate heat, add the steaks, brown on both sides, and transfer to the prepared baking dish. Discard fat from the skillet, add the vermouth and water, scraping browned bits off the bottom of the pan, and pour over the steaks.

3 In a large bowl, combine the corn, onion, raisins, salt and pepper, and bread crumbs and mix till well blended. Spoon the mixture evenly over the steaks, cover, place in the oven, and braise till the steaks are very tender, 1¼ to 1½ hours, basting the tops a couple of times.

4 Cut the steaks in half and serve with the corn topping piping hot.

PIG PICKIN'S

Hogs are the cheapest, quickest, and easiest farm animals to raise. A pig can increase its weight 150-fold in its first eight months of life.

CREOLE PORK STEAKS

3 tablespoons peanut oil

2 pork blade steaks, about
   ¾ inch thick

1 large onion, finely chopped

1 medium green bell pepper,
   seeded and finely chopped

1 garlic clove, minced

½ cup dry white wine

One 16-ounce can crushed
   tomatoes with juice

¼ teaspoon sugar

1 tablespoon Worcestershire
   sauce

Tabasco sauce to taste

1 bay leaf

Salt and freshly ground black
   pepper to taste

Sometimes called "picnic chops" in Creole Louisiana (referring to the lower part of a pig shoulder marketed as a "fresh picnic" cut of meat), blade steaks easily adapt to any of the assertive secondary ingredients and seasonings typical of Creole and Cajun styles of cooking. Even after 1½ hours of simmering, the sapid cooking liquid in this recipe will most likely still be watery (depending on the amount of juice in the canned tomatoes), so be sure to boil it down slightly at the end to a nicely thickened sauce that will cling to the steaks.

1 In a large, deep skillet, heat half the oil over moderate heat, add the steaks, and brown on both sides. Transfer the steaks to a plate and discard the fat from the skillet.

2 Add the remaining oil to the skillet, add the onion, bell pepper, and garlic and stir till lightly browned, about 8 minutes. Add the wine and bring to a boil, scraping browned bits off the bottom of the pan. Return the steaks to the pan and spoon some of the onion and bell pepper over them. Add the tomatoes and their juice, the sugar, Worcestershire, Tabasco, bay leaf, salt and pepper, and enough water to just cover. Bring to a boil, reduce the heat to low, cover, and simmer the steaks till they are very tender, about 1½ hours. If the sauce is too watery, increase the heat to high and boil down to thicken.

3 To serve, cut the steaks in half and spoon hot sauce over each portion.

PIES, LOAVES, HASHES, and BURGERS

OLD-FASHIONED PORK PIE
WITH BISCUIT CRUST

PORK, APPLE, AND RAISIN PIE

CAROLINA PORK AND SWEET POTATO PIE
WITH BISCUIT BATTER CRUST

GEORGIA BREAKFAST PIE

SPICY TENNESSEE SAUSAGE
AND VEGETABLE PIE

TEXARCANA PORK AND BEAN PIE WITH
CORNPONE TOPPING

NATCHITOCHES PORK PIES

GREAT SMOKY BACON, COUNTRY HAM,
AND SAUERKRAUT PIE

BACON AND CORN PIE WITH CORNMEAL CRUST

HOOTIE'S HAM AND CHEESE QUICHE

BACON MEAT LOAF

COUNTRY HAM, PORK, AND CHEDDAR LOAF

VIRGINIA HAM AND OLIVE LOAF
WITH SOUR CREAM SAUCE

BARBECUED PORK AND
SAUSAGE MEAT LOAF

DEVILED HAM AND PORK LOAF

CREOLE OYSTER AND BACON LOAVES

PORK, BACON, AND SAUSAGE HASH
WITH APPLES AND ALMONDS

COUNTRY HAM AND TURNIP HASH

HAM CROQUETTES WITH PARSLEY SAUCE

CURRIED PORK AND APPLE MOLD

CRACKLIN' PORK BURGERS

OPEN-FACE PIG AND PIMENTO BURGERS

TARPON SPRINGS GREEK BURGERS

Old-Fashioned Pork Pie with Biscuit Crust

Makes 6 servings

For the Filling:

2 slices bacon, coarsely chopped

1½ pounds ground lean pork

2 medium onions, finely chopped

½ small green bell pepper, seeded and finely chopped

1 garlic clove, minced

¼ teaspoon powdered sage

Salt and freshly ground black pepper to taste

1½ cups beef broth or water

For the Crust:

2 cups all-purpose flour

1 teaspoon baking powder

1 teaspoon salt

6 tablespoons (¾ stick) butter, chilled and cut into pieces

½ cup milk

1 tablespoon butter, melted

Since the crust for this popular Southern pie is made with butter instead of shortening or lard, and since the dough is kneaded and rolled instead of patted out, some might argue that it's not a genuine biscuit crust. Of course these are the same Rebs who proclaim that butter should never come near a cornbread batter, and that hush puppies must be fried only in a cast-iron pot. All I know is that the lady in Huntsville, Alabama, who taught me years ago how to make this no-nonsense, wonderful pork pie always referred to its "biscuit crust" and that I can't imagine one that turns out any better. In rural homes, the pie would typically be served with crisply fried potatoes and some variety of field peas boiled with a piece of pork side meat.

1 Grease a 9-inch pie dish and set aside.

2 To make the filling, fry the bacon in a large skillet over moderate heat till half cooked, break up the pork in the skillet, add the onions, bell pepper, garlic, sage, and salt and pepper, and stir till the pork loses all its pink color and the vegetables are soft, about 8 minutes. Add the broth, stir till slightly thickened, about 10 minutes, and remove from the heat.

3 Preheat the oven to 425°F.

4 To make the crust, combine the flour, baking powder, salt, and 6 tablespoons butter in a bowl and work the mixture with your fingers till mealy. Add the milk and stir just till the dough gathers into a ball. On a lightly floured surface, knead the dough 8 or 10 times, divide in half, and roll out one half with a floured rolling pin into a 12-inch circle. Fit the dough into the prepared pie dish, pressing the bottom and sides, then spoon the pork filling into the dish. Roll out the remaining dough into a 12-inch circle, drape it over the filling, trim and pinch together the edges, and cut several steam vents in the top with a small knife. Brush the top with the melted butter and bake for 15 minutes. Reduce the heat to 350°F and continue baking till the pie is golden, 30 to 35 minutes.

5 Serve hot.

Pork, Apple, and Raisin Pie

For the Filling:

¼ cup seedless dark raisins

¼ cup Madeira or semisweet sherry

2 tablespoons butter

1 pound ground pork

1 medium onion, chopped

2 Granny Smith apples, peeled, cored, and coarsely chopped

½ teaspoon ground cinnamon

Salt and freshly ground black pepper to taste

For the Crust:

2 cups all-purpose flour

1 teaspoon salt

8 tablespoons (1 stick) butter, chilled and cut into pieces

4 tablespoons lard, chilled and cut into pieces

½ cup ice water

My guess is that this popular sweet-tart pie harks back to colonial days in the South, when so many savory meat pies were enhanced with Madeira or sherry and when both butter and lard were used to produce a crust both rich and flaky. In all likelihood, tiny dried currants would have been used in place of raisins, and if you can find the more exotic fruit (which is actually a grape), feel free to make the substitution. Just make sure to buy the dried variety of currants, not the fresh red or white berries, which have a different flavor and tend to disintegrate when cooked for any length of time.

1 To make the filling, combine the raisins and Madeira in a small bowl and let soak for about 30 minutes.

2 In a large skillet, melt the butter over moderate heat, break up the pork in the skillet, add the onion, and stir till the pork loses all its pink color and the onion is golden, 8 to 10 minutes. Add the apples, cinnamon, and salt and pepper and stir till the apples are soft, about 8 minutes. Add the raisins and Madeira, increase the heat, and cook till the liquid is slightly reduced. Remove from the heat.

3 Preheat the oven to 400°F. Grease a 9-inch pie dish and set aside.

4 To make the crust, combine the flour, salt, butter, and lard in a bowl and work the mixture with your fingers till mealy. Stirring, gradually add enough of the ice water to form the dough into a ball. On a lightly floured surface, knead the dough several times, divide in half, and roll out one half with a floured rolling pin into a 12-inch circle. Fit the dough into the prepared dish, pressing down the bottom and sides, then spoon the pork filling into the dish. Roll out the remaining dough into a 12-inch circle and drape it over the filling. Trim and pinch together the edges, cut several steam vents in the top, and bake till the pie is golden, about 50 minutes.

5 Let cool slightly before serving.

Carolina Pork and Sweet Potato Pie with Biscuit Batter Crust

For the Filling:

3 slices bacon

1 large onion, chopped

1 celery rib, chopped

1 medium green bell pepper, seeded and chopped

1 garlic clove, minced

2 pounds lean cooked pork, cut into small cubes

2 sweet potatoes, peeled and cut into small cubes

2 cups beef broth

2 tablespoons yellow cornmeal

2 tablespoons tomato paste

2 tablespoons Worcestershire sauce

Tabasco sauce to taste

1 teaspoon salt

Freshly ground black pepper to taste

Today, North Carolina is the South's leading producer of both pork and sweet potatoes, so it's hardly surprising that home cooks all over the state pride themselves on elaborate stews, casseroles, and pies, such as this one, that utilize these two important staples. Most likely, this biscuit-batter crust can be traced back to the "loose" suet and short pastry crusts that topped the dramatic "raised" savory meat and fish pies of the first English settlers—basically the same batter crust that, when sweetened, was also used to make the South's distinctive fruit cobblers. Just make sure that the batter is not too stiff when mixed; if so, add enough extra milk to produce a very soft batter that can be easily spooned over the filling. This pie is one of the best ways I know to use the leftovers of a large roasted pork shoulder or fresh ham (trimmed of fat).

1 Preheat the oven to 350°F. Grease a 2-quart baking dish or casserole and set aside.

2 To make the filling, fry the bacon in a large skillet over moderate heat till almost crisp; drain on paper towels. Add the onion, celery, bell pepper, and garlic to the skillet and stir for about 3 minutes. Crumble the cooked bacon over the vegetables, and then add the remaining filling ingredients, stirring. Reduce the heat to low, simmer, stirring from time to time, for about 30 minutes, and then transfer to the prepared baking dish.

For the Crust:

2 cups all-purpose flour

2 teaspoons baking powder

2 teaspoons salt

3 tablespoons vegetable shortening

¾ cup milk

1 large egg, beaten

3 To make the crust, combine the flour, baking powder, salt, and shortening in a bowl and work the mixture with your fingers till mealy. Add the milk and egg and stir till well blended and smooth.

4 Spoon the batter over the top of the pork mixture and bake till golden, about 40 minutes.

5 Serve hot.

PIG PICKIN'S

Most Southern pigs belong to one of eight breeds: Berkshire, Hampshire, Duroc, Poland China, Spot, Landrance, Yorkshire, and Chester White. The rarest and most exotic Southern pig is the Ossabaw, a 500-year-old descendant of Spanish Iberico hogs that is found only on Ossabaw Island, Georgia.

Georgia Breakfast Pie

1 cup milk

2 cups water

½ teaspoon salt

½ cup regular grits

¾ pound bulk pork sausage

½ teaspoon red pepper flakes

Pinch of powdered sage

¼ pound sharp cheddar cheese, grated

4 large eggs, beaten

For breakfast, what could be more Southern than eggs, fried sausage patties, and a mess of grits, but when these three staples are combined with tangy sharp cheddar cheese and turned into a puffy pie, you have an unusual dish that couldn't be more appropriate for any casual breakfast or brunch. If you can find stone-ground grits, all the better, not only because they have more flavor than regular commercial ones but also because they maintain their creamy texture no matter how long they're cooked. I do not recommend using quick grits for this dish.

1 Combine the milk, water, and salt in a heavy saucepan and bring to a boil. Gradually add the grits, stirring, reduce the heat to moderately low, cover, and cook the grits till thick and creamy, 20 to 30 minutes, stirring often. Remove from the heat and keep covered.

2 Preheat the oven to 325°F. Grease a 9-inch pie plate and set aside.

3 In a large skillet, break up the sausage and stir over moderate heat till it loses its pink color, about 8 minutes. Remove from the heat and drain off the grease. Add the red pepper flakes, sage, and cheese and stir till the cheese melts. Add the grits and the eggs and stir till well blended. Scrape the mixture into the prepared pie plate and bake till the pie is puffy, about 45 minutes.

4 Serve hot.

Spicy Tennessee Sausage and Vegetable Pie

MAKES 6 SERVINGS

1 pound bulk pork sausage

1 small onion, finely chopped

2 cups fresh or thawed frozen corn kernels

2 cups canned crushed tomatoes, drained

1 teaspoon red pepper flakes

2 tablespoons all-purpose flour

1 teaspoon sugar

Salt and freshly ground black pepper to taste

1 cup bread crumbs

2 tablespoons butter, melted

Just about every state in the South produces at least one commercial brand of bulk pork sausage (most with just the right ratio of lean meat to fat), but never will you spot a larger variety than in the markets of Memphis, Chattanooga, and other cities in Tennessee. (Likewise, Tennessee sausage can usually be found in major Virginia, North Carolina, and Mississippi grocery stores.) For this pie (which is delicious for a summer brunch), there should be more than enough liquid in the tomatoes to keep the filling very moist, but if not, add a little canned tomato juice before scraping it into the pie plate. The pie should be firm but never dry.

1 Preheat the oven to 400°F. Grease a deep 9- to 10-inch pie plate and set aside.

2 In a large, heavy skillet, break up the sausage and fry over moderate heat, stirring, till nicely browned. Pour off all but about 1 tablespoon of fat, add the onion, and stir for 2 minutes. Add the corn, tomatoes, and red pepper flakes, stir, and let simmer for about 10 minutes. In a cup, combine and mix the flour, sugar, and salt and pepper, sprinkle over the meat and vegetables, stir, and let simmer for about 5 minutes longer.

3 Scrape the mixture into the prepared pie plate, sprinkle the bread crumbs over the top, drizzle the butter over the crumbs, and bake till golden brown, 30 to 35 minutes.

4 Serve hot.

Texarcana Pork and Bean Pie with Cornpone Topping

Makes 6 servings

For the Filling:

2 tablespoons lard

1½ pounds lean ground pork shoulder

1 medium onion, chopped

1 teaspoon chili powder

Salt and freshly ground black pepper to taste

One 15-ounce can pinto beans, drained

One 16-ounce can crushed tomatoes

One 8-ounce can tomato sauce

½ cup seedless dark raisins

2 ounces sharp cheddar cheese, shredded

Smack on the Texas border, Texarcana, Arkansas, is known to many primarily as the home of Bryce's Cafeteria, which is actually a family-style restaurant with cafeteria service that's been serving genuine, inexpensive Southern food with Texas overtones ever since the 1930s. If memory serves, the menu always includes at least a couple of distinctive pork dishes, but the one I've never forgotten was a delectable, puffy pork and bean pie that not only curiously contained raisins but also had a topping of small cornpone ovals that resembled hush puppies. (Cornpone is really no more than eggless cornbread.) My adaptation might not be exactly like the original, but it comes close enough, whether I drop the batter by spoonfuls or simply layer it evenly over the top of the filling.

1 Grease a large, deep pie plate and set aside.

2 To make the filling, melt the lard in a large, heavy skillet over moderate heat, break up the pork in the skillet, add the onion, and stir till the pork is lightly browned, about 8 minutes. Sprinkle the chili powder and salt and pepper over the top and stir well. Add the beans, tomatoes, tomato sauce, and raisins, bring to a simmer, and cook for about 20 minutes, stirring. Add the cheese and stir till melted and well blended. Scrape the mixture into the prepared pie plate and set aside.

For the Topping:

1 cup yellow cornmeal

2 tablespoons all-purpose flour

1 tablespoon sugar

2 teaspoons baking powder

1 teaspoon salt

½ cup milk

2 tablespoons vegetable
shortening, melted

3 Preheat the oven to 400°F.

4 To make the topping, combine the cornmeal, flour, sugar, baking powder, and salt in a bowl and stir till well blended. Add the milk and shortening and stir till the batter is well blended and smooth.

5 Drop the batter by oval spoonfuls over the pork and beans and bake till golden brown, 30 to 35 minutes.

6 Serve the pie hot.

PIG PICKIN'S

"Ham's substantial, ham is fat,

Ham is firm and sound.

Ham's what God was getting at

When he made pigs so round."

—Roy Blount, Jr.

Natchitoches Pork Pies

For the Filling:

2 tablespoons peanut oil

1½ pounds ground pork shoulder

½ cup chopped scallions
(part of green tops included)

1 garlic clove, minced

1 teaspoon salt

1 teaspoon freshly ground
black pepper

¾ cup all-purpose flour

For the Pastry:

2 cups all-purpose flour

1 teaspoon baking powder

½ teaspoon salt

3 tablespoons vegetable
shortening

1 large egg, beaten

⅓ cup milk

1 cup peanut oil for deep frying

Natchitoches (pronounced NACK-i-tosh) would be only a dot on the map of central Louisiana were it not for the distinctive half-moon meat pies that a place called Lasyone's has been producing since 1966 (and, more recently, shipping all over the country). The spicy fried turnovers can be made with beef, pork, or a combination of the two meats, but never have I had better luck than when using only full-flavored ground pork shoulder with just the right ratio of lean meat to fat. Of course, the original recipe is still a secret to everyone but James Lasyone and his two daughters, but he does disclose that what matters most is not the filling but the fried dough, which should never be greasy. To accomplish this, be sure to use a deep-fat thermometer, maintain the heat of the oil at 350°F, and fry the pies just till they turn golden.

1   To make the filling, heat the oil in a large skillet over moderate heat, add the pork, scallions, and garlic, and cook, stirring and breaking up the pork till it loses all traces of pink color, about 8 minutes. Add the remaining filling ingredients and continue to cook, stirring, till the mixture is almost dry, about 10 minutes. Transfer to a bowl, let cool, and then chill.

2 To make the pastry, sift the flour, baking powder, and salt into a bowl, add the shortening, and cut with a pastry cutter till the mixture resembles coarse cornmeal. Add the egg and milk and stir till a ball of dough forms. Transfer the dough to a lightly floured surface, roll out about ½ inch thick with a floured rolling pin, and, using a clean empty coffee can, cut out rounds of dough.

3 To assemble the pies, place a heaping tablespoon of filling on one side of each round of dough. With your fingertips, dampen the pie edges with water, fold the other side of the dough over the filling, and seal the edges with a fork dipped in water. Prick twice on top with a fork.

4 To fry, heat the oil in a medium cast-iron skillet to about 350°F, quickly fry each pie till golden, about 2 minutes on each side, and drain briefly on paper towels.

5 Serve hot.

Great Smoky Bacon, Country Ham, and Sauerkraut Pie

Makes 6 servings

For the Crust:

1½ cups all-purpose flour

1 teaspoon baking powder

½ teaspoon salt

4 tablespoons lard, chilled
    and cut into bits

¼ cup water

2 tablespoons Dijon mustard

For the Filling:

2 thick slices bacon, chopped

2 medium onions, thinly sliced

1 cup packed sauerkraut,
    rinsed and squeezed dry

½ teaspoon caraway seeds

⅛ teaspoon ground nutmeg

Salt and freshly ground black
    pepper to taste

1½ cups half-and-half

3 large eggs

¼ pound cooked country ham,
    chopped

3 tablespoons chopped fresh
    parsley leaves

Travel through the Great Smoky Mountains of Tennessee and you're bound to spot not only large pig farms but also vast cabbage fields, some of which were most likely first planted by the original Scotch-Irish and German settlers. From those hogs are produced some of the South's finest country hams and bacon, and from the cabbage fields barrels of briny sauerkraut (or simply "kraut"), and when everything is combined with other ingredients to make pies, puddings, loaves, and casseroles, the results can be memorable. In the region itself (and in delis all over the country) can be found succulent fresh sauerkraut curing in special containers, most of which needs to be rinsed briefly of excess salt. Otherwise, look for sauerkraut packaged in refrigerated bags or sold in jars—but not the canned product.

1 Preheat the oven to 350°F. Grease a 9-inch pie plate and set aside.

2 To make the crust, combine the flour, baking powder, salt, and lard in a bowl and work the mixture with your fingers till mealy. Add the water and stir till the dough gathers into a ball. On a lightly floured surface, roll out the dough with a floured rolling pin into a 12-inch circle and fit it into the prepared pie plate, tucking the edges under and pressing the dough. Prick the bottom and sides with a fork, bake for about 20 minutes, and then brush the interior surfaces with the mustard.

3 Meanwhile, to make the filling, fry the bacon in a large skillet over moderate heat till about half cooked, add the onions, and stir till golden, about 8 minutes. Add the sauerkraut, caraway seeds, nutmeg, and salt and pepper, stir well, reduce the heat to low, cover, and simmer for about 15 minutes.

4 Reduce the oven to 325°F.

5 In a bowl, whisk together the half-and-half and eggs till well blended.

6 Spoon the sauerkraut mixture over the bottom of the baked pie shell, sprinkle the ham and parsley evenly over the top, add the half-and-half mixture, and bake till the pie is set and golden, 45 to 50 minutes.

7 Serve hot or warm.

BACON AND CORN PIE WITH CORNMEAL CRUST

For the Filling:

8 thick slices bacon, cut into small cubes

2 medium onions, chopped

1 medium green bell pepper, seeded and chopped

One 12-ounce package thawed frozen corn kernels

1½ cups half-and-half

2 large eggs, beaten

1 cup grated Swiss cheese

¼ teaspoon ground nutmeg

Salt and freshly ground black pepper to taste

For the Crust:

1 cup yellow cornmeal

½ cup all-purpose flour

1 teaspoon baking powder

½ teaspoon salt

4 tablespoons vegetable shortening, chilled

¼ cup milk

All sorts of dishes are made with bacon and corn in the South, and if you reduced the kernels and added some lima beans in this lusty pie, it might well be called a succotash pie. What gives it distinction is the crispy cornmeal crust that is lightened by both flour and baking powder. Just be sure not to mix the dough too much and to pat (not roll) it out.

1 To make the filling, fry the bacon in a large, deep skillet over moderate heat till crisp; drain on paper towels. Pour off all but 2 tablespoons of grease, add the onions and bell pepper, and stir till softened, about 8 minutes. Add the corn, stir for 3 minutes longer, remove from the heat, and let cool for 5 minutes. Add the half-and-half, eggs, cheese, nutmeg, and salt and pepper, stir till well blended, and set aside.

2 Preheat the oven to 400°F. Grease a 9-inch pie dish and set aside.

3 To make the crust, combine the cornmeal, flour, baking powder, salt, and shortening in a bowl and work the mixture with your fingers till well blended. Add the milk and stir just till the dough gathers into a clump. On a lightly floured surface, pat the dough out into a manageable circle, fit it into the prepared pie dish, and press it firmly on the bottom and up the sides. Fold excess dough under and crimp the edges.

4 Sprinkle the bacon over the bottom of the crust, scrape the filling evenly into the dish, and bake till golden, about 50 minutes. Let the pie cool for about 20 minutes before serving in wedges.

Hootie's Ham and Cheese Quiche

MAKES 6 SERVINGS

2 cups fresh bread crumbs

3 tablespoons butter, melted

8 large eggs

1½ cups whole milk

⅛ teaspoon ground nutmeg

Salt and freshly ground black
    pepper to taste

1½ cups chopped cooked ham

1½ cups grated Swiss cheese

I don't think I was ever in my sister's house in Wilmington, North Carolina, when she didn't have some type of ham in the refrigerator—slices of cured country ham to be fried for breakfast, an enormous fresh ham to be glazed and roasted for a formal buffet, and, to be sure, an ordinary baked smoked ham butt or shank for salads, sandwiches, hashes, or one of Hootie's wildly popular Sunday-brunch quiches served with a congealed fruit salad. Hootie is the first to say that this quiche can be made also with chopped cooked country ham or lean ham hock, and by all means feel free to experiment with different interesting cheeses.

1 Preheat the oven to 350°F.

2 Place the bread crumbs in a 10-inch-round baking dish, drizzle the butter evenly over the top, and toss well. In a large bowl, beat the eggs till just blended, add the remaining ingredients, and stir till well blended. Pour the mixture over the bread crumbs and bake till golden brown and fluffy, 35 to 40 minutes.

3 To serve, allow the quiche to stand about for 10 minutes, and then cut into wedges.

Bacon Meat Loaf

MAKES 6 SERVINGS

3 slices white loaf bread

½ cup milk

1 pound ground pork (preferably shoulder)

1 pound ground beef chuck

1 medium onion, finely chopped

1 celery rib, finely chopped

1 garlic clove, minced

1 teaspoon Dijon mustard

1 tablespoon Worcestershire sauce

¼ cup ketchup

1 large egg, beaten

Salt and freshly ground black pepper to taste

8 to 10 slices bacon

Simply and frankly stated, this Southern meat loaf is probably the most delicious you'll ever put in your mouth and the most convincing testimony to the power of bacon to transform an ordinary dish into a culinary masterpiece. Be warned, however, that since the loaf is wrapped entirely in bacon, there will be no crusty surfaces, which some people expect. An obvious solution is to remove the bacon slices during the final 15 minutes of baking, then arrange a slice on top of each portion of meat loaf, but my guess is that once you've tasted the wrapped loaf, you'll forget all about a crust. Remember that if you overmix this (or any other) meat loaf, the texture can be tough.

1 Preheat the oven to 375°F.

2 In a small bowl, tear the bread into bits, add the milk, stir well, and let soak for about 10 minutes.

3 In a large bowl, combine the pork, beef, onion, celery, garlic, mustard, Worcestershire, ketchup, egg, and salt and pepper, add the soaked bread, and mix thoroughly but gently with your hands till well blended and smooth (do not overmix). Place the mixture on a heavy baking pan with raised edges and form into a loaf about 9 inches long and 4 inches wide. Wrap the bacon slices crosswise snugly around the loaf, slightly overlapping, and tuck the ends under the loaf. Bake in the upper third of the oven till the bacon is almost crisp, about 1 hour, and then, using 2 metal spatulas, transfer the loaf to a platter and let stand for about 10 minutes before serving in thick slices.

COUNTRY HAM, PORK, AND CHEDDAR LOAF

MAKES 4 TO 6 SERVINGS

1 pound ground cooked
    country ham

½ pound lean ground pork

1 small onion, minced

2 tablespoons minced fresh
    parsley leaves

2 tablespoons minced sweet
    pickles

1¼ cups crushed cracker crumbs

¾ cup milk

1 large egg, beaten

1 tablespoon ketchup

1 teaspoon dry mustard

Salt and freshly ground black
    pepper to taste

¾ cup heavy cream

¼ pound sharp cheddar cheese,
    grated

Southerners often like to add something sweet to even the most savory dishes, and nothing counters the saltiness of the country ham in this robust loaf better than a little sweet pickle. Even if ordinary baked smoked ham is substituted for the more pungent style, I still add about a tablespoon of minced sweet pickle. Served with pickled peaches and maybe some beaten biscuits, thick slices of this loaf make a simple but satisfying summer lunch. Do be sure to allow the loaf to stand for at least 10 minutes before slicing, and, in truth, I think it's just as delicious at room temperature as hot.

1 Preheat the oven to 350°F.

2 In a large bowl, combine the ham, pork, onion, parsley, pickles, and cracker crumbs and mix with your hands till well blended. In a small bowl, combine the milk, egg, ketchup, mustard, and salt and pepper, whisk till well blended, add to the meat mixture, and mix gently till well blended and smooth (do not overmix). Scrape the mixture into a 9 by 5 by 3-inch loaf pan or dish and smooth the top with a spoon.

3 In a saucepan, combine the cream and cheese, stir over moderate heat till the cheese melts, pour the sauce over the top of the loaf, and bake, uncovered, till golden brown, 1 to 1¼ hours.

4 Loosen the loaf from the pan, transfer to a platter, and let stand for about 10 minutes before serving in slices.

Virginia Ham and Olive Loaf with Sour Cream Sauce

For the Loaf:

1 pound lean cooked country ham (preferably Smithfield)

1 cup finely chopped pimento-stuffed green olives

2 tablespoons butter

1 large onion, finely chopped

1 celery rib, finely chopped

1 garlic clove, minced

¼ pound mushrooms, finely chopped

Freshly ground black pepper to taste

¾ cup chicken broth

1½ cups dry bread crumbs

2 large eggs, beaten

½ cup heavy cream

¼ teaspoon powdered sage

No doubt, the most mellow, elegant, and expensive Southern country ham is a genuine Virginia Smithfield, a truly ceremonial ham that is traditionally glazed, baked, and featured on a festive holiday table. As is true with all cured country hams, however, the problem is always what to do with the leftover ends and nubs and scraps after the ham has been sliced down to the bone. Virginia cooks come up with any number of solutions (salads, soups, hashes, pastes), but possibly the most sophisticated I've encountered is this moist, sapid loaf served with a suave cream sauce. The body of the crusty loaf is not particularly firm, so be sure to allow it to stand a while before slicing.

1 Preheat the oven to 375°F. Butter a 9 by 5 by 3-inch loaf pan or dish and set aside.

2 To make the loaf, grind the ham well in a food processor (or chop it finely), place in a bowl, add the olives, toss, and set aside.

For the Sauce:

1 tablespoon butter

1 small onion, finely chopped

1 small green bell pepper, seeded and finely chopped

1 garlic clove, minced

1 tablespoon all-purpose flour

1 cup chicken broth

1 cup sour cream

2 tablespoons finely chopped fresh parsley leaves

Freshly ground black pepper to taste

3 In a medium skillet, melt the butter over moderate heat, add the onion, celery, garlic, mushrooms, and pepper, and stir for about 10 minutes. Add the broth, stir for about 2 minutes, and add to the ham and olives. Add the bread crumbs, eggs, cream, and sage, stir till well blended, scrape the mixture into the prepared pan, and bake, uncovered, till slightly crusted, about 1 hour.

4 Meanwhile, to make the sauce, melt the butter in a saucepan over moderate heat, add the onion, bell pepper, and garlic, and stir till softened, about 8 minutes. Add the flour and stir rapidly with a fork for 1 minute. Add the broth and stir for 1 minute longer. Add the sour cream, parsley, and pepper, stir for 1 minute longer, and keep the sauce hot.

5 To serve, allow the baked loaf to stand for about 10 minutes, and then slice and serve with the hot sauce.

Barbecued Pork and Sausage Meat Loaf

1½ cups soda cracker crumbs

¼ cup milk

1 pound ground lean pork

1 pound bulk pork sausage

1 medium onion, finely chopped

½ small green bell pepper, seeded and finely chopped

¼ teaspoon dried rosemary, crumbled

Salt and freshly ground black pepper to taste

2 large eggs, beaten

½ to ¾ cup bottled barbecue sauce

This meat loaf is "barbecued" only by virtue of a little commercial barbecue sauce added to the meat mixture—a practice as common in the South as "moistening" certain casseroles with canned soup. This is one loaf that should be made free-form (as opposed to packed into a baking dish) and baked on the rack of a broiling pan, not only so the fat can drip away but also so both the top and sides will be delectably crusty. When forming the loaf, if it feels too moist and "loose," simply add a few more finely crumbled crackers without soaking them. In the South, the loaf would usually be served with extra barbecue sauce on the side.

1 Preheat the oven to 375°F.

2 In a small bowl, combine the cracker crumbs and milk, stir, and let soak for about 10 minutes.

3 In a large bowl, combine the soaked crumbs with all the remaining ingredients and mix gently with your hands till well blended and smooth (do not overmix). Transfer the mixture to the rack of a broiling pan, form it into a loaf about 9 inches long and 4 inches wide, and bake in the upper third of the oven till the top and sides are crusty, 1 to 1¼ hours.

4 Transfer the loaf to a platter and let stand for about 10 minutes before serving in thick slices.

Deviled Ham and Pork Loaf

1½ pounds ground smoked ham

½ pound ground pork loin or lean shoulder

2 cups fresh bread crumbs

1 tablespoon light brown sugar

1 teaspoon dry mustard

Salt and freshly ground black pepper to taste

2 large eggs, beaten

1 cup milk

1 tablespoon cider vinegar

Sprigs of watercress for garnish

In the South, any meat or seafood spread, ball, cake, hash, croquette, or loaf that contains mustard (and/or cayenne pepper) is called "deviled," and you simply won't find a more intriguing deviled loaf than this simple one, mysteriously enhanced by a little brown sugar and vinegar (you could also add about ½ cup of chopped green olives or even ¼ cup of drained capers). The loaf is delicious hot with only Dijon mustard on the side, but if you want something more special, serve it slightly chilled with either a sour cream–horseradish sauce or a good fruit chutney. The same loaf can be made with all ham, but be warned that it won't slice as easily and evenly as when the ground pork is included.

1 Preheat the oven to 375°F. Grease a 9 by 5 by 3-inch loaf pan or dish and set aside.

2 In a large bowl, combine all the ingredients except the watercress, mix with your hands till well blended (do not overmix), scrape the mixture into the prepared pan, and bake, uncovered, till firm, about 1 hour. Let the loaf stand for about 10 minutes, transfer to a serving platter, and garnish the edges with watercress.

3 Serve hot or warm in slices.

CREOLE OYSTER AND BACON LOAVES

4 slices bacon

Peanut oil for deep frying

1 cup yellow cornmeal

2 teaspoons salt

1 teaspoon freshly ground
   black pepper

⅛ teaspoon cayenne pepper

1½ pints freshly shucked oysters
   (about 2½ dozen medium
   oysters), drained

2 loaves French bread, about
   1 foot long each

6 tablespoons (¾ stick) butter,
   melted

½ cup mayonnaise

Considered by many locals in New Orleans to be the predecessor of the more popular po' boy sandwich, the Oyster and Bacon Loaf was often tagged the "peacemaker" in Creole Louisiana, referring to an elaborate sandwich a wayward husband would bring home to placate an angry wife. Today, only trencherman eaters can plow through a whole loaf (washed down with Dixie beer), and what you're more likely to find in New Orleans delis are half-loaves smeared with both butter and mayonnaise, packed full of fat fried Gulf oysters and smoky bacon, and quickly heated before being wrapped in butcher paper. Ideally, the oysters should be fried in the basket of a deep-fat fryer, but whether you use this piece of equipment or simply a heavy saucepan, be sure that the temperature of the oil remains between 360° and 375°F and that the oysters are fried just till golden brown to prevent toughness.

1 In a large skillet, fry the bacon over moderate heat till crisp; drain on paper towels.

2 Preheat the oven to 200°F.

3 In a deep-fat fryer or large, heavy saucepan, heat about 2 inches of oil till it registers 375°F on a deep-fat thermometer.

4 In a bowl, combine the cornmeal, salt, pepper, and cayenne and stir till well blended. Roll the oysters in the meal to coat well, and, using a deep-fry basket or a slotted spoon, lower them into the oil in batches and fry till golden brown, about 2 minutes. Place the oysters on a platter lined with paper towels and keep warm in the oven.

5 Slice the bread loaves in half lengthwise, then crosswise. Brush the inside surfaces of the bread with butter, then spread mayonnaise over the surfaces. Heap oysters on the 4 bottom pieces of bread, arrange a slice of bacon on top of each, and cover with the 4 top slices of bread. Place the loaves on a platter in the oven for about 10 minutes before serving warm.

Pork, Bacon, and Sausage Hash with Apples and Almonds

3 slices bacon

1 medium onion, minced

1 garlic clove, minced

2 medium ripe tomatoes, peeled, seeded, and chopped

1 fresh red chile pepper, seeded and chopped

1½ pounds lean pork, chopped

½ pound smoked pork sausage links, casings removed, chopped

3 tablespoons fresh lemon juice

Pinch of ground cloves

1 large hard-boiled egg, finely chopped

2 apples

2 tablespoons butter

3 tablespoons slivered or chopped toasted almonds

Southern cooks find nothing lowly about a well-made hash, and when it comes to serving one on a breakfast or brunch buffet, imaginations can run wild, as in this crusty beauty boasting three forms of pig and many different flavors and textures. When browning the hash, remember that it should be crusted without drying out the interior. To toast the almonds (as well as any pecans, walnuts, or hazelnuts), preheat the oven to 300°F, spread the nuts on a baking sheet, and bake till slightly browned, 10 to 12 minutes, stirring several times and watching them closely to prevent burning.

1 In a large, cast-iron skillet, fry the bacon over moderate heat till almost crisp; drain on paper towels and chop finely.

2 Pour off all but about 2 tablespoons of fat from the skillet, add the onion and garlic, and stir for 2 minutes. Add the tomatoes and chile pepper, stir well, and simmer till the mixture is thickened, about 8 minutes. Add the pork, sausage, chopped bacon, lemon juice, and cloves and continue cooking for about 20 minutes, stirring often. During the final 10 minutes of simmering, preheat the oven broiler.

3 Brown the hash under the broiler till slightly crusty on top, about 5 minutes; transfer to a large serving platter, sprinkle with the chopped egg, and keep warm.

4 Core the apples and slice them into thin rings. In a large skillet, melt the butter over low heat, add the apples, and sauté on both sides till golden, about 10 minutes in all.

5 Arrange the apples around the edges of the hash, sprinkle almonds over the top, and serve immediately.

 PIG PICKIN'S

"The state of Virginia produces only three things: rattlesnakes, Presidents, and razorback hogs." —Will Rogers

Country Ham and Turnip Hash

1 pound cooked country ham, cut into ½-inch cubes

1½ cups cooked diced white turnips (slightly firm in texture)

2 medium onions, minced and sautéed in 2 tablespoons butter for 2 minutes

½ large green bell pepper, cored, seeded, and finely chopped

½ teaspoon dried sage, crumbled

Salt and freshly ground black pepper to taste

¾ cup heavy cream

4 tablespoons (½ stick) butter

4 large eggs

Finely chopped fresh parsley leaves for garnish

Popularized by roadside diners, lunch counters, and cafeterias in the early twentieth century, hash made with leftover meats and various root vegetables continues to be a favorite all over the South, and none is more appreciated than one that features salty country ham and sweet Southern white turnips. When shopping, look for small but heavy young white turnips with purplish tops and brightly colored greens (especially during the winter months), avoiding the larger, older ones with withered roots and a rough, woody texture. To boil any young turnips, peel and dice them, then simmer them in boiling water, covered, just till they're barely soft, about 20 minutes.

1 In a large bowl, combine the ham, turnips, onions, bell pepper, sage, salt and pepper, and cream, stir till well blended, and, with your hands, form into a large cake.

2 In a large, heavy skillet, melt half the butter over moderately high heat, add the ham cake, and press down evenly with a spatula to form a compact oval cake. Reduce the heat to moderate and cook the hash for about 5 minutes or till the underside is browned and crusty. Loosen the hash with the spatula and invert onto a plate. Add the remaining butter to the skillet and increase the heat slightly. Slide the hash back into the skillet with the unbrowned side facing down, reduce the heat to moderate, and cook for about 5 minutes or till the other side is browned and crusty. Transfer the hash to a platter and keep warm.

3 Break the eggs gently into 1 or 2 saucepans of boiling water, poach for 2 minutes, and transfer with a slotted spoon to a clean cloth to drain. Top the hash with the poached eggs, sprinkle parsley over the top, and serve immediately.

PIG PICKIN'S

"In the South, it is fat bacon and pork, fat bacon and pork only, and that continues morning, noon, and night for all classes, sexes, ages, and conditions."

—John Wilson, Godey's Ladies Book, 1860

Ham Croquettes with Parsley Sauce

Makes 6 servings

For the Sauce:

2 tablespoons butter

2 tablespoons all-purpose flour

1 cup whole milk

Salt and freshly ground black
pepper to taste

2 tablespoons minced fresh
parsley leaves

I am still on the bandwagon to restore all croquettes (meat, poultry, and seafood) to the prominent role they once played in every country-club dining room and department-store restaurant in the South, and none do I relish more than those made with some form of ham and served with a mustard, tomato, or cream sauce, or with this subtle parsley sauce. In truth, a well-made, carefully fried ham croquette is delicious just by itself (either as an appetizer or main course), and for ideal texture, I remain convinced that the mixture for these croquettes should be chilled overnight before being formed into patties. As with all croquettes, feel free to experiment with different secondary ingredients (olives, capers, bell peppers, and so on).

1 To make the sauce, melt the butter in a small saucepan over moderately low heat, add the flour, and stir till a smooth paste forms. Gradually add the milk, stirring till thickened and smooth, 3 to 4 minutes. Add the salt and pepper and parsley, stir till well blended, and keep the sauce warm over very low heat.

4 tablespoons (½ stick) butter

3 scallions (white parts only), finely chopped

3 tablespoons all-purpose flour, plus extra for dredging

1½ cups milk

4 cups coarsely chopped cooked ham

3 large egg yolks

1 tablespoon Dijon mustard

¼ teaspoon dried sage, crumbled

Salt and freshly ground black pepper to taste

1 large egg, beaten with 2 tablespoons water

2 cups fine dry bread crumbs

Peanut oil for frying

2 To make the croquettes, melt the butter in a saucepan over moderate heat, add the scallions and flour, and whisk till soft and well blended, about 2 minutes. Whisking rapidly, add the milk till well blended; add the ham, stir well, and remove from the heat. Whisking rapidly, add the egg yolks, return to the heat, add the mustard, sage, and salt and pepper, and whisk till well blended. Scrape the mixture into a dish, cover, and refrigerate overnight.

3 With your hands, divide the mixture into 6 balls and roll lightly in the extra flour. Pat the balls into smooth oval patties, dip briefly into the egg wash, dredge in the bread crumbs, and place on a plate till ready to fry.

4 In a large, heavy skillet, heat about 1 inch of oil over moderately high heat for about 1 minute, fry the patties till golden brown, about 3 minutes on each side, and drain briefly on paper towels. Serve the croquettes with the parsley sauce on the side.

CURRIED PORK AND APPLE MOLD

4 slices white loaf bread,
   crusts trimmed

½ cup milk

1½ pounds ground pork loin
   or lean shoulder

2 Granny Smith apples, peeled,
   cored, and finely chopped

1 medium onion, minced

1 tablespoon curry powder

½ teaspoon ground cinnamon

Salt and freshly ground black
   pepper to taste

1 large egg, beaten

For formal buffets, Southerners love nothing more than to serve an attractive meat, poultry, or seafood mold, the center ring filled with fluffy mashed potatoes, steamed broccoli florets, buttered rice or corn kernels, or any other vegetable or grain that goes well with the main dish. For added flavor, three or four slices of bacon could be draped over this particular spicy mold, but remember that unless you remove the bacon during the final 15 or so minutes of baking, the top will not be fully crusty.

1 Preheat the oven to 350°F. Grease a 5-cup metal ring mold and set aside.

2 Shred the bread finely into a bowl, add the milk, and let soak for 5 minutes.

3 In a bowl, combine the bread with all the remaining ingredients and mix with your hands till well blended and smooth. Pack the mixture into the prepared mold and bake, uncovered, till crusted on top but still moist inside, 50 to 55 minutes. Let stand for about 5 minutes, loosen the edges with a small knife, and pour off any drippings. Turn the mold out onto a serving platter and fill the center with mashed potatoes, buttered rice, or a steamed vegetable. Serve in thick slices.

CRACKLIN' PORK BURGERS

MAKES 4 SERVINGS

2 tablespoons butter

2 medium onions, thinly sliced

2 slices white loaf bread, torn into small bits

¼ cup milk

¼ pound lean salt pork, rind removed, chopped

1½ pounds ground pork

1 garlic clove, minced

1 tablespoon Worcestershire sauce

Salt and freshly ground black pepper to taste

1½ cups fine dry bread crumbs

Mustard to taste

4 hamburger buns, heated in aluminum foil

I'm not going to say that this is the best burger you'll ever sample, but I'm tempted. Being either crunchy pieces of rendered pork fat or the crisp skin of roasted pork shoulder, cracklings (or cracklin's) can be found packaged in virtually all Southern markets and are used to flavor salads, stews, breads, and, indeed, something special like these succulent pork burgers traditionally smothered with plenty of caramelized onions—preferably Vidalias. Here I spread mustard over the buns to appeal to all tastes, but if you really want to eat like a Southerner, you'll also use a little mayonnaise.

1 In a medium skillet, melt the butter over low heat, add the onions, and cook slowly, stirring, till caramelized, about 20 minutes. Transfer to a plate and keep warm.

2 Meanwhile, combine the bread and milk in a bowl and let soak. In a large skillet, fry the salt pork over moderate heat till crisp, stirring; drain the cracklin's on paper towels. Remove the skillet from the heat and reserve the fat in the skillet.

3 In a bowl, combine the ground pork, garlic, Worcestershire, salt and pepper, soaked bread, and the cracklin's and mix with your hands till well blended. Form the mixture into 4 patties, and coat the patties with bread crumbs. Reheat the fat in the skillet over moderate heat, add the patties, and cook till nicely browned, about 7 minutes on each side.

4 To serve, spread mustard over the inside surfaces of the buns, place a burger on each bottom half, spoon caramelized onions generously over each burger, and cover with the bun tops.

Open-Face Pig and Pimento Burgers

Makes 4 servings

1 pound ground pork

½ teaspoon red pepper flakes

Salt and freshly ground black
    pepper to taste

One-half 10¾-ounce can cream
    of mushroom soup

¼ cup heavy cream

4 hamburger buns, lightly toasted

One 7-ounce jar pimento strips,
    drained

¼ pound sharp cheddar cheese,
    thinly sliced

It's been said that pig, pimentos, and cheddar cheese constitute one of the South's many culinary holy trinities (like onions, celery, and bell peppers, or pecans, brown sugar, and molasses), and nothing illustrates this better than these open-face burgers found in diners and cafeterias throughout the region. And here is a good example of when cooks think nothing of flavoring and moistening a dish with a little canned soup—not a lot, just enough to help bind the meat mixture till it's appropriately moist and slightly firm. The concept behind these burgers is not unlike that of Kentucky hot browns and Creole po' boy sandwiches.

1 Preheat the oven broiler.

2 In a medium skillet, break up the pork over moderate heat and stir till thoroughly cooked, about 10 minutes. Pour off any fat, add the red pepper flakes and salt and pepper, and stir well. In a small bowl, combine and mix the soup and cream till well blended, and add just enough to thoroughly moisten the meat, stirring till the mixture is moist but still slightly firm.

3 Arrange the hamburger bun halves on the rack of a large broiler pan and spoon equal amounts of the pork mixture on each half. Arrange pimento strips over the meat, arrange slices of cheese over the pimentos, and broil till the cheese melts and the tops are slightly browned.

4 Serve the burgers hot with knives and forks.

Tarpon Springs Greek Burgers

Makes 4 servings

¼ cup Greek olive oil

3 tablespoons white wine vinegar

3 tablespoons fresh lemon juice

1 teaspoon dried oregano, crumbled

1 garlic clove, minced

Salt and freshly ground black pepper to taste

2 Kirby cucumbers, peeled and coarsely chopped

8 to 10 Greek black olives, pitted and coarsely chopped

2 scallions (part of green tops included), finely chopped

1½ pounds ground lean pork

1 small onion, minced

2 mint leaves, minced

1 cup plain yogurt

On Florida's Gulf coast not far from Tampa, Tarpon Springs has long been home to a large community of Greek immigrants involved in the town's sponge industry, one result being the evolutionary development of a veritable Southern-Greek cuisine that is the same as that in Charlotte, North Carolina (where, many years ago, my own Greek grandfather operated a modest restaurant). In the Old Country, of course, these burgers (or ground steaks) would most surely be made with finely chopped lamb, but since pork is so much more readily available in Florida, cooks in Greek coffee shops and restaurants adapted to the milder meat generations ago. I've never seen the burgers served on buns, and the traditional accompaniment is fried potatoes.

1 In a bowl, combine the olive oil, vinegar, and lemon juice and whisk till well blended. Add the oregano, garlic, and salt and pepper and stir till well blended. Add the cucumbers, olives, and scallions, stir well, cover with plastic wrap, and let marinate for about 1 hour.

2 Preheat the oven broiler.

3 In a bowl, combine the pork, onion, mint, and yogurt and mix with your hands till well blended. Shape the mixture into 4 thick oval patties, place on the rack of a broiler pan, and broil about 4 inches from the heat till cooked through, about 8 minutes on each side.

4 Drain the cucumbers, olives, and scallions and serve the burgers hot with a little of the mixture spooned over the top.

Roasts

Bacon-Wrapped Pork Loin with Dates
and Walnuts

Marinated Pork Roast
with Bourbon-Lemon Glaze

Pot-Roasted Pork Loin and Leeks

Jeanne's Roast Pork with
Sausage-Cornbread Stuffing

Florida Mango- and
Prune-Stuffed Pork Loin

Paul's Cajun Vegetable-Stuffed
Pork Roast

Cold Marinated Baked Pork Loin

Roast Pork Loin with Spiced Apricots

Crown Roast of Pork with Spicy Sausage
and Raisin Stuffing

Savannah Pork Loin Baked in Milk

Baked Pork Loin with
Fig-Citrus Stuffing

Virginia Pork Tenderloin
with Blue Cheese Sauce

Seared Pork Tenderloin with
Bourbon-Molasses Glaze

Roast Pork Tenderloin Stuffed
with Honeyed Apples and Pecans

Roasted Pork Shoulder with
Applejack Gravy

Slow-Roasted Pork Shoulder
with Orange-Raisin Sauce

Hominy-Stuffed Pork Shoulder
with Rum Gravy

Mock Louisiana Cochon de Lait

Baked Pork Butt with
Home-Style Pan Gravy

Chilled Poached Pork Butt

Roasted Quail with Salt Pork
and Country Ham

BACON-WRAPPED PORK LOIN WITH DATES AND WALNUTS

MAKES 6 SERVINGS

One 3- to 3½-pound boneless pork loin

2 tablespoons olive oil

1 teaspoon ground cinnamon

1 teaspoon ground nutmeg

Salt and freshly ground black pepper to taste

10 slices applewood-smoked bacon

1 cup dry white wine

1 cup water

1 medium onion, chopped

3 garlic cloves, minced

12 pitted dates

1 cup chopped walnuts

Since pork loin is so lean and risks being dry when cooked, Southern cooks learned centuries ago to either braise the meat slowly in liquid or roast it wrapped with some form of pork fat. Today, nothing keeps a roasted loin moist or delivers delectable extra flavor like a premium wood-smoked bacon, so long, that is, as the bacon has an adequate quota of fat. Sweet dates and walnuts in this particular dish not only enhance the mildness of the pork but also balance the smokiness of the bacon. If carving the roast with the bacon is awkward and messy, simply remove the bacon slices first, and then serve a slice or two over each portion of pork.

1 Preheat the oven to 325°F.

2 Rub the pork loin all over with the oil, then rub the cinnamon, nutmeg, and salt and pepper evenly into the meat. Wrap the pork crosswise with slightly overlapping bacon slices and secure the ends with toothpicks. Position the pork on a rack in a large roasting pan and pour the wine and water around the sides. Add the remaining ingredients and roast the pork, uncovered, till well-done, 1½ to 2 hours, basting from time to time.

3 Transfer the pork, dates, and walnuts to a platter and keep warm. Spoon off as much fat from the pan as possible and make natural pan gravy by stirring the juices over moderate heat till the onion browns slightly, adding a little more hot water and stirring till the gravy is nicely thickened.

4 To serve, remove the toothpicks, carve the pork into ¼-inch-thick slices, rearrange the slices, dates, and walnuts on the platter, and spoon the gravy over the top.

PIG PICKIN'S

The Cajuns of Louisiana produce three distinctive styles or pork: andouille (smoked pork sausage), boudin (peppery-hot link sausages), and tasso (spicy smoked ham).

MARINATED PORK ROAST WITH BOURBON-LEMON GLAZE

MAKES 6 SERVINGS

One 4-pound boneless pork loin

2 garlic cloves, sliced into slivers

2 teaspoons dried rosemary, crumbled

Salt and freshly ground black pepper to taste

1 cup dry vermouth

½ cup fresh lemon juice

¼ cup bourbon

½ cup sugar

Marinating a pork loin not only contributes needed moisture to the lean meat but also allows various flavors to penetrate it much more thoroughly than a mere sprinkling or rubbing. Then, when the roast is glazed with a sweet-sour mixture of bourbon and lemon juice and cooked to a glossy brown, the result is a mouth-watering dish fit for the most sophisticated Southern buffet or dinner table. This is one pork roast that needs no gravy.

1 Tie the pork loin at several intervals with butcher's twine. With a sharp paring knife, make deep slits all over the loin, insert slivers of garlic into the slits, and season the meat all over with the rosemary and salt and pepper. Place the loin in a large, shallow baking dish, pour the vermouth around the edges, cover with plastic wrap, and let marinate for about 2 hours, turning several times.

2 Meanwhile, preheat the oven to 450°F.

3 Remove the loin from the marinade, pat dry with paper towels, position on a rack in a large roasting pan, and roast for 20 minutes. Reduce the heat to 325°F and continue roasting for about 45 minutes, basting with the pan juices.

4 Meanwhile, in a small bowl, combine the lemon juice, bourbon, and sugar, and stir till the sugar dissolves.

5 Remove the pan from the oven and carefully pour off the fat. Spoon the bourbon mixture over the loin, return it to the oven, and roast for about 45 minutes longer, basting with the glaze frequently till the roast is glossy brown.

6 Remove the roast from the oven, transfer to a serving platter, remove the twine, and let stand for about 10 minutes before carving into ½-inch-thick slices.

Pot-Roasted Pork Loin and Leeks

One 4- to 5-pound pork loin
(center cut or rib end)

3 tablespoons all-purpose flour

2 large leeks

3 garlic cloves, minced

1 cup dry white wine

1 cup chicken broth, plus more
if needed

½ teaspoon paprika

Salt and freshly ground black
pepper to taste

While most people don't think to pot-roast a large cut of pork the way they do a beef rump, shoulder, or round roast, Southern cooks learned long ago that no method assures more tender and moist meat. Naturally, a couple of coarsely chopped large ordinary onions can be substituted for the leeks, but since the fragrance and flavor of leeks (like those of Vidalia onions) are milder and subtler, given the Southern penchant for sweetness, the thick, white stalks are preferred for smothering meats and poultry—especially the smaller, more tender leeks. When dealing with any leeks, just always be sure to wash them thoroughly to release any dirt or sand trapped between the leaf layers. And if you want this dish to be even sweeter, feel free to add one or two carrots cut into rounds, the way a Southerner might do.

1 Preheat the oven to 325°F.

2 Remove excess fat from the pork loin, chop it finely, and reserve. Sprinkle the flour all over the loin and spread it evenly with your fingers. Cut off the roots and tough green leaves of the leeks and peel away any coarse outer layers of stalk. Cut the stalks into 1-inch rounds, wash thoroughly under tepid water to remove all traces of grit, and pat dry with paper towels.

3 In a large, heavy roasting pan, fry the reserved pork fat over moderate heat till all the fat is rendered; discard the bits. Place the loin in the pan and lightly brown it evenly on all sides, taking care not to burn. Transfer to a platter, add the leeks and garlic to the pan, and stir till softened, about 10 minutes. Add the remaining ingredients and bring to a boil over high heat, scraping any brown bits from the bottom of the pan.

4 Return the loin plus any juices to the pan, cover, and braise the pork and leeks in the oven for 1½ hours. Uncover and roast the pork, basting once or twice, till it shows no resistance when pierced deeply with a sharp knife, 30 to 45 minutes, adding a little more broth to the leeks if necessary.

5 Transfer the loin to a serving platter, skim as much fat as possible from the surface of the cooking liquid, and heat the leeks and gravy well.

6 To serve, carve the loin into slices and spoon the leeks and gravy over the top.

Jeanne's Roast Pork with Sausage-Cornbread Stuffing

Makes 6 servings

One 4- to 5-pound pork loin

½ pound bulk pork sausage

1 large onion, finely chopped

2 celery ribs, finely chopped

4 cups cornbread crumbs

1 teaspoon dried sage

Salt and freshly ground black pepper to taste

1½ cups beef broth

My good friend, cookbook author Jeanne Voltz, may have spent many years in New York and California, but she never forgot her Alabama roots and was the one who taught me this technique of roasting a stuffed pork loin on top of extra stuffing. The concept is not unlike the Southern practice of serving two styles of stuffing with roast turkey—a soft one cooked inside the bird and a crusty one baked outside—and all I can say is that the overall flavor and texture experience of the succulent pork with the two stuffings is pretty amazing. For a neater roast, you can attempt to tie the stuffed chops with butcher's twine the way a professional chef would do, but I personally don't think it's worth the trouble.

1 Preheat the oven to 325°F.

2 With a sharp knife, separate the ribs of the pork loin almost to the backbone, position the loin in a large roasting pan, and roast it for 1 hour.

3 Meanwhile, break up the sausage in a skillet, fry it over moderate heat till well browned, drain on paper towels, and transfer to a bowl. Pour off all but 2 tablespoons of fat from the skillet, add the onion and celery, stir till softened, about 5 minutes, and add to the sausage. Add the remaining ingredients and stir till the stuffing is well blended.

4 Remove the loin from the oven, transfer to a work surface, and drain off the fat from the pan. Gently push the chops apart and spoon part of the stuffing in the spaces between them. Spread the remaining stuffing in the pan, position the loin on top of the stuffing, and roast it till very tender, 1 to 1¼ hours longer.

5 To serve, transfer the loin to a serving platter and place the extra stuffing in a serving dish. Carve the meat completely into individual chops, top each with its own stuffing, and serve the extra stuffing on the side.

 PIG PICKIN'S

Hogs turn three pounds of grain in their feeding trough into a pound of weight gain.

FLORIDA MANGO- AND PRUNE-STUFFED PORK LOIN

8 to 10 pitted prunes, quartered

½ cup orange juice

One 3-pound boneless pork loin

1 teaspoon ground ginger

Salt and freshly ground black pepper to taste

1 firm, ripe mango, peeled and seeded

½ cup dry white wine

Since the first domesticated hogs in the United States were a herd of 13 brought from Spain to Tampa, Florida, in 1539 by Hernando de Soto, it makes sense that pork has always been a major staple throughout the Sunshine State. Add to that the influx of pig-loving Cuban and other Hispanic immigrants over the past few decades, and it's no surprise that some of the most intriguing and delectable pork dishes utilizing the state's abundance of fresh fruits are found all over southern Florida. When I was served this roasted pork loin at a book fair in Pompano Beach, it was stuffed with prunes and carambola, the firm, juicy, exotic "star fruit" that is being cultivated in Florida and can sometimes be found in gourmet grocery stores outside the region. Mango is an appropriate substitute, and, in fact, I think I like it even better when combined with the soft prunes.

1 In a bowl, combine the prunes and orange juice and let soak for about 30 minutes.

2 Sprinkle the pork all over with the ginger and salt and pepper and rub into the meat.

3 Preheat the oven to 350°F.

4 Transfer the prunes to a cutting board, reserving the orange juice, add the mango, and chop together finely to form a loose paste. Using the handle of a wooden spoon, bore a 1½-inch hole lengthwise through the middle of the pork and stuff the hole firmly with the fruit paste. Place the pork on a rack in a large roasting pan, add the reserved orange juice plus the wine, and roast, basting from time to time, till the pork is very tender, about 1½ hours.

5 Let the roast stand for about 10 minutes before carving into ½-inch-thick slices.

PIG PICKIN'S

In the nineteenth century, wealthy Southern planters, military officers, and top politicians who ate only the choice lean loin meat from a pig's back were said to live "high on the hog."

Paul's Cajun Vegetable-Stuffed Pork Roast

MAKES 6 SERVINGS

2 teaspoons freshly ground
    black pepper

1½ teaspoons salt

1 teaspoon cayenne pepper

1 teaspoon sweet paprika

1 teaspoon dried thyme, crumbled

½ teaspoon dry mustard

3 tablespoons butter

1 tablespoon lard

1 medium onion, finely chopped

2 celery ribs, finely chopped

½ green bell pepper, seeded
    and finely chopped

2 garlic cloves, minced

One 4-pound boneless pork loin

Leave it to the great Cajun chef Paul Prudhomme to come up with this bold, sumptuous, stuffed pork roast that I first sampled when he was overseeing the kitchen at Commander's Palace restaurant in New Orleans. What amazed me most was the way Paul not only stuffed the loin with the highly seasoned vegetable mixture but then also spread extra mixture all over the meat to produce a roast that was fully moist inside, with a very dark, almost crunchy crust. Do watch the loin carefully during the final 15 minutes to make sure the mixture doesn't burn. And don't even think about serving some form of gravy with this Cajun masterpiece.

1 Preheat the oven to 275°F.

2 In a small bowl, combine the black pepper, salt, cayenne, paprika, thyme, and mustard, mix till well blended, and set aside.

3 In a large skillet, melt the butter and lard over moderate heat, add the onion, celery, bell pepper, and garlic, and stir for about 3 minutes. Add the mixed seasoning, stir for about 2 minutes longer, remove from the heat, and let cool.

4 Position the pork loin on a rack in a large roasting pan fat side up and make several slits in the meat with a small knife, being careful not to cut through to the bottom. Stuff the slits with some of the vegetable mixture, then rub the mixture thoroughly over the entire loin with your hands. If any of the mixture is left, spread it evenly over the top. Roast slowly, uncovered, for 3 hours. Increase the heat to 425°F and continue roasting till dark brown on top, about 15 minutes longer.

5 To serve, transfer the roast to a serving platter and carve into ½-inch-thick slices.

COLD MARINATED BAKED PORK LOIN

One 5-pound pork loin
   (center cut)

1 tablespoon dried thyme,
   crumbled

1 tablespoon dry mustard

½ cup dry sherry

½ cup soy sauce

3 garlic cloves, minced

1 tablespoon ground ginger

Freshly ground black pepper
   to taste

8 ounces apple jelly

Sprigs of watercress for garnish

This is the type of elegant, glazed pork dish that any serious Virginia or Louisiana home cook might feature on a stylish summer buffet—accompanied by maybe a congealed vegetable salad, pickled peaches, a basket of beaten biscuits, and, for dessert, a colorful grasshopper pie. Most cold meats call for many more complex seasonings than hot ones, and this is particularly true with a lean, relatively bland pork loin that has so little natural interior fat to flavor it. When I commented on the multiple diverse seasonings that an exacting lady in Richmond, Virginia, once used for a marinated loin much like this one, she simply quipped, "Honey, if there's one thing I hate, it's dull pig."

1 Rub the pork loin all over with the thyme and dry mustard and place in a large, shallow baking dish. In a bowl, combine the sherry, soy sauce, garlic, ginger, and pepper and stir till well blended. Pour the mixture around the loin, cover with plastic wrap, and let marinate in the refrigerator for at least 6 hours, turning once and basting several times.

2 Preheat the oven to 325°F.

3 Transfer the loin to a rack in a large, heavy baking pan, add the marinade to the pan, cover, and bake till very tender, 2 to 2½ hours, basting from time to time.

4 Transfer the loin to a rack in a large, shallow, clean baking dish and let cool. In a saucepan, melt the jelly over moderate heat and let cool. Skim fat from the liquid in the baking pan, add the liquid to the jelly, and stir till well blended. Spoon the glaze over the loin, repeating as the mixture runs off into the dish to build up a glossy coating on the loin. Cover with plastic wrap and chill till ready to serve.

5 To serve, carve the loin into ¼-inch-thick slices, arrange the slices on a platter, and garnish the edges with watercress.

PIG PICKIN'S

Technically, a pig of either sex becomes a hog when it reaches 100 pounds. A young male is called a shoat, and a female who has not yet produced a litter is known as a gilt. Boars are breeding males, and sows are the females with whom they have produced offspring.

ROAST PORK LOIN WITH SPICED APRICOTS

MAKES 4 TO 6 SERVINGS

For the Apricots:

2 cups dry red wine

¼ cup sugar

¼ teaspoon ground cinnamon

¼ teaspoon ground allspice

¼ teaspoon ground nutmeg

8 to 10 fresh, firm apricots, pitted and cut in half

1 cup chicken broth

For the Pork:

One 3-pound boneless pork loin

2 tablespoons peanut oil

2 cloves garlic, minced

2 teaspoons minced fresh rosemary

Salt and freshly ground black pepper to taste

1 cup white wine

Southerners love peaches, apricots, nectarines, plums, and any number of other fruits with roast pork, and when juicy fresh apricots make their short summer appearance in the markets, cooks think up as many ways to dress them up for special dishes as they do with peaches. Remember that apricots are very delicate—even more so than peaches and nectarines—and should always be bought slightly firm so that they don't virtually disintegrate when cooked. If you can't find fresh apricots, spiced peaches or nectarines are just as delicious with this pork.

1 To prepare the apricots, combine the wine, sugar, cinnamon, allspice, and nutmeg in a large, heavy saucepan, bring to a boil, and stir till the sugar dissolves. Add the apricots, reduce the heat to low, and simmer till the apricots are tender, about 10 minutes. With a slotted spoon, transfer the apricots to a plate, add the broth to the pan, bring to a low boil, and cook till the sauce is reduced to about 1 cup, 15 to 20 minutes. Return the apricots to the pan, stir gently, remove from the heat, and let stand while the pork is cooking.

2 Position the pork loin on a rack in a large roasting pan, rub with the oil, and sprinkle with the garlic, rosemary, and salt and pepper, pressing the seasonings into the meat. Add the wine to the pan and roast till the pork is tender, about 1½ hours, basting occasionally. Remove from the oven and let stand for about 10 minutes.

3 To serve, reheat the apricots, carve the pork into ½-inch-thick slices, and spoon apricots and a little sauce over each portion.

CROWN ROAST OF PORK WITH SPICY SAUSAGE AND RAISIN STUFFING

For the Roast:

One 8- to 9-pound crown roast
of pork

1 tablespoon dried sage,
crumbled

1 tablespoon dried thyme,
crumbled

3 garlic cloves, minced

For the Stuffing:

2 pounds bulk pork sausage

1 medium onion, diced

2 celery ribs, diced

2 garlic cloves, minced

½ cup seedless golden raisins

1 cup fresh bread crumbs

2 tablespoons light brown sugar

½ cup chopped parsley leaves

½ teaspoon dried sage, crumbled

½ teaspoon ground cinnamon

1½ teaspoons salt

Freshly ground black pepper
to taste

1 large egg, beaten

Intended for a truly sumptuous occasion (a formal wedding dinner, an anniversary feast, a lavish holiday meal), a stuffed crown roast of pork is the highest tribute a Southern (or any other) cook can make to the glorious pig. The circular roast must be ordered from and prepared by a good butcher and should include between 20 and 22 ribs (chops). The stuffing can be savory or sweet, mild or spicy, and possibilities besides this typically Southern sausage and raisin stuffing would be cornbread and crabapples, ham and pecans, and spinach and apricots. Virtually all crown roasts of pork are served with a fine natural or cream gravy—spooned over both the meat and stuffing.

1 Have a butcher remove the backbone of the roast, French-cut the rib ends, and score the fat in a diamond pattern.

2 Preheat the oven to 400°F.

3 Wrap the tips of the ribs in foil, rub the meat with the sage, thyme, and garlic, and position the roast on a rack in a large roasting pan. Roast for 20 minutes, reduce the heat to 325°F, and continue roasting for 1¼ hours.

(continued)

For the Gravy:

2 tablespoons all-purpose flour

½ cup dry white wine

½ cup chicken broth

1 cup heavy cream

1 tablespoon Dijon mustard

**Freshly ground black pepper
to taste**

4 Meanwhile, to prepare the stuffing, fry the sausage in a large skillet over moderate heat, breaking it up with a fork, till well browned. Drain on paper towels and pour off all but about 2 tablespoons of fat from the skillet. Add the onions, celery, and garlic and stir till softened, about 5 minutes. Transfer the mixture to a large bowl, add the remaining stuffing ingredients, and mix till thoroughly blended.

5 Remove the roast from the oven and fill the center with the stuffing. Return to the oven and continue roasting for about 1¼ hours longer. Increase the heat to 450°F and continue roasting till beautifully browned, 15 to 20 minutes longer. Transfer the roast to a large serving platter and remove the foil from the rib ends, replacing it with decorative paper frills.

6 To prepare the gravy, pour all but 2 tablespoons of fat from the roasting pan, add the flour to the pan, and stir over moderate heat for 3 minutes. Add the wine, increase the heat to moderately high, and reduce the liquid to about 2 tablespoons. Add the broth, cream, mustard, and pepper, stir well, return the heat to moderate, and continue cooking and stirring till the gravy is smooth. Pour into a gravy boat.

7 To serve, carve the roast into individual chops and serve with the stuffing and gravy.

Savannah Pork Loin Baked in Milk

One 3-pound boneless pork loin

1 tablespoon dried sage, crumbled

Salt and freshly ground black pepper to taste

2 Vidalia onions, thinly sliced

2 cups whole milk

1 tablespoon all-purpose flour

Strips of lemon rind for garnish

Folks in Savannah, Georgia, always do things a little differently from others in the South, and my friend and colleague Damon Lee Fowler is no exception when it comes to baking his pork loin in milk atop a bed of sweet Vidalia onions. This is one of the moistest and silkiest pork roasts you'll ever taste; Damon's method of making pan gravy is exemplary, and the directions should be followed to the letter. Damon simply garnishes his thin slices of pork with strips of lemon rind, but I've discovered that actually adding about a tablespoon of grated rind to the milk before baking makes the dish even more subtle and delicious. Do not use low-fat milk in this recipe.

1 Preheat the oven to 450°F.

2 Rub the pork loin all over with the sage and salt and pepper. Layer half the onions over the bottom of a large baking pan or ovenproof casserole, position the loin on top of the onions, and roast in the oven, uncovered, till lightly browned, about 20 minutes. Cover the pork with the remaining onions and pour the milk slowly over all. Cover the pan, reduce the heat to 325°F, and bake till the pork is very tender, about 2 hours longer.

(continued)

3 Transfer the pork and onions to a platter and keep warm. Spoon off most of the fat from the pan, reserving 2 tablespoons. Pour off but reserve the pan juices. Return the reserved fat to the pan, heat over moderately high heat, sprinkle the flour over the top, and stir till it begins to brown, 3 to 4 minutes. Stirring constantly, add the pan juices and cook till the gravy is lightly thickened, about 4 minutes. Taste for salt and pepper, and then pour into a gravy boat.

4 To serve, carve the pork into thin slices, surround it with the onions, and spoon a little gravy over the meat. Garnish with strips of lemon rind and serve with the remaining gravy on the side.

FRIED COUNTRY HAM WITH RED-EYE GRAVY (PAGE 240)

Above: **AUNT BUNNY'S BACON AND SAUSAGE SOUFFLÉ (PAGE 264)**

Opposite: **SULLIVAN'S ISLAND BACON AND SHRIMP BOG (PAGE 268)**

Above: **NORTH CAROLINA EASTERN-STYLE CHOPPED OR PULLED 'CUE (PAGE 278)**

Left: **CORKY'S MEMPHIS-STYLE BARBECUED BACK RIBS (PAGE 294)**

Opposite: **OLD DOMINION SCALLOPED POTATOES WITH COUNTRY HAM (PAGE 356)**

Opposite: **CREOLE HAM, SAUSAGE, AND SHRIMP JAMBALAYA (PAGE 380)**

Above: **SKILLET CORNBREAD WITH CRACKLIN'S (PAGE 384)**

Bacon-Cheddar Biscuits (page 398)

Baked Pork Loin with Fig-Citrus Stuffing

Makes 4 to 6 servings

1 cup (about ¼ pound) finely diced fresh figs

1 orange, peel grated and juice strained

1 lemon, peel grated and juice strained

3 cups fresh bread crumbs

3 tablespoons butter, melted

¼ teaspoon ground nutmeg

Salt and freshly ground black pepper to taste

One 3-pound boneless pork loin

1 cup beer

Just the hoppy aroma of this pork baking in beer is enough to awaken the appetite, and the acid-sweet balance of the citrus and figs in the stuffing produces a taste sensation you don't soon forget. This is yet another pork loin that is so moist and flavorful that it needs no gravy. Dried figs can be used in place of the fresh, but you won't have as moist a stuffing. Do remember that fresh figs (available during the summer months) are extremely perishable and keep in the refrigerator for no more than a few days.

1 Preheat the oven to 325°F.

2 In a medium bowl, combine the figs and citrus peels and juices and stir till well blended. In a small bowl, combine the bread crumbs, butter, nutmeg, and salt and pepper, toss well, add to the figs and citrus, and stir till well blended, adding a little more orange juice if the stuffing seems too dry (it should be slightly moist).

3 With a sharp knife, carve a pocket lengthwise in the pork loin to within ½ inch of the other side, fill the pocket with the stuffing, and tie the loin securely at several intervals with butcher's twine to close completely. Position the pork on a rack in a large baking pan, add the beer, cover, and bake till very tender, about 1½ hours.

4 To serve, remove the twine and carve the pork into ½-inch-thick slices.

Virginia Pork Tenderloin with Blue Cheese Sauce

MAKES 6 SERVINGS

Two 1-pound pork tenderloins

Salt and freshly ground black pepper to taste

2 tablespoons peanut oil

½ cup water

2 ounces blue cheese

4 tablespoons (½ stick) butter, softened

¼ cup Madeira or semisweet sherry

1 tablespoon finely chopped scallions

2 cups chicken broth

2 tablespoons chopped fresh parsley

When I raved over this moist tenderloin cloaked in a sumptuous blue cheese sauce at a dinner on Long Island, it made my heart proud when the hostess informed me that the recipe came from a close friend in Richmond, Virginia, who liked to serve the pork over a bed of chopped leeks sautéed in butter. I know that during Jeffersonian days nothing was appreciated more at Monticello and other Virginia homes than pork flavored with Madeira, and while the colonial cooks might have first raised an eyebrow at the blue cheese in the sauce, I have no doubt that had they tasted this utterly modern dish, they would have been as ecstatically impressed as I was. Yes, the pork goes well with leeks, but, as I've discovered, it's even more delicious served over thin slices of Vidalia onions sautéed in butter.

1 Preheat the oven to 375°F.

2 Season the tenderloins with salt and pepper on all sides. In a large cast-iron or enameled skillet, heat the oil over moderate heat, add the tenderloins, and brown lightly on all sides. Add the water to the skillet, place in the oven, and cook till tender, 25 to 30 minutes.

3 Meanwhile, combine the blue cheese and butter in a small bowl, mash with a fork to a paste, and set aside.

4 Transfer the tenderloins to a platter and keep warm. Add the Madeira and scallions to the skillet, bring to a boil, and reduce the liquid to a thick consistency, about 8 minutes. Add the broth and continue to boil till slightly thickened, about 5 minutes. Bit by bit, swirl in the blue cheese paste to form an emulsion; add the parsley, stir, and remove the sauce from the heat.

5 To serve, carve the tenderloin into medium-thick slices and spoon sauce over each portion.

Seared Pork Tenderloin with Bourbon-Molasses Glaze

One 1½-pound pork tenderloin

2 tablespoons peanut oil

1 teaspoon powdered sage

Salt and freshly ground black
  pepper to taste

1 tablespoon butter

1 cup bourbon

2 tablespoons unsulfured
  molasses

¼ cup seedless dark raisins

2 tablespoon minced fresh chives

The idea here is to sear the tenderloin well to seal in the juices, and then roast it while basting with the thickened sauce till the outside is glazed to a mahogany finish. If the sauce thickens too quickly during the reduction, add just enough water to maintain a liquid consistency and to guarantee there will be enough glaze to be spooned over the slices when serving.

1 Preheat the oven to 375°F.

2 Rub the tenderloin with some of the oil, sprinkle with the sage and salt and pepper on all sides, and rub in the seasonings. In a large cast-iron skillet, heat the remaining oil and the butter over moderate heat, add the tenderloin, and sear on all sides till well browned. Transfer to a platter.

3 Add the bourbon, molasses, and raisins to the skillet, bring to a boil over moderately high heat, and stir till the sauce has thickened slightly. Return the pork to the skillet, baste with the sauce, transfer the skillet to the oven, and roast till the tenderloin is tender, 25 to 30 minutes, basting from time to time.

4 To serve, carve the tenderloin into thin slices, arrange the slices on the platter, spoon a little glaze from the skillet over the meat, and sprinkle chives over the top.

Roast Pork Tenderloin Stuffed with Honeyed Apples and Pecans

2 Granny Smith apples, peeled, cored, and finely chopped

½ cup finely chopped pecans

2 scallions (part of green tops included), finely chopped

3 tablespoons honey

Salt and freshly ground black pepper to taste

Two 1-pound pork tenderloins

3 tablespoons peanut oil

In the South, apples and pecans are often combined to make all sorts of salads, breads, and stuffings, and when a little honey (still another nod to the incurable Southern sweet tooth) is added, as in this subtle stuffing for roasted pork tenderloins, the flavor is nothing less than sublime. What I like to do is roast also a few small unpeeled new potatoes right next to the tenderloins, cut them in half, and saturate the tops with enough butter to run off onto the plates and provide a "sauce" for bites of pork.

1 Preheat the oven to 375°F.

2 In a small bowl, combine the apples, pecans, scallions, honey, and salt and pepper, stir till well blended, and set aside.

3 Rub the tenderloins well with the oil and place on a work surface. With a sharp knife, cut a pocket lengthwise in each tenderloin to within about ½ inch of the other side, fill the pockets with equal amounts of the apple and pecan mixture, tie the tenderloins with butcher's twine to close the pockets securely, and season both with salt and pepper. Transfer the tenderloins to a large, heavy rimmed baking pan and roast till tender, about 30 minutes. Remove from the oven, discard the twine, and let stand for about 10 minutes before carving and serving.

ROASTED PORK SHOULDER WITH APPLEJACK GRAVY

One 7- to 8-pound pork picnic shoulder

3 tablespoons all-purpose flour

1 tablespoon finely chopped fresh rosemary

¼ teaspoon cayenne pepper

Salt and freshly ground black pepper to taste

2 tablespoons peanut oil

4 tablespoons (½ stick) butter

3 medium onions, chopped

3 garlic cloves, minced

2 Granny Smith apples, cored and cut into chunks

½ cup applejack

Applejack is an aged American brandy made from apple cider, and while the spirit was certainly a favorite in colonial New England, records show that it was as popular in early Southern kitchens as bourbon, rum, and Madeira when it came to flavoring roasted meats. For this slowly cooked pork roast, a picnic shoulder is preferred over a Boston butt since it not only has more fat for natural basting but also produces a crisper skin to contrast with the soft, succulent meat. (Do not remove the skin when preparing the shoulder for roasting.) If you're unable to find a bottle of applejack, substitute apple cider.

1 Preheat the oven to 325°F.

2 Tie the pork shoulder with 2 or 3 pieces of butcher's twine. In a small bowl, combine the flour, rosemary, cayenne, and salt and pepper, mix till well blended, and rub the mixture evenly over the entire shoulder. In a large, heavy roasting pan, heat the oil and half the butter over moderate heat, position the shoulder in the pan, and brown on all sides, using 2 heavy cooking forks to turn the meat. Scatter the onions and garlic around the meat, cut up and add the remaining butter, cover with foil, and cook in the oven for 1 hour.

3 Add the apples and applejack, baste everything with the pan juices, cover, and cook for 1 hour longer. Uncover, baste the meat again, and roast, uncovered, till the skin is very crisp, about 45 minutes longer, adding a little water to the pan if necessary.

4 Transfer the roast to a cutting board and remove the twine. Drain excess fat from the pan, holding the onions and apples back with a spatula; add about 1 cup of water, and simmer over moderate heat till the gravy thickens, about 10 minutes, stirring.

5 To serve, carve the shoulder first down to the bone near the shank end, and then away from the shank and all around the roast, discarding any large chunks of fat. Arrange the slices on a platter and spoon the gravy over the top.

Slow-Roasted Pork Shoulder with Orange-Raisin Sauce

Makes 6 to 8 servings

One 7- to 8-pound pork shoulder butt

4 garlic cloves, minced

2 tablespoons chopped fresh sage leaves

2 tablespoons chopped fresh oregano leaves

Salt and freshly ground black pepper to taste

2 tablespoons peanut oil

2 cups apple cider

3 tablespoons cornstarch

1 tablespoon orange juice

1 teaspoon grated orange rind

2 tablespoons butter

1 cup seedless golden raisins

To the Southern way of thinking, there is virtually no way you can overcook a fatty pork shoulder, whether it be for barbecue or a roast such as this one that is slowly cooked all of six hours till the meat is fully succulent and the skin crisp and crackly. Although it is the fat that keeps the roast moist, what's amazing is how most of it melts away after being in the oven for so long. Not all shoulders, however, have the same quantity of fat, so do check the roast after four or five hours to make sure the meat is still soft and moist. A cup of any chopped dried fruit (apricots, currants, dates, figs, peaches) can be substituted for the raisins, and this sauce is also suitable for any other pork roast, chops, or country-style baked ribs.

1 Preheat the oven to 450°F.

2 Tie the pork shoulder with 2 or 3 pieces of butcher's twine. In a small bowl, combine the garlic, sage, oregano, and salt and pepper and mix till well blended. Rub the pork all over with the oil, then rub the herb mixture all over, pressing it into the meat. Position the pork on a rack in a large roasting pan and roast for 20 minutes. Reduce the heat to 275°F and continue to roast slowly till the meat is almost falling off the bone and the skin is crackly, about 6 hours.

3 About 30 minutes before the pork is finished roasting, combine ¼ cup of the cider and the cornstarch in a small bowl and whisk till well blended and smooth. Pour the mixture into a small saucepan, add the remaining cider plus the orange juice, rind, butter, and raisins, and simmer over moderate heat, stirring constantly, till the sauce is thickened, about 10 minutes. Keep the sauce hot over very low heat.

4 Remove the pork from the oven, transfer to a cutting board, and let stand for about 10 minutes. Remove the twine, carve the meat into ½-inch-thick slices or chunks, arrange them on a platter, and serve with the hot sauce.

 PIG PICKIN'S

"If anything could be called the national dish of the South, perhaps barbecue, even more so than fried chicken, would be it."

—Damon Lee Fowler, *Classical Southern Cooking*

HOMINY-STUFFED PORK SHOULDER WITH RUM GRAVY

MAKES 6 TO 8 SERVINGS

One 4- to 5-pound boned pork
picnic shoulder, skin left on

¾ cup dark rum

1½ cups fresh bread crumbs

½ cup milk

1 cup canned hominy, drained

1 small onion, minced

1 garlic clove, minced

2 tablespoons minced fresh
parsley leaves

½ teaspoon dried sage, crumbled

½ teaspoon dried marjoram,
crumbled

Salt and freshly ground black
pepper to taste

1 cup chicken broth

Southern hominy, which is dried corn kernels from which the hull and germ have been removed, is either ground into grits, added to various casseroles, or used in stuffings for large pork roasts such as this picnic shoulder redolent of rum and herbs. (Canned hominy is now available in most markets nationwide.) While you can bone the shoulder yourself if you're really deft with a boning knife, I strongly recommend you have a good butcher do this job, if for no other reason than to have the pocket for stuffing cut correctly. This is the style of roast you can be proud to serve on the most sophisticated buffet or dinner table.

1 Preheat the oven to 325°F.

2 Position the pork shoulder in a large, shallow baking pan or dish, pour ½ cup of the rum over the top, and let it stand while making the stuffing.

3 In a small bowl, combine the bread crumbs and milk, let soak for about 5 minutes, squeeze dry, discard the milk, and place the crumbs in a bowl. Add the hominy, onion, garlic, parsley, sage, marjoram, and salt and pepper and stir till well blended. Drain the rum from the pork over the hominy mixture and stir till well blended.

4 On a work surface, spread open the pork shoulder, cutting it further with a sharp knife if necessary to form a deep pocket. Spoon the stuffing into the pocket, then tie the meat at close intervals with butcher's twine to close securely. Position the shoulder on a rack in a large roasting pan and roast till the meat is very tender and the skin crisp and crunchy, about 3 hours.

5 Transfer the shoulder to a serving platter, pour off fat from the pan, and deglaze the pan over moderate heat with the remaining rum, scraping up all the brown bits. Add the broth, let cook till reduced to about 1½ cups, and pour into a gravy boat.

6 To serve, remove the twine from the roast, carve the meat into ½-inch-thick slices, and serve with the hot gravy.

MOCK LOUISIANA COCHON DE LAIT

One 8- to 9-pound pork shoulder, skin left on

Salt and freshly ground black pepper to taste

4 tablespoons bacon grease

2 large onions, chopped

2 celery ribs, chopped

2 carrots, scraped and chopped

4 garlic cloves, minced

½ teaspoon dried thyme

½ teaspoon dried rosemary

2 bay leaves

2 cups dry white wine

1 quart chicken broth

There are year-round pig festivals all over the South, but none can equal the Cajun cochon de lait (suckling pig) extravaganzas in central Louisiana, where 25- to 40-pound piglets are carefully seasoned and slowly roasted (not barbecued) outside in deep pits over hickory and charcoal fires. Given the impracticality of acquiring a 30-pound suckling pig, building a pit with concrete blocks at either end, and piercing the animal with a heavy steel pipe to be suspended over live embers, I've come up with this mock cochon de lait cooked in the oven that at least approximates the succulent texture of the genuine item. Either a shoulder butt or picnic shoulder can be used, but whichever you choose, just make sure the skin is left on so that there will be plenty of cracklin's. Traditionally, this pork is pulled off the bones and either piled on French bread with melted Swiss cheese (to make po' boy sandwiches) or served by itself with baked beans, coleslaw, and, always, Cajun dirty rice (enriched with and colored by ground chicken gizzards, onion, bell pepper, garlic, and bacon drippings).

1 Preheat the oven to 275°F.

2 Season the pork shoulder all over with salt and pepper. In a large, heavy roasting pan, heat the bacon grease over high heat till almost smoking, reduce the heat to moderate, and sear the pork on all sides till golden brown. Remove from the pan, add the onions, celery, carrots, garlic, and herbs to the grease, and stir till softened, about 10 minutes. Add the wine, bring to a boil, and reduce by half. Return the pork to the pan, add the broth, bring to a simmer, cover tightly with a lid or foil, and bake till the meat is falling off the bone, about 5 hours. Uncover and roast for about 1 hour longer or till the skin is crackly.

3 Remove the pan from the oven and let the pork cool to room temperature. Pull all the meat and skin off the bone, discarding any excess fat, tear into bite-size pieces, and set aside on a platter. Strain the liquid from the pan into a saucepan, bring to a boil, and reduce by half, skimming off fat as it rises to the top. Pour the hot sauce over the meat, toss well, and keep warm in the oven till ready to serve.

Baked Pork Butt with Home-Style Pan Gravy

MAKES 6 SERVINGS

One 5- to 6-pound pork shoulder butt

1 tablespoon dried oregano, crumbled

Salt and freshly ground black pepper to taste

3 garlic cloves, finely chopped

3 cups water

¼ cup all-purpose flour

This is the type of simple roast I serve at an informal, casual dinner for friends when I find pork butts on sale and don't care to go to lots of trouble in the kitchen. Like most Southerners, I like a fairly dense pan gravy with lots of browned bits scraped from the pan, but if you prefer a smooth, silky one, simply strain it into a gravy boat. Nothing goes better with this roast than fresh corn on the cob and lima beans simmered with a small piece of lean salt pork.

1 Preheat the oven to 325°F.

2 Tie the pork butt with 2 or 3 pieces of butcher's twine. Rub the butt all over with the oregano and salt and pepper and position it on a rack in a large baking pan. Scatter the garlic around the sides, add 1 cup of the water, cover, and bake till the meat is tender, 2 to 2½ hours, adding a little more water if necessary. Transfer the butt to a large platter.

3 To make pan gravy, drain the drippings from the baking pan into a large skillet, sprinkle the flour over the top, and stir over moderate heat till lightly browned. Pour the remaining 2 cups of water into the baking pan, scraping up the brown bits, and add to the skillet, stirring till thickened. Reduce the heat to low, add salt and pepper to taste, simmer the gravy for 4 to 5 minutes, and pour into a gravy boat.

4 To serve, remove the twine from the butt, carve the meat into medium-thick slices, and serve with the hot gravy.

CHILLED POACHED PORK BUTT

One 3- to 4-pound boneless pork shoulder butt, skin removed

1 large onion, chopped

1 celery rib (leaves included), chopped

1 garlic clove, chopped

3 small fresh red chile peppers, seeded and chopped

One 1-inch piece of fresh ginger

5 whole cloves

5 black peppercorns

1 bay leaf

Salt and freshly ground black pepper to taste

2 cups dry white wine

Fresh parsley sprigs for garnish

For their elaborate buffets, Southern hostesses have always loved to serve chilled or lukewarm meats (spiced beef, herbed tongue, jellied baked ham), and none qualifies more than a poached pork butt cut into thin slices and served with a tangy remoulade sauce or simply hot mustard. Since the butt is cut from the upper shoulder of the hog and is leaner and more compact than the lower picnic shoulder, be sure that this is the roast you buy. The poached pork is also delicious in composed salads with apples, orange sections, cooked corn kernels, ripe olives, capers, and the like.

1 Tie the pork butt at several intervals with butcher's twine and position it in a large, heavy baking pan or ovenproof casserole. Add the onion, celery, garlic, chiles, ginger, cloves, peppercorns, bay leaf, salt and pepper, and wine, plus enough water to barely cover the meat, and bring to a boil, skimming scum from the surface. Reduce the heat to low, cover, and poach for about 2 hours, skimming the surface from time to time. Turn the butt over and continue simmering till the meat is fork-tender, about 1 hour, basting frequently with the broth.

2 Remove the butt from the oven and let cool in the broth. Transfer to a platter, remove the twine, cover with plastic wrap, and chill in the refrigerator till ready to serve.

3 To serve, carve the butt into thin slices, arrange the slices on a platter, and garnish with parsley sprigs. Serve with a remoulade sauce or Dijon mustard.

Roasted Quail with Salt Pork and Country Ham

Makes 4 servings

8 dressed frozen quail, thawed

1 tablespoon dried tarragon, crumbled

Salt and freshly ground black pepper to taste

Thin slices lean salt pork (streak-o'-lean) as needed

½ cup gin

8 pieces of toast

Dijon mustard

8 thin slices cooked country ham

3 tablespoons minced fresh parsley leaves

Since, in the South, roasted quail would be inconceivable without some form of fatty pork to flavor the birds and keep them moist, I proffer this renegade but elegant dish only as further testimony to the pig's cardinal role in virtually all aspects of Southern cookery. Here, in addition to the quail being wrapped with salt pork for natural basting (bacon strips could also be used), the tarragon- and juniper-scented birds are given even more gustatory contrast by serving them atop slices of salty, smoky country ham. Regarding the quality of highly perishable quail, rest assured that today the frozen are just as delectable as the fresh and are much more readily available in most markets.

1 Preheat the oven to 400°F.

2 Rinse the quail well inside and out and pat dry with paper towels. Sprinkle each quail lightly with tarragon, season with salt and pepper, and wrap each one with a few slices of salt pork, tucking the ends under the bottoms. Arrange the quail on a rack in a large, shallow roasting pan, add the gin around the edges, and roast for 15 minutes, basting once. Remove and discard the salt pork, baste the birds again, and continue roasting till nicely browned, about 10 minutes, basting once more.

3 Spread each piece of toast lightly with mustard, place a slice of ham on each piece, position a quail on top of each, sprinkle parsley over the tops, and serve immediately.

Ham

Georgia Coca-Cola-Glazed Baked Ham

St. Mary's County Stuffed Ham

Mississippi Spice-Stuffed Baked Ham

Baked Fresh Leg of Pork
with Honey-Bourbon Glaze

Company Stuffed Fresh Ham

Stuffed Ham Braised in Sherry

Fresh Ham Braised in Beer
with Mustard Glaze

Basic Cooked Country Ham

Wilkes County Country Ham
Braised in Cider and Molasses

Baked Smithfield Ham with Bourbon,
Honey, and Pecan Glaze

Baked Country Ham Stuffed
with Greens and Apricots

Ham Hock Seasoning Liquid

Appalachian Braised Ham Hocks
and Cabbage

Fried Country Ham with Red-Eye Gravy

Broiled Ham Steak with
Rum-Molasses Glaze

Country Ham, Hominy,
and Turnip Green Dressing

River Road Baked Crown of Ham

Creamed Virginia Ham
and Wild Mushrooms

New Orleans Ham and Artichoke
Alexandria

Georgia Coca-Cola-Glazed Baked Ham

MAKES AT LEAST 10 SERVINGS

One 8- to 10-pound smoked ham butt

4 cups regular Coca-Cola (not Diet Coke)

2 cups fine dry bread crumbs

1 cup packed dark brown sugar

2 tablespoons mustard

No doubt the first ham to be glazed with Coca-Cola was baked not long after the pharmacist John Pemberton created the syrupy beverage in Atlanta at the end of the nineteenth century. Elsewhere in the South today, hams are glazed with every sweetened substance imaginable, but in the state of Georgia, it's still almost an unwritten law that no ham is worth its fat and sodium that's not well crumbed and transformed into a dark, glistening masterpiece by being repeatedly basted with Coke mixed with the pan juices. Do not trim off any of the fat on this ham, by no means use sugarless Diet Coke, and most Georgia cooks will tell you in no time flat that a "Coke Ham" is not authentic if it's studded with cloves. And can you substitute Pepsi for Coke? Sure you can—but don't tell any Georgia cracker I said so.

1 Preheat the oven to 325°F.

2 Position the ham fat side up on a rack in a large, shallow baking pan, pour about 3½ cups of the cola over the ham, cover, and bake for 2 hours, basting frequently with the pan juices.

3 Remove from the oven and trim off the skin. In a bowl, combine the bread crumbs, brown sugar, mustard, and enough of the remaining Coke to form a thick paste. Pat and press the paste all over the ham, return to the oven, increase the heat to 350°F, and bake, uncovered, till the paste has transformed into a dark glaze, about 45 minutes, basting frequently and adding a little more Coke if necessary.

4 To serve, transfer the ham to a platter and let stand for about 15 minutes before carving into slices.

PIG PICKIN'S

Every year, there is a Ladies' Pig-Racing Contest in Pinehurst, North Carolina.

St. Mary's County Stuffed Ham

2 green cabbages, cored and finely chopped

2 bunches watercress (stems removed), rinsed

3 medium onions, finely chopped

4 celery ribs (leaves included), finely chopped

1 teaspoon dry mustard

1 teaspoon salt

½ teaspoon freshly ground black pepper

½ teaspoon cayenne pepper

One 10- to 11-pound ham shank

When Southerners speak of Maryland stuffed ham, they are referring more precisely to the tangy, braised ham stuffed with any variety of greens served in southern Maryland's St. Mary's County. Either a fresh or lightly cured ham can be used, but what contributes most to this dish's unique flavor is the way the ham is left to soak overnight in its broth. In local taverns and small restaurants, the ham is almost always served in thick slices with beaten biscuits.

1 Place the cabbage, watercress, onions, celery, mustard, salt, pepper, and cayenne in a roasting pan large enough to fit the ham. Add enough water to reach within 1 inch of the top of the vegetables, stir, and bring to a boil. Turn off the heat, cover the pan, and let the vegetables stand for 10 minutes in the hot water. Drain the vegetables in a large colander over a bowl to catch the broth, let cool, and reserve the broth.

2 With a sharp knife, cut Xs about 1 inch square and 2 inches deep all over the ham and fill each X with vegetable stuffing. Wrap the ham in a wide double thickness of cheesecloth and tie the ends to secure it tightly.

3 Place the ham in the pan along with the reserved broth and add enough water to cover. Cover, bring the liquid to a boil, reduce the heat to low, and simmer the ham for 2½ to 3 hours, adding water as needed to keep it covered. Turn off the heat and let the ham cool in the liquid, preferably overnight.

4 When ready to serve, reheat the ham in its liquid, transfer to a cutting board or large platter, remove and discard the cheesecloth and skin from the ham, and carve the meat into thick slices.

Mississippi Spice-Stuffed Baked Ham

**MAKES AT LEAST
12 SERVINGS**

One 10- to 12-pound smoked
   ham butt

2 cups water

1 cup cider vinegar

3 cups crumbled cornbread

3 cups fresh bread crumbs

1 teaspoon ground allspice

1 teaspoon ground cloves

1 teaspoon ground ginger

1 teaspoon garlic salt

1 teaspoon freshly ground
   black pepper

½ cup molasses

1 tablespoon Dijon mustard

2 large eggs, beaten

3 tablespoons butter, melted

Spiced meat dishes abound in the Deep South, and none is
more distinctive than the large spice-stuffed hams served
warm or cold on buffet tables for all sorts of informal events.
Cooks might well add about half a cup of golden raisins or
chopped pecans to this stuffing, but however you modify
the mixture, just be sure to reserve enough to press over the
outside of the ham to form a slight crust during the final half
hour of baking. Naturally, you can always have a butcher bone
the ham for you, but if you've never boned a butt or shank,
all you need is a good boning knife and a bit of patience.
(Boning really involves little more than carefully following
the bone with the knife as you lift off the meat.)

1 Preheat the oven to 325°F.

2 Position the ham on a rack in a large baking pan, add the
water and vinegar, cover, and bake for 1½ hours, basting
several times.

3 Meanwhile, combine all the remaining ingredients in a large
bowl, mix till thoroughly blended, and set the stuffing aside.

4 Transfer the ham to a work surface, retaining the liquid in the pan. Remove and discard the skin and all but about ½ inch of the fat on the ham. Using a sharp boning knife, cut the meat from the bone in one piece, following the bone carefully with the knife. Fill the cavity of the ham with as much stuffing as necessary, re-form the ham as neatly as possible, skewer the openings shut, and tie the ham securely with butcher's twine.

5 Reposition the ham in the pan fat side up, cover, and bake for 1 hour longer. Remove the ham from the oven again, press as much of the remaining stuffing as possible over the top with your fingers, return the ham to the oven, and bake, uncovered, for 30 minutes longer.

6 To serve, transfer the ham to a serving platter, remove the skewers and twine, and let stand for about 15 minutes before carving into thin slices and serving with a little of the stuffing.

Baked Fresh Leg of Pork with Honey-Bourbon Glaze

MAKES 8 TO 10 SERVINGS

One 11- to 12-pound fresh ham
  (butt or shank)

2 tablespoons salt

2 teaspoons dried thyme

2 teaspoons dried sage

1 cup honey

2 tablespoons bourbon

Freshly ground black pepper
  to taste

2 cups water

While fresh, unsmoked hams are not that popular in most areas of the country, in the South a "leg of pork" is perceived (justifiably) as one of the finest cuts of pig and is often treated almost as a ceremonial joint of meat fit for the most stylish table or buffet. Most cooks simply bake the hams with an orange juice or cola and brown sugar glaze, but since the meat can be relatively bland, here the leg is simmered initially with aromatics, then baked slowly with a honey glaze spiked with bourbon. If you can't take the time to brush the ham fairly often with the glaze, add a little water to the bottom of the pan to catch the drippings and use a bulb baster instead. Traditionally, a ham such as this one would be served with roast potatoes or spoon bread and either boiled field peas or squash soufflé.

1 Place the ham in a large baking pan or pot with enough water to almost cover and add the salt, thyme, and sage. Bring the water to a boil, reduce the heat to low, cover, and simmer the ham for 1 hour.

2 Meanwhile, combine the honey, bourbon, and pepper in a small saucepan, stir over low heat till hot and well blended, and remove from the heat.

3 Preheat the oven to 325°F.

4 Transfer the ham to a work surface and drain the liquid from the pan. Remove and discard the skin and part of the surface fat of the ham, position the ham on a rack in the baking pan, and add the water to the pan. Brush the top and sides of the meat with the honey glaze and bake for about 2 hours, basting periodically with the pan juices.

5 To serve, transfer the ham to a serving platter and carve into medium-thick slices.

COMPANY STUFFED FRESH HAM

1 large onion, minced

1 medium green bell pepper,
   seeded and minced

1 celery rib, minced

3 garlic cloves, minced

1 teaspoon dry mustard

Salt and freshly ground black
   pepper to taste

Cayenne pepper to taste

One 11- to 12-pound fresh ham
   (butt or shank), skin left on

Peanut oil

2 cups water

Southerners love a baked or roasted fresh ham as much as a smoked one, not only because of the porky flavor but also because the fresh skin transforms so beautifully into crunchy, succulent cracklin's when cooked. (Another important consideration, to be sure, is that a fresh ham is usually much less expensive than a loin roast.) While baking the ham, make sure there are always at least two cups of juices in the pan to be used as basting liquid and gravy—typically spooned over both the meat and mounds of boiled rice. As for the strips of cracklin's, in the South they would probably be eaten with the fingers.

1 Preheat the oven to 425°F.

2 In a bowl, combine the onion, bell pepper, celery, garlic, mustard, salt and pepper, and cayenne, mix till well blended, and set the stuffing aside.

3 With a sharp knife, make deep slits all over the ham several inches apart and rub oil over the surface. Using your fingers, fill the slits with the stuffing, then position the ham fat side up on a rack in a large baking pan, add the water, and roast, uncovered, till the ham browns, about 45 minutes, adding more water if the pan becomes too dry.

4 Reduce the heat to 325°F, cover, and bake till the ham is very tender and the skin crunchy, about 2 hours, adding more water if necessary and basting periodically with the pan juices. Remove the ham from the oven, let cool slightly, and pour the pan juices into a bowl.

5 To serve, remove the skin, place on a cutting board, and slice into thin strips. Carve the meat into medium slices, arrange on a serving platter, spoon a little pan juice over the slices, and scatter the strips of skin (cracklin's) over the top.

PIG PICKIN'S

"Smithfield ham, granddaddy of all dry-cured country hams produced in half a dozen Southern states, bears about as much resemblance to your pink, watery, run-of-the-mill brine-cured ham as a horse chestnut does to a chestnut horse." —R.W. Apple, Jr., *New York Times*

Stuffed Ham Braised in Sherry

One 10- to 11-pound smoked ham butt

1½ cups fresh bread crumbs

1 teaspoon ground cinnamon

½ teaspoon ground nutmeg

½ teaspoon ground cloves

¾ cup finely chopped pecans

6 pitted prunes, finely chopped

1¼ cups sweet sherry

½ cup packed light brown sugar

2 cups water

Sprigs of watercress for garnish

If there's not too much bone on this butt, the ham does not necessarily have to be boned to be successfully stuffed. (A large shank, on the other hand, really needs boning.) Also, if you like, you may choose to fill the boned ham with the stuffing and tie it securely instead of cutting and filling pockets. If you do fill pockets as directed, just be sure to pack the stuffing as compactly as possible so that as little as possible oozes out during the baking.

1 Have a butcher bone and tie the ham securely, or do the job yourself with a boning knife and butcher's twine. Using an apple corer, make 8 to 10 deep incisions all over the ham, turning the corer so that small pockets are formed.

2 Preheat the oven to 325°F.

3 In a bowl, combine the bread crumbs, spices, pecans, prunes, and ¼ cup of the sherry and mix thoroughly with your hands to make a compact stuffing. Force the stuffing with your fingers into the pockets on the ham, pushing firmly so that the stuffing is as compact as possible. Rub the ham well with the brown sugar, pressing it down with your fingers. Position the ham on a rack in a large, shallow baking pan, add the water and remaining 1 cup of sherry, cover, and bake for 2 hours, basting frequently with the pan juices. Uncover and bake till the ham is nicely glazed, 30 to 45 minutes, basting once or twice.

4 To serve, transfer the ham to a platter and let stand for about 15 minutes before carving into thick slices, making sure each has some stuffing. Garnish with sprigs of watercress.

FRESH HAM BRAISED IN BEER WITH MUSTARD GLAZE

MAKES AT LEAST 10 SERVINGS

One 11- to 12-pound fresh ham (butt or shank)

1 medium onion, chopped

1 celery rib (leaves included), chopped

3 garlic cloves, chopped

1 teaspoon dried thyme

1 teaspoon dried rosemary

2 tablespoons salt

8 black peppercorns

Four 12-ounce bottles of lager beer or light ale

½ cup firmly packed light brown sugar

2 tablespoons Dijon mustard

2 tablespoons corn syrup

The idea behind this fresh ham is to flavor the meat throughout in a highly aromatic braise, then bake it with a tangy sweet glaze till the exterior is almost a glistening mahogany color. Since this ham is glazed, it's best to remove the skin and any excess fat before the final baking. I know of no dish that better illustrates how beer enhances the flavor of pig than this one.

1 Position the ham in a large baking pan or kettle, add the onion, celery, garlic, thyme, rosemary, salt, and peppercorns, and pour the beer over the top. Bring to a low boil, reduce the heat to low, cover, and braise the ham for 1 hour. Turn the ham over, return to a simmer, cover, and cook for 1 hour longer.

2 Preheat the oven to 350°F.

3 Transfer the ham to a work surface and let cool slightly. Strain the contents of the pan, discard the solids, return the liquid to the pan, and place a rack on the bottom. Remove and discard any skin and excess fat on the ham. In a small bowl, mix together the brown sugar, mustard, and corn syrup to form a paste and rub the paste all over the ham. Position the ham on the rack in the pan, cover, and bake till the ham is nicely glazed, about 1 hour, basting several times with the pan juices.

4 To serve, carve the ham into medium-thick slices or chunks, arrange on a serving platter, and spoon a little hot pan juice over the top.

Basic Cooked Country Ham

**MAKES AT LEAST
15 SERVINGS, WITH
LEFTOVERS**

One 12- to 15-pound dry-cured,
    aged country ham

1 cup packed dark brown sugar

10 to 12 whole cloves, ground

The South's most famous country hams are produced in Virginia (including especially the Smithfield hams), North Carolina, Tennessee, and Kentucky, and the finest are dry-cured with only salt and seasonings and aged from six to nine months till the meat is almost mahogany colored. All genuine country hams are salty, and while many Southerners (myself included) would never dream of soaking a ham before cooking it for fear of losing some of its distinctive flavor along with the saltiness, most people object to intensely salty ham (which, I'm the first to admit, is an acquired taste). This is the basic method of soaking and cooking a large country ham, and since the more aged a ham is, the less cooking it needs, the cooking times are approximate. Ideally, country ham should be simmered just till it is tender but still slightly firm and moist when tested with a sharp knife inserted in the thickest area of the meat. Traditionally, a cooked country ham is always carved into thin slices (as opposed to an uncooked one that is cut into thick slices for frying).

1 Scrub the ham thoroughly with a stiff brush under running water to remove all traces of mold and place in a large roasting pan. Add enough cool water to cover and let soak for 6 to 12 hours (depending on salt tolerance), changing the water twice.

2 Drain the pan, scrub the ham again under running water, and return it to the pan. Add fresh water to cover, bring the water very gradually to a gentle simmer, cover, and simmer very gently for 3 to 3½ hours (or about 15 minutes per pound), adding more water to keep the ham covered.

3 Preheat the oven to 425°F.

4 Drain the water from the pan, transfer the ham to a work surface, remove and discard the skin, and trim all but ½ inch of the fat. Score the fat in diamonds, cover with the brown sugar and cloves, and rub the seasonings well into the ham. Return the ham to the pan fat side up and bake, uncovered, till nicely glazed, about 30 minutes.

5 To serve, carve the ham into thin slices with an electric or serrated knife.

WILKES COUNTY COUNTRY HAM BRAISED IN CIDER AND MOLASSES

One 14- to 16-pound dry-cured
country ham

1 cup molasses

1 cup firmly packed light brown
sugar

1 gallon apple cider, as needed

3 medium onions, chopped

3 medium carrots, scraped and
chopped

2 cups dry bread crumbs

2 cups firmly packed light brown
sugar

High in the mountains of North Carolina, Wilkes County is
prime country ham territory, and you simply won't encounter
finer cured country hams than those aged naturally for
nine months in the ham house of Clayton Long on his
farm in Glendale Springs. Unlike most producers, Clayton
cures his hams with only salt and brown sugar, he uses no
preservatives or coloring agents, and since he refuses to
subject his superlative hams to excessive federal regulations
and thus can't ship them over the state line, customers like
me have to travel to the farm if they want a Long ham. Over
the years, Clayton must have taught me a dozen ways to
cook a country ham, one of the most memorable being this
simple braise using apple cider and molasses. A large ham
such as this usually has to be simmered for about 3 hours,
but do test it after 2½ hours with a sharp knife inserted in
the thickest area to make sure the meat is still slightly firm
before the final glaze.

1 Scrub the ham well with a stiff brush under running water,
then position it in a large roasting pan. Add cool water to
cover and let the ham soak for about 6 hours, changing the
water twice.

2 Remove the ham from the pan, rinse the pan well, return the ham to the pan, and add enough fresh water to come halfway up the sides. Add the molasses and brown sugar to the water, stir as well as possible, then add enough cider to just cover the ham. Add the onions and carrots and bring the liquid to a very low simmer. Cover partially and simmer slowly for 3 hours. Let the ham cool completely in the liquid.

3 Preheat the oven to 425°F.

4 Place the ham on a work surface, remove and discard the skin and all but ¼ inch of the fat, and score the fat in squares or diamonds. Rinse the roasting pan well after discarding the contents, then place the ham fat side up on a rack in the pan. Mix the bread crumbs and brown sugar and coat the top and sides with the mixture, pressing down with your fingers. Bake, uncovered, till the crumbs are browned, 20 to 30 minutes.

5 To serve, position the ham on a large wooden or ceramic platter and carve into thin slices with an electric or serrated knife.

Baked Smithfield Ham with Bourbon, Honey, and Pecan Glaze

MAKES AT LEAST
12 SERVINGS, WITH
LEFTOVERS

One 12- to 14-pound Smithfield ham

2 cups water

½ cup bourbon

½ cup apple juice

1½ cups packed dark brown sugar

1 cup ground toasted pecans

¼ cup honey

⅛ teaspoon cayenne pepper

Hams dry-cured, hickory-smoked, and aged in and around Smithfield, Virginia, have been legendary since the days Thomas Jefferson and Queen Victoria ordered them special, and today there is still no more ceremonial ham for the formal buffet table. Lean, dark-colored, delicate, and richly flavored, a Smithfield is so beautifully processed that it can be sliced paper thin and served raw like prosciutto. On the other hand, when the ham is slowly baked, and then subjected to a luscious glaze such as this one with bourbon, honey, and pecans, the result is a culinary masterpiece. If you're truly offended by saltiness in foods, you can soak a Smithfield for no longer than about six hours before baking it, but remember that you do so at the expense of distinctive flavor. Unlike other country hams, Smithfield ham is very rarely fried with red-eye gravy for breakfast in the South and is always served in thin slices.

1 Preheat the oven to 325°F.

2 Scrub the ham well with a stiff brush under running water, position it on a rack in a large baking pan, add the water, cover, and bake for 2½ hours, adding a little more water if necessary.

3 Meanwhile, combine the bourbon and apple juice in a saucepan and boil over moderately high heat till reduced to about ½ cup. In a bowl, combine the brown sugar, pecans, honey, and cayenne and stir till well blended. Add the bourbon mixture and stir to form a paste.

4 Remove the ham from the oven and increase the heat to 400°F. Remove and discard the skin and all but about ½ inch of fat, score the surface fat in diamonds, and rub the paste evenly over the top and sides. Return the ham to the oven and bake, uncovered, till the surface has a glossy mahogany glaze, about 30 minutes.

5 To serve, let the ham stand for about 30 minutes on a platter before carving into thin slices.

Baked Country Ham Stuffed with Greens and Apricots

Makes at least 12 servings, with leftovers

5 slices bacon

½ cup finely chopped scallions (part of green tops included)

¼ cup finely chopped celery

¼ cup chopped fresh parsley leaves

1 cup chopped turnip greens, mustard greens, or kale

1 cup chopped spinach

1 cup chopped dried apricots

1 teaspoon dry mustard

¼ teaspoon dried marjoram, crumbled

1 teaspoon minced dried red chile pepper

Freshly ground black pepper to taste

One 12- to 14-pound country ham

2 cups bourbon

1 cup water

Sprigs of watercress for garnish

Nothing is more Southern and festive than a country ham stuffed with any variety of piquant greens offset by some sweet fruit, and when you glaze the ham with bourbon, the result is a glistening masterpiece worthy of the most elegant holiday table. Here the stuffing almost disintegrates during the long baking, imparting its bittersweet essence throughout the meat while, at the same time, enriching the basting liquid as some of it oozes from the pockets. Like all ceremonial country hams, this one should be carved in delicate slices so thin they can be eaten with the fingers, if preferred. When I serve this stuffed ham for Christmas, I like to wrap the hock with colorful foil frills and decorate the platter with sprigs of holly instead of watercress.

1 In a skillet, fry the bacon over moderate heat till crisp. Drain on paper towels, crumble, and pour all but 3 tablespoons of fat from the skillet. Add the scallions and celery and stir for about 3 minutes. Add the crumbled bacon, parsley, greens, spinach, apricots, mustard, marjoram, chile pepper, and black pepper, toss the mixture, cover, reduce the heat to low, and cook till the greens are soft, about 20 minutes, stirring. Transfer the stuffing to a large bowl and set aside.

2 Preheat the oven to 325°F.

3 Scrub the ham well with a stiff brush under running water, remove and discard the skin, and trim all but about ¼ inch of the fat. With a sharp paring knife, cut about 10 deep X-shaped incisions over the surface of the ham, spread the incisions apart with your fingers, and force stuffing deeply into each pocket. Position the ham in a large roasting pan, pour the bourbon and water over the top, cover, and bake for 3 hours, basting occasionally and adding a little more water to the pan if necessary. Uncover and continue baking for about 30 minutes, basting frequently to produce a nice glaze on the ham.

4 To serve, transfer the ham to a large platter, carve into thin slices, and garnish the edges with sprigs of watercress.

Ham Hock Seasoning Liquid

Makes 6 cups of seasoning liquid and 2 cooked ham hocks

2 ham hocks

6 cups water

½ teaspoon dried thyme, crumbled

1 bay leaf

Salt and freshly ground black pepper to taste

Few dashes of Tabasco sauce

In the South, it's unimaginable to boil beans, peas, or greens without seasoning them with some form of pork, or "side meat." While the simplest method is just to add a piece of fatback, bacon, lean salt pork (streak-o'-lean), or country ham to the simmering water in the pot, serious Southern cooks know there's nothing more practical and delicious than a full-flavored seasoning liquid made with hocks sawed off ham shanks (or bought in the market). Fat, of course, is what gives the vegetables the most flavor, but if you're squeamish or on a restricted diet, it's easy enough to chill the simmered seasoning liquid, then lift off all or part of the fat from the top. In any case, you end up not only with a good amount of simmering liquid but also with two cooked ham hocks that can be chopped and used to enhance any number of soups, stews, casseroles, salads, and even breads.

Scrub the hocks well with a stiff brush under running water, scrape the skin with a sharp knife to remove any hairs, and split the hocks in half with a cleaver or heavy, sharp knife. Place in a large saucepan, add the water, and bring to a boil, skimming scum off the surface. Reduce the heat to low, add the thyme, bay leaf, salt and pepper, and Tabasco, cover, and simmer the hocks till very tender, about 2 hours, adding enough water to maintain a measure of about 6 cups.

Appalachian Braised Ham Hocks and Cabbage

4 meaty ham hocks (fresh or smoked)

2 medium onions, chopped

2 celery ribs, chopped

2 carrots, scraped and diced

2 teaspoons salt

Freshly ground black pepper to taste

Paprika to taste

1 medium head green cabbage, wilted leaves discarded, cut into wedges

In West Virginia and throughout the Appalachians, meaty ham hocks simmered with cabbage and other vegetables is generally known as a "pig hock dinner," served almost always with some type of pickle and a big pan of cornbread. The fat from the hocks provides much of the dish's succulent flavor, but chilling the hocks and cooking liquid for a few hours before adding the cabbage not only allows you to remove all or part of the hardened fat on the surface but also yields a more intensive jellied broth that gives the cabbage a delightfully silky quality.

1 Scrub the hocks with a stiff brush under running water and scrape the skin with a heavy, sharp knife to remove any hairs. Place the hocks, onions, celery, and carrots in a large casserole or pot with enough water to cover, add the salt, pepper, and paprika, bring to a boil, and skim off the scum. Reduce the heat to low, cover, and simmer till the hocks are tender, about 2 hours.

2 Add the cabbage, return to a simmer, cover, and cook till the hocks and cabbage are very tender, about 30 minutes longer.

3 To serve, transfer the hocks with a slotted spoon to a large serving platter and spoon the cabbage around the edges.

FRIED COUNTRY HAM WITH RED-EYE GRAVY

MAKES 6 SERVINGS

Three ¼-inch-thick center slices cured country ham

1 cup water or brewed coffee

Fried cured country ham with red-eye gravy is as sacred a breakfast treat for Southerners as hot buttered grits and baking powder biscuits, and throughout the South, grocery stores carry numerous packaged brands of sliced ham (some respectable, some not so hot) for just that purpose. It's an unwritten creed that center slices of country ham are meant to be fried, semi-center used for ham biscuits, and end pieces used to season boiled beans, peas, turnip greens, and other vegetables. It's also believed that reddish country ham that's not been properly cured and aged will not make good red-eye gravy, and that notion is correct. Remember that only raw country ham with sufficient fat can be fried successfully; that the color of the meat should actually be a dark pink or light brown; that soaking the ham in water leaches out not only salt but flavor; that, by far, the preferred skillet is cast iron; and that overcooking the ham will make it hard and tough. As for the red-eye gravy, you can deglaze the pan with either water or brewed coffee, depending on how intense a flavor you prefer. (Only a Yankee would try to make red-eye gravy by deglazing with wine.)

1 Trim off pieces of fat from the edges of the ham and score the remaining fat at intervals with a sharp knife to keep the slices from curling. Place the pieces of fat in one or two cast-iron skillets, render the fat over moderately low heat, and discard the pieces. Add the ham slices to the skillet, slowly fry till they are just lightly browned on each side, and transfer to a platter just large enough to hold the slices.

2 Increase the heat to moderate, pour the water or coffee into the skillet, scrape the bottom with a spatula to loosen the browned bits, and let boil till the liquid is reduced almost to a glaze. Pour the gravy over the ham slices, cut the slices into 2- to 3-inch serving pieces, and serve hot.

Broiled Ham Steak with Rum-Molasses Glaze

¼ cup molasses

3 tablespoons dark rum

½ teaspoon ground ginger

One 1½- to 2-pound bone-in ham steak, about 1 inch thick, trimmed of excess fat

Once was the time in the South when nothing was more popular at informal dinners than broiled ham steaks brushed with pineapple juice and served topped with glazed crushed pineapple. I still think these simple steaks can be delicious (especially when fresh pineapple is used), but what you'll most likely find today in sophisticated kitchens are steaks enhanced by more complex glazes like this one composed of molasses, rum, and ground ginger. Just be sure to slash the fatty edges so the steak doesn't curl, and, for heaven's sake, don't overcook the steak or burn the glaze.

1 Preheat the oven broiler and lightly grease the rack of a broiler pan.

2 In a small saucepan, combine the molasses, rum, and ginger and stir over moderate heat till well blended, about 8 minutes. Slash the fatty edges of the steak at 1-inch intervals, place the steak on the prepared boiler pan, brush the top lightly with the glaze, and broil 4 inches from the heat for about 8 minutes. Turn the steak, brush the other side with the glaze, and broil till glossy brown, 6 to 7 minutes.

3 To serve, cut the steak into 4 equal portions and serve immediately.

Country Ham, Hominy, and Turnip Green Dressing

MAKES 6 SERVINGS

4 tablespoons (½ stick) butter

1 medium onion, chopped

3 cups crumbled cornbread

2 cups dry bread crumbs

¾ cup diced cooked country ham

One-half 10-ounce package frozen chopped turnip greens or kale, thawed

½ dried thyme, crumbled

Freshly ground black pepper to taste

2 cups chicken broth

Southerners use end pieces of a cooked country ham for flavoring everything from salads to soups to boiled vegetables and peas, but one of the best ideas is to incorporate the leftovers in a dressing that can be either baked as a side dish or stuffed into a roasted chicken, turkey, duck, or boneless pork loin. When baked on its own, this dressing should be moist but slightly crusty on the outside.

1 Preheat the oven to 375°F. Butter a 1½- to 2-quart baking dish or pan and set aside.

2 In a large skillet, melt the butter over moderate heat, add the onion, and stir till softened, about 5 minutes. Scrape the onion into a large bowl, add all the remaining ingredients, and stir till the dressing is well blended and moist. Scrape into the prepared baking dish and bake till golden brown but still slightly moist, 35 to 40 minutes.

3 Serve the dressing hot, cut into squares (or use unbaked as a stuffing for meats or fowl).

RIVER ROAD BAKED CROWN OF HAM

MAKES AT LEAST 8 SERVINGS

1 cup whole milk

3 large eggs

3 cups fresh bread crumbs

½ cup dry red wine

2 teaspoons Worcestershire sauce

1 small onion, minced

Freshly ground black pepper
  to taste

3 pounds diced smoked ham

1 pound diced veal shoulder

½ cup currant jelly, melted

When, why, and how this baked crown of ham became a specialty in the grand River Road mansions that dot the countryside from Baton Rouge, Louisiana, to New Orleans is a mystery, but even today the beautiful dish is popular at gracious garden parties, formal buffets, and other "socials." Typically, a little veal is always added to the ham for more delicacy, the meats might be ground instead of diced for a finer texture, and the platter is garnished with both apples and hominy sautéed in brown butter. The crown is just as delicious chilled as hot.

1 Preheat the oven to 350°F. Grease a 10-inch tube pan and set aside.

2 In a large bowl, whisk together the milk and eggs till well blended, add the bread crumbs, and let soak for 10 minutes. Add the wine, Worcestershire, onion, and pepper and stir till well blended. Add the ham and veal, stir till well incorporated, pack the mixture into the prepared pan, and bake for 2 hours.

3 Unmold the crown in a shallow baking pan, brush the top and sides well with the jelly, and bake till the crown is fully glazed, about 30 minutes longer.

4 To serve, transfer the crown to a serving platter, let stand for about 10 minutes, and cut into large wedges.

CREAMED VIRGINIA HAM AND WILD MUSHROOMS

6 tablespoons (¾ stick) butter

½ pound chanterelle or shiitake
  mushrooms, thinly sliced

3 tablespoons all-purpose flour

2 cups whole milk

½ cup half-and-half

2 cups diced cooked country ham

2 tablespoons dry sherry

Freshly ground black pepper
  to taste

6 slices toast, or mounds of
  soft boiled rice or grits

3 tablespoons minced fresh
  parsley leaves

Popular for generations at Southern country clubs, bridge luncheons, and quaint department store tea rooms and restaurants, creamed ham and mushrooms on toast used to be made exclusively with ordinary smoked ham and button mushrooms. Today, however, I've noticed that, more often than not, both professional and some home cooks are prone to use more assertive Virginia ham (like Smithfield) and wild mushrooms for the dish, and that luscious mixture tends to be served over mounds of soft rice or grits instead of toast. Personally, I love the old version as much as the new, and I continue to believe that nothing goes better with the rich dish redolent of sherry than a simple cold congealed fruit or vegetable salad.

1 In a medium skillet, melt 3 tablespoons of the butter over moderate heat, add the mushrooms, stir till they absorb the butter and are golden, about 10 minutes, and set aside.

2 In a heavy saucepan, melt the remaining butter over moderately low heat, add the flour, and stir till a smooth paste forms. Gradually add the milk, stirring till thickened and smooth, 3 to 4 minutes. Add the half-and-half, ham, mushrooms, sherry, and pepper and stir till well blended and hot.

3 To serve, place a slice of toast, or a mound of hot boiled rice or grits, on each of 6 serving plates, spoon equal amounts of the ham and mushroom mixture over the top, and sprinkle with the parsley.

New Orleans Ham and Artichoke Alexandria

6 tablespoons (¾ stick) butter

½ pound mushrooms, thinly sliced

Two 14-ounce cans artichoke hearts, drained and quartered

3 tablespoons all-purpose flour

2 cups milk

2 tablespoons dry sherry

Salt and freshly ground black pepper to taste

2 cups grated Swiss cheese

6 English muffins, split and toasted

12 medium slices baked ham

24 pimento strips, drained

This is one of those toothsome breakfast or brunch specialties for which New Orleans is so renowned, and while I've never learned the origins of the name *Alexandria*, rest assured that the dish will inspire sighs of ecstasy from any and every guest at the table. Other than possibly substituting slices of mildly cured country ham for the traditional baked smoked style, I wouldn't dream of altering the recipe someone at Broussard's restaurant in New Orleans gave me years ago. If you have trouble finding seven-ounce jars of whole pimento strips, the four-ounce ones of diced pimentos can be made to work just as well.

1 In a large, heavy saucepan, melt 2 tablespoons of the butter over moderate heat, add the mushrooms, and stir till softened, about 5 minutes. Add the artichokes, stir for about 7 minutes longer, and transfer the mixture to a bowl.

2 Melt the remaining butter in the pan, sprinkle the flour over the top, and whisk till smooth, about 3 minutes. Gradually add the milk, whisking till thickened, and then add the sherry and salt and pepper and stir till blended. Add the cheese and stir till it has melted. Add the mushrooms and artichokes, stir till well blended, and keep hot over very low heat.

3 To serve, arrange 2 muffin halves on each of 6 serving plates, place a slice of ham on each half, top each with 2 pimento strips, and cover each with equal amounts of the hot artichoke mixture.

SAUSAGE and BACON

Fresh Bulk Pork Sausage Meat

Savannah Spiced Country Sausage

Cajun Boudin Rice Sausage

Creole Chaurice Sausage

Blue Ridge Pork and Bacon Sausage

Breakfast Sausage Biscuits
with Cream Gravy

Hickory-Smoked
Country Sausage Links

Sausage and Pecan Stuffing
for Roast Fowl

Kentucky Scramble

Country-Style Sausages and Apples

Canadian Bacon Breakfast Sandwiches
with Molasses

Bacon Waffles

Tennessee Fried Streak-o'-Lean

Aunt Bunny's Bacon and Sausage Soufflé

Bacon, Cream Cheese, and Horseradish
Cocktail Dip

Bacon and Chicken Succotash

Bacon and Squash Soufflé

Sullivan's Island Bacon and Shrimp Bog

Fried Catfish with Bacon and Pecan-
Tarragon-Butter Sauce

Mississippi Bacon Spaghetti

Fresh Bulk Pork Sausage Meat

MAKES 3 POUNDS

- 2 pounds boneless pork shoulder
- 1 pound fresh pork fat, chilled for about 30 minutes in the freezer
- 2 tablespoons salt
- 1 teaspoon freshly ground black pepper
- 2 teaspoons ground sage
- 1 teaspoon red pepper flakes
- 2 tablespoons cold water

Southern cooking would be inconceivable without bulk sausage meat, and to view the staggering array of brands in markets is a lesson that outsiders don't soon forget. Traditionally, sausage making (usually by women) has always been part of the fall hog-killing ritual throughout the South, and sausage fanatics like myself will drive fifty miles out of the way when word comes that a certain market is carrying "whole-hog sausage" made with numerous different cuts of pig. Since today, unfortunately, much of what you find in markets away from (and sometimes within) the South is frozen rolls of fatty, underseasoned, disgusting sausage meat, I strongly urge you to buy a good meat grinder, follow this basic recipe, and get in the habit of grinding your own bulk sausage the way I've been doing for decades. It's not absolutely essential to chill the pork fat in the freezer, but this does make the grinding much easier and neater. (Except in rare instances, sausage should never be ground in a food processor.) This sausage keeps well in the refrigerator for up to about four days, and it can be frozen for up to three months.

Cut the pork and pork fat into 2-inch cubes and pass first through the coarse blade, then through the fine blade of a meat grinder into a large bowl. Add the remaining ingredients, moisten both hands with water, and knead the mixture till well blended and smooth. Wrap the sausage in plastic wrap and store in the refrigerator for at least 2 hours before using.

Savannah Spiced Country Sausage

**Makes 2 pounds;
6 to 8 servings**

1½ pounds ground pork shoulder

½ pound fresh ground pork fat

1 teaspoon salt

½ teaspoon freshly ground
black pepper

½ teaspoon red pepper flakes

¼ teaspoon ground allspice

⅛ teaspoon ground ginger

⅛ teaspoon ground cinnamon

Pinch of ground cloves

3 tablespoons cold water

The important role of herbs and spices in the distinctive cuisine of Savannah goes back to the first colonial merchant ships to arrive in the Carolina and Georgia Lowcountry in the early eighteenth century, and while today sausage making in most of the South usually involves little more seasoning than salt and pepper, sage, and perhaps some hot red pepper flakes, many Savannah home cooks still heavily spice their sausage just the way their ancestors did. Ideally, you should get in the habit of grinding your own sausage meat (remembering always to grind the chunks of pork and pork fat together to prevent clogging the blades with fat), but if this is a problem, any good butcher can do the job for you. The risky alternative, of course, is to use two pounds of commercial sausage and hope that the ratio of lean to fat is about right.

1 Cut the pork and pork fat into 2-inch cubes and pass first through the coarse blade, then through the fine blade of a meat grinder into a large bowl. Add all the remaining ingredients and mix with your hands till thoroughly blended. Form the mixture into a ball, wrap in plastic wrap, and refrigerate for at least 2 hours before using.

2 When ready to cook, form the mixture into 6 to 8 patties and fry in a large skillet over moderate heat till cooked through and browned, 15 to 20 minutes, turning once and keeping the cooked patties hot till ready to serve.

CAJUN BOUDIN RICE SAUSAGE

**MAKES ABOUT 3 POUNDS;
AT LEAST 10 SERVINGS**

2 pounds boneless pork shoulder
    butt

½ pound fresh pork fat
    (cheek, jowl, or salt pork)

½ pound pork liver

1 medium onion, chopped

1 carrot, scraped and chopped

1 celery rib, chopped

3 cups cooked rice

½ cup chopped scallions
    (part of green tops included)

2 garlic cloves, minced

½ teaspoon dried thyme,
    crumbled

Salt and freshly ground black
    pepper to taste

Tabasco sauce to taste

About 6 feet of medium hog
    casings, rinsed well

Peanut oil for frying

In Cajun Louisiana, it is custom in the fall at hog-killing time for home cooks (especially women) to make two styles of rice sausages with the pork trimmings: sturdy boudin noir with liver (and often pig's blood), and the more delicate boudin blanc with chopped chicken and heavy cream added to the pork. Both types of sausage (widely available throughout Louisiana and, in links, at some upscale markets in major cities outside the state) are unique and utterly delectable, and each is relatively easy to make once you have the right meats. Never use smoked bacon in place of fresh pork fat to make boudin, and trim only excess gobs of surface fat from the shoulder butt. Hog casings are available at butchers and online. The sausage keeps well for up to about four days in the refrigerator, but because of the rice, it should not be frozen.

1 In a large pot, combine the pork butt, fat, liver, onion, carrot, and celery and add enough water to cover. Bring to a boil, reduce the heat to low, cover, and simmer till the meats are very tender, about 1½ hours. Transfer the meats to a platter, strain the broth into a bowl, discard the solids, and reserve the broth.

2 Cut the meats into chunks, place in a meat grinder or food processor, grind coarsely, and scrape into a large bowl. Add the rice, scallions, garlic, thyme, salt and pepper, and Tabasco and mix with your hands till well blended, adding just enough of the reserved broth to keep the mixture moist.

3 Either form the mixture into patties with your hands or, using the sausage-stuffing attachment on the meat grinder, stuff it into a casing according to machine instructions and twist into 3- to 4-inch links, tying the ends of the casing. Fry the patties or links in a little oil in a heavy skillet over moderate heat just till browned and drain on paper towels.

PIG PICKIN'S

"A real, salt-cured, aged country ham is history and art. Don't call it salty. Call it Southern prosciutto."

—Kathleen Purvis, *The Charlotte Observer*

CREOLE CHAURICE SAUSAGE

2 pounds boneless lean pork,
  cut into chunks

1 pound pork fatback, cut
  into chunks

2 medium onions, finely chopped

3 garlic cloves, minced

½ cup finely chopped fresh
  parsley leaves

2 teaspoons red pepper flakes

1 teaspoon dried thyme, crumbled

½ teaspoon ground allspice

½ teaspoon ground bay leaves

Salt and freshly ground black
  pepper to taste

About 6 feet of medium hog
  casings, rinsed well

Peanut oil for frying

Dating back to the nineteenth century, this garlicky, spicy Creole sausage can be used to enrich gumbos, jambalayas, or bean dishes, but more often than not in Louisiana, it is simply grilled as a breakfast sausage. An easy alternative to stuffing the sausage meat into casings is to form it into cylinders about two inches in diameter, wrap in foil, chill well, and, when ready to serve, slice into ½-inch-thick rounds and fry till nicely browned on both sides. Hog casings are available at butchers and online. The sausage keeps in the refrigerator for up to about four days and freezes well for up to about three months.

1 Using a meat grinder with a sausage-stuffing attachment, grind the pork and fatback together through the coarse blade into a large bowl. Add the onions, garlic, parsley, red pepper flakes, thyme, allspice, bay leaves, and salt and pepper, mix with your hands till well blended, cover with plastic wrap, and chill overnight in the refrigerator. Wash the grinder.

2 Return the sausage mixture to the grinder, this time stuffing it into a long casing according to machine instructions and twisting the casing into 4-inch links, tying both ends of the casing. Chill the links for at least 2 hours, and when ready to cook, cut the links apart with a sharp knife, prick them all over, and fry in a little oil in a heavy skillet over moderate heat till nicely browned, 15 to 20 minutes.

BLUE RIDGE PORK AND BACON SAUSAGE

**MAKES 2½ POUNDS;
6 TO 8 SERVINGS**

2 pounds pork shoulder, cut into chunks

½ pound slab bacon (rind removed), cut into chunks

2 scallions (white parts only), minced

2 tablespoons minced fresh parsley leaves

1 teaspoon ground fennel seeds

1 teaspoon white vinegar

Salt and freshly ground black pepper to taste

Cayenne pepper to taste

Sausage making is a major enterprise (indeed, industry) in the Blue Ridge Mountains of Virginia, North Carolina, and Tennessee, and I know of no other region in the South where some producers not only include a little cured bacon in their sausage mixtures but also flavor them with ground fennel seeds (as in Italian-style sausage found throughout the North). Since the texture of this sausage should be quite fine, this is one time the meats can be ground in a food processor—so long, that is, as they're not reduced to a paste.

1 In a meat grinder or food processor, finely grind together the pork and bacon into a large bowl. Add all the remaining ingredients, mix with your hands till well blended, cover with plastic wrap, and refrigerate for at least 2 hours.

2 When ready to cook, form the mixture into 6 to 8 patties and fry in a large skillet over moderate heat till cooked through and browned, 15 to 20 minutes, turning once and keeping the cooked patties hot till ready to serve.

Breakfast Sausage Biscuits with Cream Gravy

Makes 4 servings

For the Biscuits:

1½ cups all-purpose flour

2 teaspoons baking powder

½ teaspoon salt

3 tablespoons chilled vegetable shortening

¾ cup milk

1 pound bulk pork sausage

For the Gravy:

4 tablespoons (½ stick) butter

¼ cup all-purpose flour

2½ cups half-and-half

Salt and freshly ground black pepper to taste

Once a breakfast staple at every roadside diner and family restaurant in the South, sausage biscuits with milk or cream gravy are no longer found on as many menus as before, and I suspect the main reason is because younger cooks simply don't know how (or don't want to go to the extra trouble) to make gravy. All of which, of course, is absurd, since, as this recipe illustrates, nothing is simpler or quicker than whipping up a little pan gravy to adorn one of the most delectable combinations in the entire Southern breakfast repertoire. One point I can't emphasize enough is using a cast-iron skillet for this dish so that as much browned sausage debris as possible can be scraped off the bottom to give the gravy real character. Butter the extra biscuit halves and serve them on the side with plenty of fruit preserves.

1 Preheat the oven to 475°F.

2 To make the biscuits, whisk together the flour, baking powder, and salt in a large bowl. Add the shortening and cut it in with a pastry cutter or rub with your fingertips till the mixture is mealy. Gradually add the milk and stir just till the dough holds together and is still sticky. Transfer to a lightly floured work surface, knead about 8 times, and form the dough with your hands into 8 smooth rounds about 1 inch thick. Arrange the rounds on a baking sheet about 1 inch apart, bake in the upper third of the oven till golden brown, about 15 minutes, and keep warm.

3 With your hands, form the sausage meat into 8 patties, fry the patties on both sides in a large cast-iron skillet over moderate heat till cooked through and nicely browned, about 15 minutes, drain on paper towels, and keep warm on a plate.

4 To make the gravy, pour off about half the fat from the skillet, add the butter to the skillet, and stir over moderate heat till the fats are incorporated, scraping the browned bits off the bottom of the pan. Gradually add the flour, stir till it has absorbed the fats, and cook, stirring constantly, till the flour turns golden brown, about 2 minutes. Gradually add the half-and-half, stirring constantly till the gravy is thickened, smooth, and slightly browned. Season with salt and pepper and stir well.

5 To serve, split 4 of the biscuits in half and place 2 halves on warm serving plates. Top each half with a sausage patty, spoon hot gravy over the tops, and serve immediately with extra split biscuits and fruit preserves on the side.

HICKORY-SMOKED COUNTRY SAUSAGE LINKS

**MAKES ABOUT 2½ POUNDS;
AT LEAST 8 SERVINGS**

2 pounds boneless pork shoulder
  butt, cut into chunks

½ pound pork fatback, cut
  into chunks and chilled for
  30 minutes in the freezer

2 tablespoons light brown sugar

1 tablespoon sweet paprika

2 teaspoons red pepper flakes

1 teaspoon ground sage

½ teaspoon dried thyme,
  crumbled

Pinch of ground allspice

Salt and freshly ground black
  pepper to taste

About 6 feet of medium hog
  casings, rinsed well

Small bag of hickory wood chips

While anyone in the South who smokes country hams most likely also smokes bacon and sausage links in the same ham house, most people must depend on a metal gas or electric home smoker for that wonderful hickory flavor that makes smoked country sausage so special. (I've also had pretty good luck using an ordinary kettle grill with charcoal embers and soaked hickory chips.) For the very best flavor, the sausage meat should be chilled and allowed to mellow overnight. Hog casings are available at butchers and online. The uncooked links keep for up to about four days in the refrigerator and for up to three months in the freezer.

1 Using a meat grinder with a sausage-stuffing attachment, grind the pork and fatback together through the coarse blade into a bowl. Add the sugar, paprika, red pepper flakes, sage, thyme, allspice, and salt and pepper, mix with your hands till well blended, cover with plastic wrap, and allow to mellow overnight in the refrigerator. Wash the grinder.

2 Return the sausage mixture to the grinder, this time stuffing it into a long casing according to machine instructions and twisting the casing into 3- to 4-inch links, tying both ends securely.

3 Hang or arrange the links on the rack of a home smoker and smoke according to the manufacturer's instructions, using the hickory chips as needed.

4 When ready to cook, cut the links apart with a sharp knife, prick them all over, and fry in a heavy skillet over moderate heat till lightly browned, about 15 minutes.

Sausage and Pecan Stuffing for Roast Fowl

Makes enough stuffing for a 12-pound turkey or goose or a large roaster chicken, with extra for baked dressing

1 pound bulk pork sausage

2 medium onions, chopped

2 celery ribs, chopped

10 cups crumbled cornbread (or fresh bread crumbs)

3 tablespoons minced fresh parsley leaves

3 teaspoons dried sage, crumbled

Salt and freshly ground black pepper to taste

2 large eggs, beaten

1½ cups chicken broth

1 cup crumbled toasted pecans

In the South, what is cooked inside the cavity of a roast turkey, goose, or large chicken is called "stuffing," but when all or part of this same stuffing is baked in a separate pan, it's called "dressing." Southerners love both moist stuffing and crusty dressing, both are typically prepared and served at the same festive dinner (with, of course, giblet gravy), and none is more popular than one made with cornbread, sausage, and pecans. To bake part of this stuffing as dressing, add a little more chicken broth to the mixture, spoon the mixture into a medium shallow baking pan, and bake in a preheated 350°F oven till crusty, 35 to 40 minutes. To prevent food poisoning, never fill any fowl with stuffing till ready to cook.

1 In a large skillet, break up the sausage and cook over moderate heat till lightly browned, about 10 minutes, stirring. Drain all but about 2 tablespoons of fat from the skillet, add the onions and celery, and cook till the vegetables soften, about 5 minutes. Transfer the mixture to a large bowl, add the cornbread, parsley, sage, and salt and pepper, and toss well. Add the eggs and broth and mix till the stuffing is well blended and moist. Add the pecans and stir till well incorporated, adding a little more broth if the stuffing seems at all dry.

2 Cover the stuffing with plastic wrap and refrigerate till ready to use.

Kentucky Scramble

½ pound bulk pork sausage

6 slices lean bacon, chopped

1 cup fresh or thawed frozen corn kernels

1 small green bell pepper, seeded and finely chopped

One 4-ounce jar pimentos, drained and chopped

Salt and freshly ground black pepper to taste

8 large eggs, beaten

Frankly, I'd never heard of a Kentucky scramble till, while visiting a couple of bourbon distilleries in Louisville, I noticed the item on the breakfast menu at my motel, ordered it, and declared it one of the most sumptuous dishes I'd ever encountered. In the restaurant, it was served with hash-brown potatoes, fried green apples, and one single enormous buttermilk biscuit, and since that momentous morning, I've learned that elsewhere in the state, the scramble itself can include only the corn, bell pepper, pimentos, and eggs, with fried bacon strips and/or sausage patties served alongside on the plate. Personally, I much prefer the meats incorporated in the scramble.

1 In a large, heavy skillet, break up the sausage, add the bacon, and fry over moderate heat till the bacon is crisp and the sausage browned; drain both on paper towels. Drain all but about 3 tablespoons of fat from the skillet, add the corn, bell pepper, pimentos, and salt and pepper, and stir till the vegetables soften, about 5 minutes. Return the sausage and bacon to the skillet and stir till well blended with the other ingredients. Add the eggs, reduce the heat to low, and stir slowly and steadily till the eggs begin to form soft, creamy curds (do not overcook the eggs).

2 Transfer the scramble to a heated platter and serve immediately.

Country-Style Sausages and Apples

2 tablespoons bacon grease

1 pound pork sausage links (fresh or commercial)

1 large onion, thinly sliced

3 Granny Smith apples, peeled, cored, and thinly sliced

1 tablespoon fresh lemon juice

2 tablespoons light brown sugar

¼ teaspoon ground cinnamon

⅛ teaspoon ground cloves

Salt and freshly ground black pepper to taste

Looking for a simple but eminently satisfying dish to serve a couple of friends for Sunday-night supper? These spicy sausages with meltingly soft onions and apples fill the bill on every count and need nothing more than a skillet of fresh cornbread and, for dessert, maybe some hot fruit cobbler with scoops of vanilla ice cream. The small amount of bacon grease contributes a good deal more Southern flavor than you might expect, so don't substitute butter or margarine in this particular dish.

1 In a large, heavy skillet, heat the bacon grease over moderate heat, add the sausages, brown on all sides, and transfer to a plate. Add the onion and apples to the skillet and stir till golden, about 8 minutes. Add the lemon juice, brown sugar, cinnamon, cloves, and salt and pepper and stir till well blended. Return the sausages to the skillet, spoon the onion and apples over the sausages, cover, reduce the heat to low, and simmer slowly for about 30 minutes.

2 Serve hot.

Canadian Bacon Breakfast Sandwiches with Molasses

8 tablespoons (1 stick) plus
   3 tablespoons butter

Eight to ten ¼-inch-thick slices
   Canadian bacon

12 large eggs

1 cup whole milk

Salt and cayenne pepper to taste

8 to 10 slices white loaf bread,
   crusts removed

Unsulphured molasses, heated

Canadian bacon (which is more like ham than bacon) has been a popular breakfast and brunch staple in the South for generations, and cooks are forever coming up with new ways to serve it, as in this unusual variation on French toast. For a long time, I served maple syrup with these clever sandwiches, but after I once substituted light, unsulphured molasses (available in most grocery stores), I knew there was no turning back. Do notice that the bacon slices should be cooked only till they're lightly browned on each side; any more and they'll be tough.

1 In a large skillet, melt the 3 tablespoons of butter over moderate heat, add the bacon slices, brown lightly, about 2 minutes on each side, and keep warm on a plate.

2 In a shallow bowl, whisk together 6 of the eggs with the milk, salt, and cayenne till well blended. In another bowl, whisk the remaining 6 eggs till frothy.

3 Cut each slice of bread in half diagonally. Soak each slice momentarily in the milk mixture, and then, using two forks or large spoons, carefully coat both sides of each slice in the beaten egg, placing the slices on a plate as they are coated.

4 In a large skillet, melt about ⅓ of the stick of butter over moderate heat, add about ⅓ of the coated slices, cook for about 3 minutes on each side till golden, and transfer the toast to a plate with a spatula. Repeat the procedure with the remaining butter and slices.

5 Cut the bacon into approximately the same size triangles as the toast, sandwich 1 bacon slice between 2 pieces of toast, arrange the sandwiches on a large heated platter, and drizzle them liberally with molasses.

PIG PICKIN'S

The basic technique today for curing genuine Southern country hams is the same as the one that Captain John Smith and the original Jamestown settlers observed Indians using to cure venison 400 years ago.

Bacon Waffles

8 slices smoked bacon

2 large eggs, separated

2 cups cake flour

3 teaspoons baking powder

¼ teaspoon salt

1¼ cups whole milk

6 tablespoons vegetable shortening, melted

Warmed maple syrup or molasses for topping

Like all Southerners, I never miss a chance to add a little cooked bacon to all sorts of salads, eggs, dips, spreads, savory pies, and breads when I think the dish might be enhanced, but not till a friend's mother in Huntsville, Alabama, served these amazing waffles with bacon incorporated into the batter itself was I aware of such a clever possibility. You don't actually have to whisk the egg yolks and whites separately, but if you do so and fold them into the batter, you will have noticeably lighter waffles.

1 Preheat a waffle iron according to the manufacturer's instructions.

2 In a large skillet, fry the bacon over moderate heat till crisp. Drain on paper towels and crumble.

3 In a small bowl, whisk the egg yolks till light and set aside. In another bowl, whisk the egg whites till stiff and set aside.

4 In a bowl, sift together the flour, baking powder, and salt, add the egg yolks and milk, and stir till well blended. Add the shortening and bacon and stir till well blended. Fold the egg whites into the batter till well blended, pour batter into the hot waffle iron according to the manufacturer's instructions, bake till the waffles are golden, and serve hot with maple syrup or molasses.

Tennessee Fried Streak-o'-Lean

1-pound slab of streak-o'-lean
(lean salt pork), rind removed

1½ cups buttermilk

1 cup cornmeal

½ teaspoon freshly ground black
pepper

¼ pound lard

For the Gravy (Optional):

2 tablespoons all-purpose flour

2 cups whole milk

Often called "Tennessee fried chicken" or "poor man's bacon" throughout the state of Tennessee, fried streak-o'-lean is a long strip of lean salt pork that is cut from pig belly like bacon, soaked in buttermilk, battered, fried till crisp, and served for breakfast or supper with eggs, grits with milk gravy, and maybe fried green tomatoes. Some cooks might initially boil the meat in water for a few minutes to leach out part of the salt, but whether this extra step is taken or not, true pork fanatics consider fried streak-o'-lean to be far superior to ordinary bacon in both flavor and texture.

1 Cut the streak-o'-lean into long, ¼-inch-thick slices, place in a shallow pan or bowl, pour the buttermilk over the top, and let soak for 30 minutes.

2 In a shallow baking pan, combine the cornmeal and pepper, mix well, and dredge the pork slices well in the mixture. In a large cast-iron skillet, melt the lard over moderate heat, add the slices in batches, fry till golden brown and crisp, 5 to 7 minutes on each side, and drain on paper towels.

3 Serve the slices with or without milk gravy.

4 To make milk gravy, pour off all but about 2 tablespoons of drippings from the skillet, add flour, and stir over moderate heat till browned. Slowly add milk and stir steadily till the gravy thickens slightly.

Aunt Bunny's Bacon and Sausage Soufflé

MAKES 6 SERVINGS

½ pound hickory-smoked bacon, cut into small pieces

½ pound bulk pork sausage

6 slices white loaf bread, crusts removed

3 tablespoons butter, melted

1½ cups grated sharp cheddar cheese

2 cups half-and-half

5 large eggs

2 teaspoons dry mustard

Salt and freshly ground black pepper to taste

While growing up in Charlotte, North Carolina, I could religiously count on my Aunt Bunny serving this tasty soufflé each and every time my family would go to her house for breakfast after early church on Sunday. The menu was always the same: bacon and sausage soufflé, a huge bowl of fresh fruit compote, pecan-cinnamon coffee cake, and Aunt Bunny's homemade peach preserves in a small cut-crystal bowl. I always thought it was the fanciest breakfast on earth and can still hear Aunt Bunny warning, "I don't want to see one scrap of that soufflé left in the dish." (And, in case you're wondering, any savory dish in the South that contains eggs can be called a soufflé.)

1 Place the bacon in a large skillet, break up the sausage in the skillet, and fry the two meats over moderate heat till fully cooked, stirring. Drain on paper towels.

2 Brush the bread with the butter, cut into small cubes, and arrange the cubes in a buttered 13 by 9-inch or round baking dish. Spoon the bacon and sausage evenly over the cubes and sprinkle the cheese evenly over the top. In a bowl, whisk together the remaining ingredients till well blended, pour over the cheese, cover with plastic wrap, and chill overnight.

3 When ready to bake, preheat the oven to 350°F, bake the soufflé till golden, 40 to 45 minutes, and serve hot.

Bacon, Cream Cheese, and Horseradish Cocktail Dip

MAKES ABOUT 3 CUPS

6 thick slices lean corncob-
smoked bacon

Two 8-ounce packages cream
cheese, at room temperature

1 cup half-and-half

2 tablespoons minced fresh chives

2 tablespoons prepared
horseradish

1 teaspoon fresh lemon juice

1 teaspoon Worcestershire sauce

Salt and freshly ground black
pepper to taste

Bacon finds its way into countless Southern cocktail dips and spreads, and today I never make this classic dip without trying to experiment with various styles of smoked bacon now available on the market. Corncob-smoked bacon has a distinctive, delightfully assertive flavor, but if you don't want to go to the trouble of ordering some from one of the number of sources on the Internet, any wood-smoked bacon can be substituted.

1 In a large skillet, fry the bacon over moderate heat till crisp; drain on paper towels and crumble finely.

2 In a bowl, blend the cream cheese and half-and-half till smooth, add the bacon, chives, horseradish, lemon juice, Worcestershire, and salt and pepper, and mix till well blended. Cover the dip and let stand for about 1 hour before serving with assorted crackers.

Bacon and Chicken Succotash

2 cups fresh or frozen lima beans

5 thick slices maple-smoked bacon

2 medium onions, finely chopped

½ green bell pepper, seeded and finely chopped

1½ cups shredded cooked chicken

2½ cups whole milk

Salt and freshly ground black pepper to taste

Tabasco sauce to taste

2 cups fresh or thawed frozen corn kernels

½ cup heavy cream

Classic corn, lima bean, and bacon succotash is as popular a side dish at Southern barbecues as Brunswick stew, but when, years ago, I decided to add some shredded leftover chicken to the concoction I planned to serve with Carolina pulled pork, almost every guest at the event asked for the recipe. Since then, I've transformed the concept into a full-fledged main course and never stop testing different artisanal smoked bacons—usually with stunning results.

1 Place the lima beans in a saucepan with enough water to cover. Bring to a boil, reduce the heat to moderate, cover, cook for 10 minutes, and drain.

2 Meanwhile, fry the bacon over moderate heat in a large, deep skillet till crisp; drain on paper towels and crumble. Drain off all but 2 tablespoons of fat from the skillet, add the onions and bell pepper, and stir till softened, about 5 minutes. Add the lima beans, chicken, milk, salt and pepper, and Tabasco, stir, and simmer till the milk is reduced, about 10 minutes. Add the corn and cream, stir, return to a simmer, and cook till the mixture has thickened but is not dry, watching carefully. Sprinkle on the bacon, stir, and serve hot in bowls.

Bacon and Squash Soufflé

Makes 4 to 6 servings

½ pound hickory-smoked bacon, cut into small pieces

8 medium yellow squash (about 3 pounds), cut into 1-inch pieces

2 large onions, coarsely chopped

2 garlic cloves, chopped

6 tablespoons (¾ stick) butter, softened

2 large eggs, beaten

½ cup minced fresh parsley leaves

½ cup dry bread crumbs

½ teaspoon salt

Freshly ground black pepper to taste

Pinch of ground nutmeg

1 cup grated extra-sharp cheddar cheese

Almost every Southern cook has his or her version of squash soufflé, but not many transform the vegetable concept into a main dish by adding some form of pork. I've made the soufflé with both bulk sausage and chopped ham hock, but when I lay hands on a beautiful hickory- or applewood-smoked artisanal bacon, there's really nothing better. And to gild the porcine lily, I love to serve the dish with large country ham biscuits smeared with plenty of pungent mustard. For the right texture, do not use a food processor for the vegetables. This is one dish that, for some reason, is not very good reheated and must be served as soon as it's baked.

1 In a large skillet, fry the bacon over moderate heat till crisp; drain on paper towels and reserve.

2 In a large saucepan, combine the squash and onions, add enough salted water to cover, and bring to a boil. Reduce the heat to low, cover, and simmer till the squash is tender, about 30 minutes. Drain in a colander and mash well in the colander with a potato masher or heavy fork to extract excess liquid.

3 Preheat the oven to 350°F. Butter a 1½- to 2-quart baking dish and set aside.

4 Place the vegetables in a large bowl, add the bacon and all remaining ingredients except for about 3 tablespoons of the cheese, and mix thoroughly with a heavy spoon. Transfer the mixture to the prepared baking dish, sprinkle the remaining cheese over the top, and bake till golden, about 30 minutes.

5 Serve immediately.

Sullivan's Island Bacon and Shrimp Bog

Makes 6 servings

½ pound double-smoked bacon, diced

2 medium onions, finely chopped

1½ cups long-grain rice, rinsed well and drained

2¼ cups chicken broth

2 medium ripe tomatoes, peeled, finely chopped, and juice reserved

2 teaspoons fresh lemon juice

1½ teaspoons Worcestershire sauce

1 teaspoon salt

¼ teaspoon freshly ground black pepper

¼ teaspoon cayenne pepper

¼ teaspoon grated nutmeg

2 pounds medium fresh shrimp, shelled and deveined

¼ cup minced fresh parsley leaves

A close cousin to the jambalayas of Louisiana in composition if not texture, the bogs of the Carolina and Georgia coastal Lowcountry are an almost soupy rice specialty enriched with everything from seafood to chicken to smoked meats. I don't think there's a style I haven't encountered, but surely one of the most memorable was this beauty made with thick, double-smoked bacon and fresh local shrimp and served at a friend's summer cottage on Sullivan's Island near Charleston, South Carolina. Feel free to experiment with different types of bacon, sausage, ham, and other pork products, remembering only that the overly moist texture of a genuine bog (unlike that of a fluffy perloo) must be maintained throughout the cooking.

In a large, heavy pot, fry the bacon over moderate heat till crisp; drain on paper towels and set aside. Pour off all but about 3 tablespoons of fat from the pot, add the onions, and stir for 3 minutes. Add the rice and stir well. Add the broth, tomatoes with their juice, lemon juice, Worcestershire, salt, black pepper, cayenne, and nutmeg, bring to a low simmer, cover, and cook for 20 minutes. Stir in the bacon and the shrimp and continue cooking, uncovered, for 10 minutes, adding a little more broth if the rice seems to be drying out in the least (the texture should be almost soupy). Stir the bog with a fork, taste for seasoning, sprinkle the parsley on top, and serve immediately.

Fried Catfish with Bacon and Pecan-Tarragon-Butter Sauce

Makes 4 to 6 servings

6 slices hickory-smoked bacon

1 cup white cornmeal

¼ cup all-purpose flour

¼ teaspoon salt

¼ teaspoon freshly ground black pepper

6 tablespoons (¾ stick) butter

1 teaspoon fresh lemon juice

1 teaspoon dried tarragon, crumbled

1 cup chopped toasted pecans

2 pounds fresh catfish fillets, rinsed and patted dry with paper towels

Sweet catfish is loved all over the South, and while Southerners will debate endlessly the virtues of large channel versus smaller bullhead catfish (most of which are farmed today), all agree that the fish is best battered and fried and that it has a natural affinity with bacon. Fried catfish simply topped with crumbled smoky bacon is hard to beat, unless, that is, you raise the dish's pedigree by serving it also with this buttery pecan-tarragon sauce I came up with years ago. The thickness of catfish fillets can vary considerably, and while I indicate an approximate frying time, watch the fillets carefully to make sure they don't overcook and remain soft and moist.

1 In a large skillet, fry the bacon over moderate heat till crisp; drain on paper towels, crumble, and reserve the fat in the skillet.

2 Meanwhile, combine the cornmeal, flour, salt, and pepper in a shallow pan and set aside. In a saucepan, melt the butter over low heat, add the lemon juice, tarragon, and pecans, stir till well blended, and keep the sauce hot.

3 Dredge the catfish fillets in the cornmeal mixture, fry the fillets in the bacon fat for about 6 minutes on each side (do not overcook), and transfer to a serving platter. Spoon the pecan sauce over the fillets, sprinkle the bacon on top, and serve hot.

Mississippi Bacon Spaghetti

MAKES 6 SERVINGS

8 ounces dried spaghetti

1 pound sliced bacon

1 medium onion, chopped

1 small green bell pepper, seeded and chopped

One 14½- to 16-ounce can crushed tomatoes with juice

1 teaspoon dried oregano

1 teaspoon sweet paprika

Salt and freshly ground black pepper to taste

1 cup grated Parmesan cheese

I'd always known about chicken spaghetti being a specialty up and down the Mississippi Delta, but not till somebody in Jackson gave me this recipe did I ever have any idea that some local cooks pride themselves equally on bacon spaghetti boasting the same (if much less complicated) Italian flair and often served with a tart spinach salad and beer after . . . football games. For a delectable textural contrast, be sure to crisp the bacon under the broiler after the dish has finished baking.

1 Preheat the oven to 350°F. Butter a 2-quart baking dish and set aside.

2 Bring a large pot of salted water to a rolling boil, add the spaghetti, reduce the heat slightly, cook till tender, about 10 minutes, and drain in a colander.

3 Cut all but 5 slices of bacon into ½-inch pieces and reserve the slices. Fry the pieces in a large skillet over moderate heat till lightly browned, add the onion and bell pepper, stir till the vegetables are softened, about 5 minutes, and drain on paper towels.

4 In a bowl, combine the spaghetti, bacon and vegetables, tomatoes, oregano, paprika, and salt and pepper and toss till well blended. Transfer the mixture to the prepared baking dish, sprinkle the cheese over the top, and cover with the reserved 5 slices of bacon. Bake for 45 minutes, and then, to make the bacon crispier, place the dish under the oven broiler for a few minutes longer.

5 Serve hot.

BARBECUE and RIBS

Basic Barbecue Table Sauce

Basic Vinegar Barbecue Moppin' Sauce

Basic Dry-Rub Barbecue Mix #1

Basic Dry-Rub Barbecue Mix #2

North Carolina Lexington-Style Chopped 'Cue

North Carolina Eastern-Style Chopped or Pulled 'Cue

South Carolina Mustard Barbecue

A Pig Pickin'

Barbecued Leg of Pork with Tennessee Table Sauce

Louis's Barbecued Shredded Pork

Smoky Oven-Roasted Spareribs

Beer-Braised Spiced Barbecued Spareribs

Oriental Barbecued Spareribs

Mama Dip's Baked Spareribs with Sauerkraut

Cajun Dry-Rub Barbecued Spareribs

Baked Spareribs Stuffed with Apples and Raisins

Corky's Memphis-Style Barbecued Back Ribs

Roasted Back Ribs with Rum Barbecue Sauce

Arkansas Black Barbecued Back Ribs

Oven-Barbecued Country-Style Ribs

Gentleman Jack Barbecued Country-Style Ribs

Louisiana Braised Country-Style Ribs and Sweet Potatoes

Young Sylvia's Barbecued Pork Chops

Georgia-Style Barbecued Pork Chops

Churchyard Honey-Barbecued Pork Loin

Montgomery Oven-Barbecued Prune-Stuffed Pork Loin

Barbecued Pork, Peach, and Red Onion Kabobs

Barbecued Bourbon Ham Steaks

BASIC BARBECUE TABLE SAUCE

2 cups cider vinegar

1 cup water

1 cup ketchup

¼ cup molasses

1 tablespoon Worcestershire
sauce

1 tablespoon paprika

1 teaspoon dry mustard

1 teaspoon garlic salt

½ teaspoon freshly ground
black pepper

½ teaspoon red pepper flakes

1 small onion, minced

Serve this sauce with any form of cooked pork. While it
is basically a table sauce, it can also be used to baste pork
cooked on an outdoor grill. Be warned, however, that, due to
the ketchup and molasses, the sauce tends to burn if used
over coals that are too hot, meaning that the meat being
basted should be cooked at least four inches from the heat.
The sauce keeps well in a sealed jar in the refrigerator for
about one month.

In a stainless-steel or enameled saucepan, combine all the
ingredients, bring to a boil, reduce the heat to low, and simmer,
stirring frequently, till the sauce is slightly thickened, 20 to
30 minutes. Let cool to room temperature before using.

Basic Vinegar Barbecue Moppin' Sauce

MAKES ABOUT 3 CUPS

1 cup white vinegar

1 cup cider vinegar

4 tablespoons (½ stick) butter, cut into pieces

1 tablespoon sugar

1 tablespoon salt

1 tablespoon red pepper flakes

1 teaspoon dry mustard

1 tablespoon Worcestershire sauce

Tabasco sauce to taste

Use this tangy all-purpose sauce to baste, mix into, and serve with any form of chopped, shredded, or pulled barbecued pork. It is the style of sauce found at a typical Southern pig pickin', where a whole hog is barbecued slowly outdoors over a wood fire. Stored in a sealed jar, the sauce keeps for up to two months in the refrigerator.

In a stainless-steel or enameled saucepan, combine all the ingredients over low heat and simmer, stirring, for about 15 minutes. Remove from the heat and let cool.

BASIC DRY-RUB BARBECUE MIX #1

½ cup packed light brown sugar

½ cup paprika

¼ cup coarse salt

¼ cup crushed black peppercorns

1 tablespoon onion powder

1 tablespoon garlic powder

2 teaspoons cayenne pepper,
    or to taste

½ teaspoon ground allspice

Sprinkled on pork before grilling, baking, or roasting, this zesty rub acts as a seasoning, but for more complex layers of barbecue flavor, apply it to ribs, chops, shoulders, and fresh hams several hours or even a day in advance so that the rub both seasons and cures the meat.

In a bowl, combine all the ingredients and mix well with your fingers, breaking up any lumps of brown sugar. Store the rub in an airtight jar for up to 3 months.

Basic Dry-Rub Barbecue Mix #2

MAKES ABOUT 2 CUPS

½ cup salt

½ cup packed dark brown sugar

½ cup freshly ground black pepper

¼ cup hot paprika

1 tablespoon dry mustard

1 tablespoon freshly grated lemon rind

1 teaspoon garlic powder

1 teaspoon chili powder

This sturdy rub is especially effective at seasoning large cuts of barbecued pork and sealing the juices of thick chops, ribs, and even ham steaks. Use two to three teaspoons of rub per pound of meat.

In a bowl, combine all the ingredients and mix well with your fingers, breaking up any lumps of brown sugar. Store the rub in an airtight jar for up to 3 months.

North Carolina Lexington-Style Chopped 'Cue

**MAKES AT LEAST
10 SERVINGS**

1 small (1½ to 2-pound) bag hickory or oak wood chips

One 10-pound bag charcoal briquets

One 9- to 10-pound pork shoulder butt (all skin and fat left on)

3 cups cider vinegar

¾ cup packed light brown sugar

½ cup ketchup

1 tablespoon Worcestershire sauce

1 tablespoon red pepper flakes

1 teaspoon onion powder

1 teaspoon salt

1 teaspoon freshly ground black pepper

Few savvy Southerners (even the rib fanatics of Memphis) will deny that North Carolina is the barbecue capital of the South (if not the world). Within the state, however, tempers flare when there's (never-ending) debate over whether the dry, spicy, vinegar-sauced chopped or pulled whole-hog 'cue in the east is superior to the moister, slightly sweet version in the west (mainly around the town of Lexington) made from only pork shoulders with a tomatoey sauce (or "dip"). Being a transplanted Tarheel myself, I declare that I love both styles equally and, years ago, I perfected a method whereby I can periodically produce on an ordinary kettle grill virtually the same eastern- or Lexington-style 'cue that, on home ground, would be made over outdoor wood-burning pits or in huge enclosed gas or electric ovens. Just be sure to follow the directions to the letter—though do feel free to experiment with the sauce for this particular style of barbecue.

1 In a pan of water, soak 6 handfuls of the chips for 45 minutes.

2 Open one bottom and one top vent on a kettle grill, place an aluminum drip pan in the bottom of the grill, stack charcoal briquets evenly around the pan (not in the center), and ignite the coals. When the coals are ashen (30 to 45 minutes), sprinkle 2 handfuls of the soaked chips evenly over the hot coals. Place the grate on the grill about 6 inches over the coals.

3 Position the pork shoulder fat side up in the center of the grate directly over the drip pan (not over the hot coals), close the lid, and cook slowly for 2 hours, replenishing the coals and chips as they burn up. Turn the pork over, close the lid, and cook for 2 hours longer.

4 Meanwhile, prepare the sauce by combining all the remaining ingredients in a large stainless-steel or enameled saucepan. Stir well, bring to a simmer over moderate heat, and cook for about 10 minutes. Remove from the heat and let stand for about 2 hours.

5 Transfer the pork to a large cutting board, make deep gashes in the meat with a sharp knife, and baste liberally with the sauce. Replenish the coals and chips as needed, replace the pork fat side down on the grate, close the lid, and cook for 2 to 3 hours longer or till the meat is very tender when stabbed with a large fork, basting with the same sauce from time to time.

6 Transfer the pork to the chopping board, remove and discard most (but not all) of the crisp skin and excess fat, and either chop the meat coarsely with a hatchet or cleaver or pull into shreds. Add just enough sauce to moisten the meat, toss till well blended, and either serve the barbecue immediately with the remaining sauce on the side or refrigerate and reheat in the top of a double boiler over simmering water when ready to serve.

North Carolina Eastern-Style Chopped or Pulled 'Cue

Makes at least 10 servings

One small (1½- to 2-pound) bag hickory wood chips

One 10-pound bag charcoal briquets

2 cups white vinegar

1 cup cider vinegar

1 tablespoon sugar

1 tablespoon red pepper flakes

1 tablespoon Tabasco sauce

1 tablespoon salt

1 tablespoon freshly ground black pepper

One 9- to 10-pound pork shoulder butt (all skin and fat left on)

This is the relatively dry, spicy style of pork barbecue (with a little skin crackling) for which eastern North Carolina is so renowned and that is featured at hundreds of barbecue joints and social pig pickin's throughout the region. Traditionally, whole hogs are slowly smoked on huge grates over hickory and/or oak fires; the cooked meat is either chopped or pulled; and, unlike the sweeter, tomatoey sauces (or "dips") used for Lexington-style barbecue in the western part of the state, the vinegar moppin' sauce here is not unlike the simple hot pepper sauces of Thomas Jefferson's day. Given the impracticality of digging a large pit in the ground (or acquiring an enormous metal smoker) and roasting a whole pig, a very good approximation of eastern-style Carolina 'cue can be accomplished with pork shoulder and an ordinary kettle grill. Typically, this barbecue is served with coleslaw, Brunswick stew, maybe baked beans, hush puppies, and either beer or iced tea. Since the chopped barbecue freezes well in airtight bags or containers, you really should consider roasting two shoulders.

1 Soak the chips, set up a kettle grill, and make a charcoal fire following the directions for North Carolina Lexington-Style Chopped 'Cue on page 276.

2 In a nonreactive bowl, combine the vinegars, sugar, red pepper, Tabasco, salt, and pepper and stir till the sugar is dissolved and the sauce well blended. When the coals are ready on the grill, position the butt fat side up on the grate over indirect heat, mop it with the sauce, close the lid, and cook for 3 hours, mopping the meat every hour and replenishing the coals and chips as they burn up. Turn the butt over, close the lid, and cook till the meat is very tender, 2 to 3 hours longer, mopping every hour and replenishing the coals and chips as needed.

3 Transfer the butt to a chopping board, remove and discard excess fat, and either chop the meat and crisp skin coarsely or pull into shreds. Transfer the meat to a roasting pan, drizzle about 1 cup of the sauce over the top, toss well, cover with foil, and keep warm.

4 To serve, mound the barbecue on plates or hamburger buns and serve with the remaining sauce on the side.

South Carolina Mustard Barbecue

One small (1½- to 2-pound) bag hickory or oak wood chips

One 10-pound bag charcoal briquets

1½ cups prepared yellow mustard

½ cup ketchup

½ cup packed light brown sugar

¼ cup white vinegar

1 tablespoon Worcestershire sauce

1 teaspoon garlic salt

1 teaspoon freshly ground black pepper

½ teaspoon cayenne pepper

One 9- to 10-pound pork shoulder butt or shank

The only basic difference between North Carolina Lexington-style 'cue and South Carolina barbecue is the mustard included in the thick sauce of the latter, but that small difference is so important that Tarheels don't so much as acknowledge this meat as barbecue, much less cook or eat it. The truth is that when mustard barbecue is prepared carefully (as the pulled pork is at the venerable Piggy Park in Columbia, South Carolina, and at Willard's in Gaffney), it can be delicious. Unlike North Carolina barbecue, mustard barbecue rarely includes any cracklin's (crisp skin), and while North Carolina 'cue is often served with cups of Brunswick stew on the side, the South Carolina pork usually calls for another unique regional dish of thick meat gravy over rice or grits, simply called "hash."

1 Soak the chips, set up a kettle grill, and make a charcoal fire following the directions for North Carolina Lexington-Style Chopped 'Cue on page 276.

2 In a small saucepan, combine the mustard, ketchup, brown sugar, vinegar, Worcestershire, garlic salt, black pepper, and cayenne and stir over low heat till the sugar dissolves and the sauce is thick. Brush the pork all over with the sauce, and when the coals are ready, position the pork on the grate of the grill over indirect heat, close the lid, and cook slowly for 3 hours, replenishing the coals and chips as they burn up and basting the meat from time to time with the sauce. Turn the pork over, baste, close the lid, and cook till the meat is very tender when stabbed with a fork, 2 to 3 hours, basting from time to time.

3 Transfer the pork to a chopping board, remove and discard the skin and excess fat, and chop the meat coarsely or pull into shreds. Add enough sauce just to flavor the meat, toss till well blended, and serve hot.

A Pig Pickin'

For the Vinegar Shake:

About 4 cups white vinegar

About 4 cups cider vinegar

About ¼ cup sugar

About ¼ cup red pepper flakes

About 2 tablespoons Tabasco
sauce

One 80- to 100-pound hog,
split in half and eviscerated

Double recipe for Basic Dry-Rub
Barbecue Mix #2 (page 275)

Okay, so you really want to take the plunge, go whole hog, produce Southern pork barbecue the way expert Q-masters do, and throw a genuine pig pickin' (not "pig pullin'") for a mob of famished fiends? I wish I had the definitive recipe, but the truth is that, while I've attended the 'cue ritual dozens of times from the Carolinas to the bayous of Louisiana and Mississippi to the backwoods of Tennessee, the methods governing this centuries-old tradition vary so radically and dramatically from region to region that the best I can do is defer, once again, to my barbecue guru, Louis Osteen, and let him outline the overall technique in his own words. What's lacking in explicit details is made up for in spirit, and, after all, barbecuing an awkward whole hog for a pig pickin' is more about spirit and passion and trial and error than precise ingredients and cooking times. How you acquire an 80- to 100-pound dressed hog, whether you dig a pit covered with chicken wire or invest in a large steel cooker like Louis's, and who all you round up to help maneuver and baste the huge carcass are problems you'll have to work out yourself. All I can promise is that once you've been through the operation maybe half a dozen times, you'll begin to get the hang of it; and once you've tasted this pig, you may begin to understand Southern barbecue.

1 "The first thing to know if you're going to have a pig pickin' is that you have to start *real* early in the day (if not the night before), have lots of cold beer nearby, and be absolutely certain that there is a fine stereo system with a good stack of bluegrass music on hand. It's just no fun otherwise.

2 "Combine all the ingredients for the shake in a large stainless-steel or plastic container, whisk till well blended, cover, and let stand at for least 6 hours and preferably overnight for the flavors to develop.

3 "Massage the insides of the hog with a barbecue rub. Barbecuing means low heat and slow cooking, so begin by setting a fire in your cooker using slow-burning coals. When the fire has reached the appropriate low heat, you can spread the split pig, skin side down, over the grill. Although some people turn the pig halfway through cooking, I have found that you can eliminate this difficult step by keeping the heat low enough throughout the entire process.

4 "You should have lots of vinegar shake on hand to baste and flavor the pig, a squirt bottle filled with water to subdue the flames from pig drippings, and a clean rag that has been tied to the end of a four-foot-long stick for the barbecue mop. The rag is for dipping into the shake and basting, and the long stick enables you to reach all sides of the pig without getting burned. That dipping-and-basting action is what we call 'doing the barbecue mop dance.'

5 "Eight to twelve hours later, or when the internal temperature registers 155° to 160°F on a meat thermometer, your pig will be ready. Ready, that is, to have its meat picked from its bones and dunked into more of the shake or your favorite barbecue sauce. I guarantee you that the first time you put this meat into your mouth, chewing it slowly, savoring the succulent meat and the smoky, vinegary flavors, you will finally understand that food doesn't get better than this. And know this to be true: There are only two things to serve with this pig—coleslaw and cornbread."

BARBECUED LEG OF PORK WITH TENNESSEE TABLE SAUCE

One 11- to 12-pound leg of pork
(fresh ham butt or shank)

¾ cup ketchup

¼ cup vegetable oil

2 tablespoons cider vinegar

2 tablespoons Worcestershire
sauce

1 small onion, chopped

1 garlic clove, chopped

2½ tablespoons sugar

1½ tablespoons molasses

1½ teaspoons spicy brown
mustard

1½ teaspoons Tabasco sauce

Salt and freshly ground black
pepper to taste

Southern Q-masters who specialize mainly in chopped or pulled pork barbecue made from whole hogs or shoulders will also often add a leg of pork (or fresh ham) to the pit or grill for those who prefer sliced meat. And almost never is this style of barbecue basted with a moppin' sauce, but rather it is simply smoked slowly for hours, carved in medium-thick slices, and served with a thick, sweet, tomatoey sauce. This particular sauce recipe was tracked down to a remote barbecue joint in Piney Flats, Tennessee by, ironically, none other than the acknowledged dean of North Carolina barbecue, John Sheldon Reed (co-author with his wife of the book *Holy Smoke*), and I can't imagine any sauce that would go any better with sliced barbecued leg than this one. Just be warned that it is strictly a table sauce and will blacken quickly if used for basting.

1 Set up a kettle grill with hot coals and wood chips following the quantities and directions for North Carolina Lexington-Style Chopped 'Cue on page 276.

2 Oil the grill's grate, and when the coals are ready, position the leg of pork on the grate over indirect heat, close the lid, and cook slowly for 2½ hours, replenishing the coals and chips as they burn up. Turn the pork over, close the lid, and continue cooking till the meat is fork-tender, about 2½ hours longer.

3 During the last hour of cooking, combine all the remaining ingredients in a blender or food processor and reduce to a thick liquid. Scrape into a saucepan, bring to a low boil, reduce the heat to low, simmer the sauce for 15 or 20 minutes, stirring, and keep warm.

4 To serve, carve the pork into medium-thick slices and serve with the sauce.

PIG PICKIN'S

"Barbecuing a pig is like performing a song: Once you start it, the expectation is that you will carry things to a conclusion. You cannot half-barbecue a pig. You must see the process through, and though it requires little in the way of technology—just meat and heat—it does require attention and a time commitment." —Peter Kaminsky, *Pig Perfect*

Louis's Barbecued Shredded Pork

Makes about 4 cups

3 pounds boneless pork shoulder (skin removed but fat left on), cut into 2-inch cubes

2 garlic cloves, minced

1 tablespoon salt

2 tablespoons freshly ground black pepper

3 cups water

1½ cups cider vinegar

1 cup ketchup

1 medium onion, minced

3 tablespoons dark brown sugar

2 tablespoons Worcestershire sauce

1 teaspoon chili powder

Salt and freshly ground black pepper to taste

Tabasco sauce to taste

Over the years, I sampled virtually every dish that came out of Louis Osteen's kitchen at his renowned restaurant, Louis's, on Pawleys Island, South Carolina, but none impressed me more than this innovative version of barbecued pulled pork served on toast as a cocktail appetizer or as a first course with bell pepper coleslaw. Notice that the pork must be made a day in advance for the right flavor and texture to develop, and remember that the consistency of the meat should be slightly coarse, almost stringy.

1 The day before you plan to serve the dish, combine the pork, garlic, salt, pepper, and water in a large, heavy pot and bring to a low boil, skimming scum from the surface. Reduce the heat to low, cover, and simmer for 2 to 2½ hours, stirring from time to time to prevent the pork from browning on the bottom of the pot.

2 Meanwhile, combine all the remaining ingredients in a stainless-steel or enameled saucepan, bring to a boil, reduce the heat to low, and simmer, stirring, till the sauce is slightly thickened. Set the barbecue sauce aside.

3 When the pork starts to come apart, tear it into shreds with a fork. When the water and other juices have evaporated, transfer the pork and rendered fat to a large bowl and shred the pork into very small pieces. Add the barbecue sauce and stir till well blended with the pork. Let cool, cover with plastic wrap, and refrigerate overnight.

4 Place the pork in a large baking pan and, using 2 heavy forks, shred it further in long pulling motions till it is bound by its own fat and the mixture is slightly coarse. Scrape into a crock or bowl, cover again, and refrigerate for at least 4 hours.

5 Remove the pork from the refrigerator about 1 hour before serving on toasted bread or in small mounds with coleslaw. Tightly covered, the pork will keep in the refrigerator for up to 1 week.

SMOKY OVEN-ROASTED SPARERIBS

MAKES 4 TO 6 SERVINGS

1½ cups cider vinegar

½ cup water

1 cup ketchup

2 tablespoons Worcestershire
    sauce

3 tablespoons light brown sugar

1 teaspoon salt

1 teaspoon freshly ground
    black pepper

1 teaspoon liquid smoke

½ teaspoon red pepper flakes

4 to 6 pounds spareribs,
    cut in half

Since liquid smoke (available in bottles at all markets) is such a powerful seasoning that's easy to overuse, I generally steer clear of it except when barbecuing certain ribs in the oven. If you don't care too much for smoky flavor, use just enough liquid smoke to taste for this sauce, placing a thumb over the mouth of the bottle to control the flow of the liquid as it's added.

1 Preheat the oven to 325°F.

2 In a small saucepan, combine all the ingredients except the ribs, bring almost to a boil, reduce the heat to low, and stir till the sugar dissolves and the sauce is smooth. Simmer for about 10 minutes longer, and set aside.

3 Position the spareribs in a large, shallow roasting pan, baste well with the sauce, and roast, uncovered, till very tender, about 2 hours, basting the ribs with the sauce every 30 minutes.

4 To serve, cut the ribs into serving portions, heat the remaining sauce, and serve it on the side.

Beer-Braised Spiced Barbecued Spareribs

Makes 4 servings

2 tablespoons peanut oil

4 pounds meaty spareribs,
   cut into smaller racks

1 small onion, minced

2 garlic cloves, minced

2 teaspoons minced lemon rind

2 teaspoons ground ginger

1 teaspoon ground allspice

1 teaspoon dry mustard

1 teaspoon cayenne pepper

Salt and freshly ground black
   pepper to taste

Two 12-ounce bottles lager or ale

Like short ribs of beef, pork spareribs intended to be barbecued or grilled are most succulent when they're first braised or simmered in some well-seasoned liquid till fork-tender. Although plain water, of course, can be used for these spicy ribs, any full-bodied beer does give the ribs a much more interesting flavor. These ribs really don't need a sauce, but if you want one for dipping, simply reduce the liquid in the pan to the desired consistency and strain it into one or more small bowls.

1 Preheat the oven to 325°F.

2 In a large roasting pan, heat the oil over moderate heat, add the ribs, and brown on both sides. Add all the remaining ingredients, bring to a boil, reduce the heat to low, cover, and simmer till the meat is tender, 1½ to 2 hours.

3 Meanwhile, light a charcoal fire in a kettle grill and let the coals burn down to a medium heat.

4 When the ribs are cooked, drain them momentarily on paper towels, place on the grate of the grill about 4 inches from the heat, and brown for about 5 minutes on each side.

5 Serve hot.

ORIENTAL BARBECUED SPARERIBS

MAKES 4 SERVINGS

½ cup soy sauce

½ cup dry sherry

½ cup water

¼ cup packed dark brown sugar

4 garlic cloves, peeled and crushed

4 pounds lean spareribs, cut into smaller racks

Virtually anything cooked in the South that involves soy sauce can be quaintly called "oriental," and these barbecued spareribs are no exception. Do try to find ribs that are meaty between the bones with also a little meat over the bones. While finishing the baked ribs on a charcoal grill does give them a perfect glaze, they can also just be simply baked and basted in the roasting pan for 1½ to 2 hours, or till they turn a glossy brown.

1 In a small saucepan, combine all the ingredients except the spareribs, bring to a simmer, stir till the sugar dissolves, remove the pan from the heat, and let the marinade cool.

2 Arrange the spareribs in a large, shallow roasting pan, pour the marinade over the top, cover, and let the ribs marinate for about 1 hour.

3 Preheat the oven to 350°F. In a kettle grill, light a charcoal fire and let the coals burn down to a medium heat.

4 Place the ribs in the oven, covered, and bake till almost tender, about 1¼ hours, turning once or twice.

5 Reserving the marinade, transfer the ribs to the grate of the grill and cook about 6 inches from the heat till glossy brown and fork-tender, about 30 minutes, turning and basting frequently with the marinade to produce a nice glaze and prevent dryness.

6 Serve hot.

Mama Dip's Baked Spareribs with Sauerkraut

Makes 6 servings

4 pounds meaty spareribs

1½ teaspoons dried thyme

1½ teaspoons dried sage

1 teaspoon salt

Freshly ground black pepper
to taste

½ teaspoon red pepper flakes

Two 16-ounce cans sauerkraut,
drained and rinsed in a
colander

3 tablespoons all-purpose flour

At her no-nonsense restaurant in Chapel Hill, North Carolina, Mildred Council is known to lovers of authentic Southern food far and wide as Mama Dip, and while Mama Dip's Kitchen turns out possibly the best fried chicken, chitlins, and turnip greens in the entire South, these luscious baked spareribs with sauerkraut served with mellow sweet potatoes are also in a class by themselves. One unusual trick to making the ribs crispy while maintaining their moisture is broiling them momentarily far enough from the heat to prevent them from drying out. If ever a dish were created for a cold-night supper, this is it.

1 With a sharp knife, cut the ribs apart, trim and discard the excess fat, and place the ribs in a large pot with enough water to cover. Add the thyme, sage, salt, black pepper, and red pepper flakes, bring to a boil, reduce the heat to low, cover, and simmer for 1 hour.

2 Transfer the ribs to a large baking pan. Skim the fat from the liquid in the pot, strain the liquid into a bowl, and pour about 2 cups of it back into the pot. Add the sauerkraut, bring to a simmer, cook for 30 minutes, and set aside.

3 Preheat the oven broiler.

4 Sprinkle the flour over the ribs, place on the lower rack of the oven, and cook till the ribs brown, about 10 minutes. Reduce the heat to 350°F, move the ribs to the sides of the pan, add the sauerkraut to the middle, cover, and bake for 30 minutes.

5 Serve the hot ribs and sauerkraut directly from the pan.

Cajun Dry-Rub Barbecued Spareribs

MAKES 4 TO 6 SERVINGS

3 tablespoons paprika

2 teaspoons dry mustard

2 teaspoons onion powder

2 teaspoons garlic powder

2 teaspoons cayenne pepper

1 teaspoon dried thyme, crumbled

1 teaspoon dried oregano, crumbled

1 teaspoon ground coriander

1 teaspoon salt

1 teaspoon freshly ground black pepper

4 to 6 pounds spareribs, cut into smaller racks

Cajun cooks throughout the Louisiana bayou tend to favor highly seasoned dry rubs over sauces when barbecuing any style of pork ribs, convinced that the rubs not only provide maximum flavor but also seal moisture into the meat. These same cooks also insist that what gives their rubs such robust, distinctive savor is the liberal use of granulated and powdered seasonings instead of fresh herbs, spices, and the like. Although these ribs, can, of course, be cooked on a charcoal grill for the final 30 minutes for a crusty finish, if you do so, watch them carefully to make sure they don't dry out.

1 Preheat the oven to 325°F.

2 In a small bowl, combine all the ingredients except the ribs and stir till well blended. Rub the mixture thoroughly all over the ribs, pressing it with your fingers, then position the ribs in a large, shallow roasting pan and roast, uncovered, till very tender, about 2 hours, basting with a little fat from the pan from time to time.

3 To serve, cut the ribs into serving portions.

Baked Spareribs Stuffed with Apples and Raisins

Makes 4 servings

2 racks of meaty spareribs
   (about 2 pounds each)

Salt and freshly ground black
   pepper to taste

4 Granny Smith apples, peeled,
   cored, and cut into ½-inch-
   thick slices

2 cups seedless dark raisins

¼ cup packed light brown sugar

1 teaspoon dry mustard

1 teaspoon powdered sage

1 teaspoon ground cinnamon

Pinches of ground cloves to taste

If you have the time, these spareribs are even better if, the night before cooking, the stuffing is spread over the meaty sides of the racks and they are covered and refrigerated so that the seasonings penetrate the meat more fully. Then, afterward, scrape off the stuffing, spread it on the other sides of the ribs, and proceed according to the recipe directions. Yes, it's a bit messy, but what about great ribs is not messy?

1 Preheat the oven to 325°F.

2 On a work surface, season the meaty sides of the ribs with salt and pepper. Place one rack meat side down and spread the apples and raisins evenly over the top. Sprinkle with the brown sugar, the mustard, sage, cinnamon, and cloves, cover with the other rack meat side up, and tie the two together crosswise and lengthwise with butcher's twine to secure the stuffing.

3 Place the tied ribs on a rack in a large, shallow roasting pan and bake till very tender, 1½ to 2 hours, basting several times with the fat in the pan.

4 To serve, cut away the twine, cut the racks in half, and serve the ribs with the stuffing.

CORKY'S MEMPHIS-STYLE BARBECUED BACK RIBS

For the Grill:

1 small bag hickory wood chips

One 10-pound bag charcoal briquets

Vegetable oil for brushing

For the Dry Rub:

¼ cup firmly packed dark brown sugar

2 tablespoons chili powder

2 tablespoons paprika

2 teaspoons dried thyme, crumbled

2 teaspoons dried oregano, crumbled

1 teaspoon ground cumin

1 teaspoon dry mustard

1 teaspoon cayenne pepper

Salt and freshly ground black pepper to taste

Pit masters in every Southern state will try to claim top honors for the best chopped pork barbecue or pulled pork, but when it comes to barbecued pork ribs, even North Carolinians are forced to admit that the undisputed capital is Memphis, Tennessee, and the ultimate prize a "First Place Ribs" at the annual Memphis in May World Championship cook-off. Memphis is all about smoky barbecued ribs—spare- or baby back, wet or dry, oven- or pit-cooked—and, at least in my experience, the city's major exponent for the past 30 years has been Corky's barbecue house, where both a dry rub and a tangy-sweet moppin' sauce are used to produce some of the world's greatest pit-cooked ribs. Naturally, the recipes for the rub and sauce are big secrets, but my approximations come pretty close to the originals. If you prefer to substitute larger, tougher, but (many experts feel) more flavorful spareribs for the baby backs, the overall cooking time will be about 30 minutes longer. In either case, the ribs should be very tender without being mushy, smoky but slightly sweet, messy but not the least slimy with too much barbecue sauce.

1 To set up the grill, soak 2 to 3 handfuls of hickory chips in a pan of water for 45 minutes. Arrange a thick layer of charcoal briquets over the bottom of an outdoor grill, ignite, and when the coals are ashen (30 to 45 minutes), sprinkle the soaked chips evenly over the coals.

For the Moppin' Sauce:

½ cup cider vinegar

½ cup tomato sauce

2 tablespoons fresh lemon juice

1 tablespoon molasses

1 tablespoon Worcestershire sauce

1 teaspoon Tabasco sauce

For the Ribs:

3 racks of baby back ribs (4 to 4½ pounds)

Salt and freshly ground black pepper to taste

2 Meanwhile, combine all the ingredients for the dry rub in a bowl and mix till well blended. In another bowl, combine all the ingredients for the moppin' sauce and whisk briskly till well blended. Using a sharp knife and, if necessary, a pair of pliers, cut and pull off the membrane from the back of each rack of ribs. Season the ribs with salt and pepper, then rub each with about 2 tablespoons of the dry-rub mixture.

3 When ready to barbecue, position the grate of the grill 4 to 5 inches from the heat, brush the grate with oil, place the ribs on the grate bone side down, and grill for about 15 minutes. Turn the ribs over with tongs and grill for 15 minutes longer. Brush with a little moppin' sauce, turn the ribs over, and grill for 15 minutes more. Brush again with the sauce, turn, and grill for 15 minutes longer or till very tender and glossy. (Replenish the coals and chips if necessary, and if the dripping fat or sauce causes flare-ups, move the ribs around or flick a little water over the coals.)

4 Transfer the ribs to a cutting board, brush them with more sauce, and then sprinkle enough dry rub over the surfaces to form a crust. Serve as whole racks or cut into sections, with extra dry rub on the side.

ROASTED BACK RIBS WITH RUM BARBECUE SAUCE

½ cup cider vinegar

¼ cup soy sauce

¼ cup light rum

2 tablespoons fresh lemon juice

1 tablespoon Worcestershire sauce

¼ cup packed dark brown sugar

2 scallions (white parts only), minced

Salt and freshly ground black pepper to taste

3 racks of baby back ribs (about 4 pounds)

Southerners flavor barbecue marinades and sauces with every spirit from bourbon to rum to Southern Comfort, and when it comes to barbecuing ribs, it's common practice to make a moppin' sauce from the same boozy marinade used to tenderize the meat. If you decide to barbecue tougher spareribs instead of baby backs, they're best if marinated for five to six hours and preferably overnight. Either type of the marinated ribs can also be cooked and basted over a charcoal fire on an open grill till very tender and glossy brown, so long, that is, as they're kept at least four or five inches from the heat and not allowed to burn.

1 In a saucepan, combine all the ingredients except the ribs, stir over low heat till the sugar dissolves, remove from the heat, and let the marinade cool.

2 Place the ribs in a large nonreactive baking or roasting pan, pour the marinade over the top, cover with plastic wrap, and let marinate for at least 3 hours or overnight in the refrigerator, turning several times.

3 Preheat the oven to 325°F.

4 Oil the rack of a large broiler pan, remove the ribs from the marinade (reserving the marinade), arrange the ribs on the rack, cover with foil, and roast for 30 minutes. Uncover, brush the ribs well with the marinade, and continue roasting, uncovered, till very tender and glazed, about 1 hour, brushing frequently with the marinade.

5 To serve, cut the ribs into serving portions, boil the remaining marinade, and serve it on the side.

PIG PICKIN'S

Headquartered in Winston-Salem and dedicated to promoting North Carolina as the "Cradle of 'Cue," the North Carolina Barbecue Society sponsors a "Historic Barbecue Trail" featuring select barbecue houses across the state that have been in business for at least 15 years, that pit-roast pigs, and that make their own sauces. Membership is $35 a year and includes an official newsletter on pig.

ARKANSAS BLACK BARBECUED BACK RIBS

MAKES 4 SERVINGS

4 pounds baby back ribs, separated

¼ cup fresh lemon juice

Salt and freshly ground black pepper to taste

¼ cup white vinegar

¼ cup water

¼ cup ketchup

¼ cup packed dark brown sugar

2 to 3 tablespoons Worcestershire sauce

2 tablespoons chili powder

Arkansans seem to love thick sauces for everything they barbecue, and when they refer to "black" ribs, they're speaking of spare- or back ribs that are literally covered with a relatively sweet sauce that has been reduced almost to a glaze, added after the ribs have baked, and cooked to a blackened finish. The trick is to produce ribs that have an intense barbecue flavor without tasting at all burnt—which explains why they're not basted with the sauce throughout the entire cooking process.

1 Preheat the oven to 350°F.

2 Arrange the ribs in a large roasting pan or baking dish, drizzle the lemon juice over the top, season with salt and pepper, cover loosely with foil, and bake for 1 hour. Turn the ribs over, cover, and bake till tender, about 30 minutes longer.

3 Meanwhile, combine all the remaining ingredients in a saucepan, bring to a boil, reduce the heat, and simmer till the sauce is thickened and almost syrupy, about 30 minutes, stirring frequently.

4 Remove the ribs from the oven, spoon the sauce evenly over the top, and continue baking, uncovered, till the ribs are very tender and almost blackened, 15 to 20 minutes, basting frequently.

5 Serve hot.

OVEN-BARBECUED COUNTRY-STYLE RIBS

8 meaty country-style pork ribs
(about 3 pounds)

¼ cup vegetable oil

1 medium onion, finely chopped

1 celery rib, finely chopped

1 garlic clove, minced

1½ cups water

1 cup ketchup

½ cup cider vinegar

3 tablespoons Worcestershire
sauce

1 tablespoon chili powder

1 tablespoon dark brown sugar

1 teaspoon dry mustard

1 teaspoon salt

1 teaspoon freshly ground black
pepper

Since country-style pork ribs have the highest meat-to-bone ratio and the least fat of all ribs, one of the most successful ways to prepare them is to simmer them slowly till fork-tender, then finish them off in the oven with a tangy barbecue sauce. (If you simply plop these ribs on a charcoal grill and brush them with sauce, rest assured they'll be tough as leather.) Do be careful not to burn the sauce by baking the ribs too long—they should be just slightly browned.

1 Arrange the ribs in a large pot with enough water to cover and bring to a boil, skimming the surface of any froth. Reduce the heat to low, cover, and simmer the ribs till fork-tender, about 2 hours.

2 Meanwhile, heat the oil in a large, heavy, stainless-steel or enameled saucepan over moderate heat, add the onion, celery, and garlic, and stir for about 5 minutes. Add all the remaining ingredients and stir till well blended. Bring the sauce to a simmer and cook, uncovered, for 20 minutes, stirring from time to time to prevent sticking.

3 Preheat the oven to 350°F.

4 With a slotted spoon, transfer the ribs from the water to a large, shallow baking dish, pour the sauce over the top, and bake till slightly browned, about 20 minutes. Turn the ribs over and bake till the other sides are slightly browned, 15 to 20 minutes, basting several times with the sauce.

5 Serve the hot ribs and sauce on a large, deep platter.

Gentleman Jack Barbecued Country-Style Ribs

MAKES 6 SERVINGS

6 country-style pork ribs
(3 to 4 pounds)

1/3 cup Jack Daniel's whiskey

1/3 cup orange marmalade, gently
heated till liquefied

2 garlic cloves, minced

2 tablespoons orange juice

2 tablespoons dark brown sugar

Salt and freshly ground black
pepper to taste

Meaty, country-style pork ribs are a cross between a bone-in pork chop and a true pork rib, and this unusual way of cooking them comes from my old friend, colleague, and barbecue expert in Raleigh, North Carolina, Fred Thompson. Since Jack Daniel's happens to be my long-time sipping whiskey of choice, I suppose I am a bit prejudiced, but the truth is that Fred's marinade for these ribs, which he also uses as a moppin' sauce, is one of the most sensational creations you'll ever taste. Also, his practice of marinating ribs in a zip-top plastic bag is a clever technique we'd all do well to adopt. Because of the long marinating time, the ribs don't need to be cooked but about an hour—or till fork-tender.

1 Place the ribs in a large zip-top plastic bag. In a small bowl, combine all the remaining ingredients and stir till well blended. Pour the marinade over the ribs, seal the bag, squish to coat the ribs evenly, and let marinate in the refrigerator for 6 to 8 hours. Bring back to room temperature before cooking.

2 Preheat the oven to 350°F. In a kettle grill, light a charcoal fire and let the coals burn down to a medium heat.

3 Remove the ribs from the marinade and place in a 13 by 9-inch baking dish, reserving the marinade. Bake the ribs for 45 minutes, basting occasionally with some of the marinade.

4 Pour the remaining marinade into a small saucepan, bring to a boil, reduce the heat to low, and simmer till slightly thickened, about 10 minutes.

5 To finish the ribs, arrange them on the grate of the grill about 4 inches from the heat and grill till browned, glazed, and tender, 8 to 10 minutes, brushing them with the marinade and turning once or twice.

6 Serve piping hot.

PIG PICKIN'S

"The best thing to do with a book about barbecue is to wipe your hands on it."

—Greg Johnson and Vince Staten, *Real Barbecue*

Louisiana Braised Country-Style Ribs and Sweet Potatoes

8 meaty country-style pork ribs (about 3 pounds)

1 cup cider vinegar

1½ cups orange juice

1 medium onion, minced

2 garlic cloves, minced

1 tablespoon grainy brown mustard

1 teaspoon Worcestershire sauce

1 teaspoon dried sage, crumbled

3 tablespoons peanut oil

1 cup water

3 large winter sweet potatoes, peeled and quartered

Nothing is more Southern than pork and sweet potatoes, and when friends outside of Baton Rouge, Louisiana, showed me the way they braise thick country-style ribs with the region's very special, honey-like Beauregard potatoes that are actually cured for ultimate sweetness, I adopted the dish instantly for my own repertory. Given the fact, unfortunately, that the supply of Beauregards is so limited, I can only remind you never to buy freshly harvested, starchy, "green" sweet potatoes during the summer months, but to wait till winter, when the most succulent aged tubers are available almost everywhere. Also, make every effort to find ribs that are really meaty for this dish.

1 Trim and discard any excess fat from the ribs and, using a hatchet or meat cleaver, whack the ribs in half.

2 In a baking dish or large bowl, combine the vinegar, ½ cup of the orange juice, the onion, garlic, mustard, Worcestershire, and sage and whisk till well blended. Arrange the ribs in the marinade, baste several times, cover with plastic wrap, and let marinate for about 6 hours in the refrigerator, basting from time to time.

3 Remove the ribs from the marinade and pat dry with paper towels, reserving the marinade. In a large, heavy pot, heat the oil over moderate heat, add the ribs, and brown on all sides. Add the reserved marinade plus the water and scrape the bottom of the pot for any browned bits. Bring to a boil, reduce the heat to a gentle simmer, cover, and cook for 1 hour. Add the sweet potatoes and the remaining 1 cup of orange juice, return to a simmer, and cook till the ribs and sweet potatoes are very tender, about 1 hour longer.

 PIG PICKIN'S

There are seven different varieties of hickory wood for Southern barbecue, and each provides a different flavor.

YOUNG SYLVIA'S BARBECUED PORK CHOPS

6 pork loin chops, about
¾ inch thick

1 teaspoon salt

1 teaspoon freshly ground
black pepper

1 medium onion, finely chopped

¼ cup water

1 teaspoon bottled steak sauce
(such as A.1.)

1 cup barbecue sauce of
your choice

2 tablespoons sugar

1 teaspoon Tabasco sauce

Born and raised in Hemingway, South Carolina, Sylvia Woods has been serving her family's soul food at Sylvia's Restaurant in New York City since 1963, and while visitors flock from around the world to taste her fried chicken, cornbread, and fruit cobblers, a dish that has always drawn me and others back over the years are these thick barbecued pork chops created by Sylvia's daughter-in-law ("young Sylvia"). One ingredient that gives the dish its special flavor is ordinary bottled steak sauce, and if anybody raises an eyebrow, Sylvia is quick to point out that "the chops are one of the reasons my son Kenneth fell in love."

1 Preheat the oven to 350°F.

2 Season the pork chops with the salt and pepper, let stand for 20 minutes, arrange them in a 13 by 9 by 2-inch baking pan, and sprinkle the onion over the top. In a small bowl, mix together the water and steak sauce, pour around the chops, cover, and bake for 1 hour.

3 In a medium bowl, combine 2 tablespoons of the pan drippings, the barbecue sauce, sugar, and Tabasco and stir till well blended, discarding any remaining pan drippings. Pour the sauce over the chops, turning to coat them evenly, and bake, uncovered, for 10 minutes. Turn the chops, baste with the sauce, and bake for about 10 minutes longer.

4 Serve hot.

Georgia-Style Barbecued Pork Chops

MAKES 6 SERVINGS

1 cup cider vinegar

1 cup ketchup

½ cup peanut oil

2 tablespoons Worcestershire sauce

½ cup packed light brown sugar

2 tablespoons prepared mustard

1 garlic clove, minced

Salt and freshly ground black pepper to taste

6 center-cut pork loin chops, about 1 inch thick

If pit masters in eastern North Carolina condemn South Carolinians for their mustard barbecue, the ridicule only intensifies when it comes to both the mustard *and* ketchup found in virtually all Georgia barbecue sauces. As always, I refuse to argue the issue, insisting only that the barbecue sauce slathered on all forms of pig at the venerable Johnny Harris restaurant in Savannah is still something to whistle "Dixie" about. Don't overcook these chops, and remember that any barbecue sauce with both ketchup and brown sugar tends to burn if not watched carefully.

1 Ignite a layer of charcoal briquets in an outdoor grill, let them burn till ashen (30 to 45 minutes), place the grill grate about 6 inches from the coals, and brush it with oil.

2 In a stainless-steel or enameled saucepan, combine all the ingredients except the pork chops and stir till well blended. Bring to a simmer over low heat, stirring, let simmer for about 15 minutes, and pour the sauce into a wide bowl to cool.

3 Dip the pork chops into the sauce, place on the grill, and cook till both sides are nicely browned, about 30 minutes in all, turning and basting with a little sauce from time to time. Transfer the chops to a platter and serve immediately.

Churchyard Honey-Barbecued Pork Loin

1 cup peanut oil

1 cup soy sauce

½ cup honey

¼ cup packed light brown sugar

1 small onion, minced

2 garlic cloves, minced

Salt and freshly ground black pepper to taste

One 3-pound boneless pork loin

Come fall every year, churches throughout the South sponsor huge pork barbecues to meet expenses and raise funds for various causes, and one of the most festive I've attended (a country-western band, a corn-eating contest, and pig wrestling) was in Marietta, Georgia. Generally, pork loin is not the best cut of meat for barbecuing since it's so lean and tends to dry out quickly, but, as I learned at this weekend affair, when a loin is butterflied, marinated, cooked just till the meat is nicely glazed with this honeyed sauce, and sliced thinly, both the taste and texture are amazing. Just remember that with a barbecued loin, the meat should be tender but not falling apart as with other styles of barbecue.

1 In a saucepan, combine all the ingredients except the pork, whisk over low heat till the marinade is well blended, about 10 minutes, and set aside.

2 Place the pork loin on a cutting board and butterfly it with a sharp knife by cutting through it widthwise to within ½ inch of the other side. Open the loin and place in a large, shallow dish or pan. Pour the marinade over the top, cover with plastic wrap, and marinate in the refrigerator for 2 hours, turning once.

3 Ignite a layer of charcoal briquets in an outdoor grill, let them burn till ashen (30 to 45 minutes), and place the grate of the grill about 6 inches over the coals.

4 Remove the loin from the marinade and place, opened up, on the grate. Brush with the marinade and cook for 30 to 40 minutes, turning twice and basting often.

5 Transfer the loin to a large platter, let rest for about 5 minutes, and then carve into fairly thin slices. Serve hot.

PIG PICKIN'S

In Southern barbecue lingo, the metal contraption with hot coals in the backyard is a "grill," *not* a "barbecue." Hamburgers and hot dogs are grilled, never barbecued, in the South.

Montgomery Oven-Barbecued Prune-Stuffed Pork Loin

Makes 6 servings

For the Barbecue Sauce:

1 cup cider vinegar

½ cup ketchup

2 tablespoons fresh lemon juice

2 tablespoons peanut oil

2 tablespoons Worcestershire sauce

¼ cup packed light brown sugar

1 garlic clove, minced

1 teaspoon dry mustard

¼ teaspoon salt

¼ teaspoon freshly ground black pepper

While barbecued pork is perceived generally throughout the South as the main feature of ultra-casual outdoor affairs involving scores of hungry people, in some of the more staid, formal dining rooms of Montgomery, Alabama, the meat can approach a level of sophistication that recalls plantation days, when cooks had the time and imagination to do more than smoke a few pigs in open pits. A stuffed loin such as this is appropriate not only for the most elegant dinner table but also for an elaborate buffet, the irony being that the handsome, succulent dish is really quite simple to prepare once you assemble all the ingredients.

1 To make the sauce, combine all the ingredients in a small saucepan, bring to a boil, reduce the heat to low, and stir till the sugar dissolves and the sauce is well blended, about 15 minutes. Let cool.

2 To make the stuffing, combine all the ingredients with about ¼ cup of the sauce in a bowl and mix till well blended.

3 Preheat the oven to 325°F.

For the Stuffing:

¼ **pound ground pork shoulder**

6 **prunes, pitted and chopped**

6 **fresh mushrooms, chopped**

1 **small onion, chopped**

1 **garlic clove, minced**

¼ **cup dry bread crumbs**

¼ **cup grated Parmesan cheese**

**Salt and freshly ground black
    pepper to taste**

**One 3-pound boneless pork loin,
    butterflied (see Churchyard
    Honey-Barbecued Pork Loin,
    page 306)**

4 On a work surface, pound the pork loin into a 15 by 10-inch rectangle about ¾ inch thick and brush with about ¼ cup of the sauce. Spread the stuffing evenly over the meat, roll up the meat as tightly as possible, and tie securely with butcher's twine. Place the loin on a rack in a shallow roasting pan and roast, uncovered, till very tender, about 2½ hours, basting from time to time with some of the sauce.

5 To serve, transfer the loin to a platter, boil the remaining sauce, carve the meat into medium-thick slices, and spoon a little sauce over the top of each portion.

Barbecued Pork, Peach, and Red Onion Kabobs

Makes 4 servings

½ cup peach jam

2 tablespoons fresh lemon juice

2 tablespoons ground ginger

1 tablespoon Dijon mustard

Salt and freshly ground black pepper to taste

One 1-pound pork tenderloin, cut into 1-inch cubes

5 medium fresh firm-ripe peaches (about 1 pound), peeled, pitted, and sectioned into wedges

1 medium red onion, cut into 2-inch wedges and layers separated

Hot buttered rice

While you don't want to grill the pork in these kabobs till it's dry, part of the pleasant taste sensation is the slightly charred flavor of all three main ingredients. To accomplish this, start the kabobs about four inches from the fire, and if they appear to be browning too quickly, simply raise the grate another inch or so and cook till the pork is still rather soft and dark edges begin to appear on the peaches and onions. If you use wooden instead of metal skewers, be sure to soak them in a little water for about five minutes.

1 In a kettle grill, light a charcoal fire and let the coals burn down to a medium heat. Oil the grate.

2 In a saucepan, combine the jam, lemon juice, ginger, mustard, and salt and pepper, stir over low heat till the jam melts, and remove the glaze from the heat.

3 On each of 4 metal skewers (or 4 wooden skewers soaked in water), thread alternating pork cubes, peach wedges, and onion layers, beginning and ending with pork and skewering an equal number of pieces on each kabob. Place the kabobs on the grate about 4 inches from the heat and cook till the pork is cooked through and the peaches and onions begin to char, about 12 minutes, turning once and basting several times with the glaze.

4 Serve the kabobs hot over mounds of rice.

Barbecued Bourbon Ham Steaks

1 cup cider vinegar

2 to 3 tablespoons bourbon

3 tablespoons light brown sugar

1 tablespoon dry mustard

½ teaspoon ground allspice

½ teaspoon ground cloves

2 center-cut smoked ham steaks, about 1 inch thick

Only in the South have I ever seen thick ham steaks barbecued on a grill, and when they're seasoned correctly, not overcooked, and served with hot corn on the cob, a big fresh fruit salad, and buttered corn sticks, nothing is better for a summer supper. For the right flavor, don't fail to marinate the steaks briefly before grilling them to a glossy finish, and be sure to slash any fat around the edges so the steaks don't curl.

1 In a kettle grill, light a charcoal fire and let the coals burn down to a medium heat.

2 In a small bowl, combine all the ingredients except the steaks, stir well till the sugar dissolves, and set the marinade aside.

3 Arrange the steaks in a large stainless-steel or enameled skillet and add enough water to cover. Bring to a low boil, simmer for 5 minutes, pour off the water, and remove pan from the heat. Pour the marinade over the hot steaks and let soak for 15 minutes.

4 Remove the steaks from the marinade, slash the fat around the edges, and reserve the marinade. Oil the grate of the grill, place the steaks on the grate about 4 inches from the heat, and cook for about 10 minutes, basting with the marinade. Turn the steaks over and cook till lightly browned and glazed, 10 to 15 minutes, basting with the marinade.

5 Serve hot.

VARIETY and SPECIALTY MEATS

Pork Cracklin's

Louisiana Pickled Pork

Country-Style Boiled
and Fried Chitlins

Horry County Chitlin Croquettes

Stewed Pigs' Feet

Deviled Pigs' Feet

Cajun Pigs' Tails with Ham
and Field Peas

Alabama Hog Pot

Hog's Head Stew

Deviled Pork Liver

Miss Edna's Pork Liver and Jowl Pudding

Mississippi Crusted Pigs' Ears

Orlando Stuffed Pork Belly
with Cream Gravy

Palmetto Scrapple

Brains and Eggs

Pork Sweetbreads, Bacon,
and Mushroom Skewers

PORK CRACKLIN'S

MAKES ABOUT 2 CUPS

1 pound fresh fatback

Sometimes confused with the streaky fat and lean meat from the sides and belly of a hog that's transformed into salt pork (streak-o'-lean), fatback is the fresh, unsalted, unsmoked layer of fat along the pig's back most often used to make lard and these tasty rendered, crunchy morsels called cracklin's. (*Cracklin'* also refers to the crisp skin of roasted or barbecued pork.) Kept in an airtight container in the refrigerator, cracklin's are delicious not only in salads and as a flavoring for stews but also in certain Southern breads. Although packaged cracklin's can be found in markets all over the South, never are these so good as homemade ones.

Cut the fatback into small dice and place in a large, heavy skillet with enough water to barely cover. Bring to a boil, cook till the water evaporates, reduce the heat to low, and continue cooking, stirring frequently, till all the fat is rendered and the morsels are browned and very crisp, 30 to 40 minutes. Drain the cracklin's on paper towels, let cool, and store in an airtight container in the refrigerator for up to 2 weeks.

LOUISIANA PICKLED PORK

MAKES ½ POUND

1 quart white vinegar

½ cup mustard seeds

4 garlic cloves, peeled and
   smashed

1 bay leaf

10 black peppercorns

2 tablespoons Tabasco sauce

½ pound boneless pork shoulder
   butt, cut into 2-inch cubes

Used throughout Louisiana to season numerous gumbos and bean dishes, pickled pork is a shoulder cut of meat that is marinated in an aromatic brine for up to a week and kept in the refrigerator for up to a month. Widely available today in all local markets, pickled pork is rarely made in homes anymore, but if you live outside the region and want to prepare certain Creole dishes that depend on the seasoning meat, you must make your own—a simple enough procedure.

1 In a large saucepan, combine all the ingredients except the pork, bring to a boil, reduce the heat to moderate, and simmer for about 5 minutes. Remove the pan from the heat and let the marinade cool.

2 Place the pork in a large bowl, pour the marinade over the top, stir well, cover with plastic wrap, and let marinate in the refrigerator for 3 to 5 days, stirring from time to time.

3 When ready to use, remove the pickled pork from the marinade and pat dry with paper towels. Store any leftover pork in the marinade for up to 1 month in the refrigerator.

COUNTRY-STYLE BOILED AND FRIED CHITLINS

10 pounds chitlins (chitterlings), fresh or thawed frozen

1 large onion, quartered

1 large celery rib, cut into thirds

1 garlic clove, peeled and smashed

¼ cup cider vinegar

1 teaspoon salt, plus more to taste

1 teaspoon freshly ground black pepper, plus more to taste

1 cup all-purpose flour

¼ cup peanut oil

Hot pepper vinegar (available in bottles)

Chopped red onions

Considered a soul food delicacy through the Mid- and Deep South, boiled and/or fried chitlins (or chitterlings) are the cooked small intestines of hogs, and if you don't think Southerners take chitlins seriously, you've never attended a "chitlin strut" festival, held every November in the small town of Salley, South Carolina. Many enthusiasts love chitlins simply boiled and served with pepper vinegar, chopped onions, mustard, corn relish, or other condiments, but since the offal can be an acquired taste for some, the best bet is to batter and fry the chitlins till well browned and crispy. Chitlins are widely available in Southern markets and at some butcher shops around the country.

1 Under cold running water, clean the chitlins to remove fat and any foreign matter, place them in a large kettle or casserole, and add the onion, celery, garlic, cider vinegar, and a sprinkling of salt and black pepper. (Do not add water, since the chitlins will create their own liquid.) Bring to a boil, reduce the heat to low, cover, and simmer till tender, 2½ to 3 hours, adding a little water if the liquid level begins to drop. Test the chitlins for tenderness, and, if necessary, continue simmering for about 30 minutes longer.

2 To fry the chitlins, drain them and pat dry with paper towels; combine the flour, 1 teaspoon salt, and 1 teaspoon pepper on a plate, and coat the chitlins in the mixture. In a large skillet, heat the oil over moderate heat, add the chitlins, brown till crispy, about 10 minutes on each side, and drain on paper towels.

3 Serve the chitlins hot with hot pepper vinegar and chopped red onions on the side.

PIG PICKIN'S

Smithfield Foods, in Tarheel, North Carolina, is the world's largest hog producer and pork processor.

HORRY COUNTY CHITLIN CROQUETTES

2 tablespoons lard

1 small onion, finely chopped

½ small green bell pepper, seeded and finely chopped

4 cups minced boiled chitlins (page 316)

2 cups bread crumbs

2 large eggs, beaten

2 tablespoons fresh parsley leaves

1 teaspoon prepared mustard

1 teaspoon soy sauce

Salt and freshly ground black pepper to taste

¼ cup vegetable or peanut oil

Although pork chitlins are loved all over South Carolina, they seem to be a veritable passion in small farming towns around Horry County west of Myrtle Beach. Typically, a home cook will boil up pounds of chitlins (especially after a hog killing in the fall), and those that are not served with vinegary greens and cornbread are used to make all sorts of loaves, hashes, pot pies, stews, and crusty croquettes like these that an old friend's black cook used to pride herself on when he was growing up in Conway. If you want the croquettes to be super crispy, dip them in beaten egg and dredge them lightly in cornmeal or flour after they have been chilled.

1 In a large cast-iron skillet, melt the lard over moderate heat, add the onion and bell pepper, and stir till softened, about 5 minutes. Add the chitlins and stir till slightly browned, about 10 minutes. Scrape the contents of the skillet into a bowl, add the bread crumbs, eggs, parsley, mustard, soy sauce, and salt and pepper, and mix till well blended, adding a little milk if the mixture is too stiff. Using your hands, form the mixture into 6 oval croquettes, place on a plate, and chill in the refrigerator for 30 minutes.

2 Heat the oil in the skillet over moderate heat, add the croquettes, and fry till golden brown on both sides, 8 to 10 minutes total. Drain briefly on paper towels, and serve hot.

Stewed Pigs' Feet

6 fresh pigs' feet (about 1 pound each), dressed

2 medium onions, quartered

2 celery ribs, cut into thirds

1 large carrot, scraped and cut into thirds

1 teaspoon ground allspice

1 bay leaf

1 tablespoon salt

6 black peppercorns

Pigs' feet, also called hogs' trotters or mud stompers in different regions of the South, are bony and full of gristle and tendons, but when slowly simmered with aromatics for a long time, the feet are transformed into a tender, gelatinous, truly wonderful treat. Since the feet have lots of tiny bones and tend to fall apart while cooking, it's best to always wrap them in cheesecloth, and while folks in coastal areas seem to prefer the feet with boiled rice or potatoes, elsewhere they're generally served with turnip greens and cornbread. Packaged pigs' feet (fresh, smoked, and pickled) are widely available in Southern markets, but if you have trouble finding them, a good butcher should be able to fill your order.

1 Wrap and tie the pigs' feet in cheesecloth and place in a large pot or kettle with enough water to cover. Bring to a boil, skimming any scum off the top, reduce the heat to low, cover, and simmer for 1 hour.

2 Add all the remaining ingredients to the pot plus additional water to keep the feet just covered, return to a simmer, cover, and cook till the feet are very tender, 2½ to 3 hours longer.

3 To serve, remove the feet from the broth, discard the cheesecloth and any tiny loose bones, and save the broth for soups and stews.

DEVILED PIGS' FEET

4 fresh pigs' feet (about 1 pound each), dressed

1 medium onion, studded with 3 whole cloves

2 celery ribs, cut into quarters

2 carrots, scraped and cut into quarters

2 garlic cloves, peeled and smashed

2 sprigs fresh parsley

10 black peppercorns

1 bay leaf

Salt to taste

¼ cup Dijon mustard

3 tablespoons red wine vinegar

Tabasco sauce to taste

Freshly ground black pepper to taste

2 cups dry bread crumbs

½ cup peanut oil

While nothing is more delicious than tender, gelatinous, stewed pigs' feet, this method of deviling and then baking them to a crusty finish that I learned from a friend in Georgia gives the trotters an exciting new dimension that elevates the earthy dish to a gourmet level. Remember that since the feet are bony and sinewy, they do require an initial long, slow simmering before they're tender enough to be crumbed and baked. Pigs' feet (fresh, smoked, and pickled) are widely available throughout the South and in finer markets elsewhere, and any good butcher will provide them with a little advance notice.

1 Wrap and tie the pigs' feet in cheesecloth, place them in a large pot or kettle with enough water to cover, and add the onion, celery, carrots, garlic, parsley, peppercorns, bay leaf, and salt. Bring to a boil, reduce the heat to low, cover, and simmer till the feet are tender, 2½ to 3 hours.

2 Preheat the oven to 400°F.

3 Transfer the feet to a platter, discard the cheesecloth and any tiny loose bones, split the feet in half with a cleaver or heavy knife, and discard the contents of the pot. In a small bowl, whisk together the mustard, vinegar, Tabasco, and salt and pepper till well blended, and brush the feet with equal amounts of the mixture. Roll the feet in the bread crumbs, arrange them on a rack in a large baking pan, drizzle each with oil, and bake till very tender and crisp, about 30 minutes.

4 Serve hot.

Cajun Pigs' Tails with Ham and Field Peas

1 pound dried field peas (black-eyed, crowder, cow, or lady)

2 pounds meaty pigs' tails, dressed, scrubbed under running water, and cut up

1 pound baked ham, cut into 1-inch cubes

1 meaty smoked ham bone

2 large onions, chopped

2 celery ribs (leaves included), chopped

1 green bell pepper, seeded and chopped

2 garlic cloves, minced

1 small fresh red chile pepper, seeded and chopped

½ teaspoon dried thyme

½ teaspoon dried basil

3 bay leaves

2 teaspoons salt

1 teaspoon freshly ground black pepper

2½ quarts water

Boiled rice

If you have a good butcher with access to all cuts of pork, by all means tell him to find a few meaty pigs' tails so you can use them in this traditional Cajun dish and see that they're as delicious as pigs' feet or hocks. Down around Lafayette, Louisiana, the tails are also barbecued or simmered with sauerkraut or turnip greens, to which they add a seductive gelatinous savor, but no matter how they're prepared, much eating with the fingers is required to pick the sweet meat from lots of small bones.

1 Place the peas in a bowl with enough cold water to cover and let soak overnight.

2 Drain the peas, picking out any hulls, place in a heavy 8-quart pot or kettle, and add all the other ingredients except for the rice. Bring to a boil, skimming any scum off the top, reduce the heat to low, cover, and simmer till the peas and tails are very tender and a natural, slightly gelatinous gravy has formed, about 2 hours. Remove the ham bone, cut off the lean meat and return to the pot, discard the bone, and stir the pot till the contents are well heated.

3 Serve hot over mounds of rice.

Alabama Hog Pot

2 fresh pigs' feet, dressed

2 pigs' ears, dressed

¼ pound lean salt pork (streak-o'-lean)

¼ cup vegetable oil

1 pound boneless pork shoulder, trimmed of excess fat and cut into 1-inch cubes

1 large onion, chopped

1 celery rib, chopped

1 carrot, scraped and chopped

Salt and freshly ground black pepper

1 medium head green cabbage (discolored leaves discarded), cored, quartered, and coarsely chopped

½ pound andouille sausage (or other smoked sausage), sliced

1 cup dry white wine

Hog pots are part of the old Southern pig-slaughtering tradition, as well as a major feature at church suppers, political rallies, and charity cookouts. Unfortunately, you don't encounter that many hog pots today, since fewer and fewer farmers and small pig producers slaughter their own animals, but when a church like one I know in Huntsville, Alabama, simmers one up for a big benefit, the experience is memorable. Although a genuine hog pot should include at least four types of pork and always cabbage, feel free to experiment with whatever cuts of meat are most readily available. Just make sure to simmer the pork till it is all fork-tender, and, for heaven's sake, serve also plenty of coleslaw and hot buttered cornbread.

1 Place the pigs' feet in a large, heavy pot with enough water to cover, bring to a simmer, skimming off any scum from the surface, cover, and cook for 1½ hours. Add the pigs' ears and salt pork to the pot, add more water to cover if necessary, return to a simmer, and cook till the feet and ears are tender, 1 to 1½ hours. Drain and, when cool enough to handle, discard any loose bones from the feet, cut the ears and salt pork into thin strips, and set aside.

2 Wash and dry the pot. Add the oil over moderate heat, brown the pork cubes in the oil on all sides, and add to the pigs' feet and other meats. Add the onion, celery, and carrot to the pot, season with salt and pepper, and cook, stirring, till the vegetables soften, about 5 minutes. Add the meats to the vegetables, scatter the cabbage over the top, arrange the sausage slices over the cabbage, and season with salt and pepper. Add the wine plus enough water to cover the ingredients, bring to a simmer, and cook till the pork cubes are tender and the cabbage very soft, about 1 hour.

3 Serve hot.

Hog's Head Stew

1 small hog's head

½ hog liver

½ hog heart

½ hog spleen

1 hog kidney

1 hog ear

Salt and freshly ground black
  pepper to taste

Cayenne pepper to taste

Boiled rice

Once was the time when all Southern farmers held a hog killin' every winter, a ritual that was followed by butchering, sausage making, maybe a barbecue, and a hog's head stew event to which neighbors from all around were invited. Today, a few rural families in the coastal Carolinas or western Tennessee and Kentucky might still practice the old tradition, but the only time I remember eating hog's head stew was when my family's dentist in Charlotte, North Carolina, once invited us to his farm to celebrate a pig killin' and pick up some whole-hog sausage he'd made. No doubt the pungent stew is an acquired taste for many, but, strangely enough, I recall wolfing it down as fast as I did that inimitable sausage that Mother would fry up later on. To get this recipe (if you want to call it that), I had to depend on my friend/colleague "Hoppin'" John Taylor in Charleston, South Carolina, who, in turn, got it from a lady in Hampton, South Carolina. If you're really serious about making the stew, have a long talk with your butcher, as I plan to do one of these days.

1 Have a butcher dress a hog's head and remove the brains and eyeballs. (Save the brains to scramble with eggs for breakfast.) Also have the butcher trim and clean the liver, heart, spleen, kidney, and ear.

2 When all the parts have been dressed, combine them with enough water to cover in a large pot or kettle and add the salt and pepper and cayenne. Bring to a boil, skimming scum from the surface, reduce the heat to low, cover, and simmer till the meat falls off the head, the other parts are very tender, and the water is cooked down low, 3 to 4 hours. Discard the skull and chop the head meat and other parts with a hatchet or cleaver. Return the meats to the broth, stir well, and simmer till piping hot.

3 Serve the stew over mounds of rice in deep soup plates.

DEVILED PORK LIVER

4 tablespoons (½ stick) butter, melted

2 teaspoons cider vinegar

2 teaspoons Worcestershire sauce

2 large egg yolks

2 teaspoons dry mustard

1½ teaspoons salt

½ teaspoon paprika

¼ teaspoon cayenne pepper

1 pound fresh pork liver, cut into 4 to 6 slices

1 cup dry bread crumbs

3 tablespoons bacon grease, or more as needed

Make no mistake: Pork liver has neither the delicate texture nor the mellow flavor of calf's liver. But for Southerners accustomed to its assertive, distinctive nature, other forms of liver pale by comparison. The best way to tame pork liver is to devil it with bold seasonings before panfrying it slowly in bacon drippings, and nothing goes better with this meat than onions sautéed in plenty of sweet butter. When shopping, make sure the liver is impeccably fresh and has a moist, smooth surface. Pork liver is also available frozen in certain markets.

1 In a bowl, combine the butter, vinegar, Worcestershire, egg yolks, mustard, salt, paprika, and cayenne and whisk till well blended. Dip the liver slices in the mixture and dredge lightly in the bread crumbs.

2 In a large, heavy skillet, heat the bacon drippings over moderately low heat, add the liver slices, and panfry slowly till the meat is tender and browned on both sides, about 20 minutes in all, turning frequently.

3 Serve piping hot.

Miss Edna's Pork Liver and Jowl Pudding

Makes 6 to 8 servings

1½ pounds pork liver

1½ pounds pork jowl

1 medium onion, quartered

Salt and freshly ground black pepper to taste

1 teaspoon dried sage

Created by the grande dame of Southern cooking, Edna Lewis, this pudding is proof of how delectable pork liver can be when combined with the right ingredients and prepared with care. I first tasted the pudding as a first course when Miss Edna was chef at Fearrington House restaurant in Pittsboro, North Carolina, near Chapel Hill, but since then, I've also served it, like liver pâté, on toast as a cocktail appetizer. Pork jowl, which is the fleshy cheek of the hog, is what gives the pudding its slightly sweet flavor, but if your butcher is unable to lay hands on some jowl, substitute either fresh pork belly or uncured bacon.

1 Place the liver, jowl, and onion in a large pot and add enough water to cover. Bring to a boil, skimming any scum off the top, reduce the heat to low, cover, and simmer for 2 hours.

2 Preheat the oven to 275°F.

3 Transfer the meats and onion to a platter and reserve 2 cups of the broth. Cut the meats into small pieces, place in a food processor along with the onion, and grind coarsely. Scrape the mixture into a bowl, add the salt and pepper, sage, and reserved broth, and stir till well blended and smooth. Scrape into a 2-quart casserole or baking dish, smooth the top with a rubber spatula, and bake till firm, 2¼ to 2½ hours. Let cool completely, cover with plastic wrap, and chill in the refrigerator for at least 2 hours before serving.

4 Serve the pudding sliced with buttered toast or spooned over cornbread.

Mississippi Crusted Pigs' Ears

Makes 6 servings

6 pigs' ears, dressed and well rinsed

2 medium onions, quartered

2 celery ribs, cut into thirds

2 medium carrots, scraped and cut into thirds

2 teaspoons dried thyme

6 black peppercorns

4 whole cloves

1 bay leaf

Salt to taste

3 tablespoons prepared mustard

4 tablespoons (½ stick) butter, melted

½ cup dry bread crumbs

Contrary to popular impressions, pigs' ears are not just dried and processed for dog snacks. Available dressed and packaged in most Southern country markets (and from good butchers elsewhere), the ears are a gelatinous, mild, sweet cut of pork that can be utterly delicious baked, broiled, or battered and deep fried—as well as added to stews and hog pots to enrich the textures. Why Mississippians have a knack with pigs' ears I don't know, but some of the best I've eaten have been around Jackson and Greenville, and nobody produced crustier ears than my famous friend and neighbor, Craig Claiborne, who was from Sunflower. Whether baked, broiled, or fried, all pigs' ears must first be simmered and tenderized in liquid for a couple of hours, then weighed down till fully flattened, so plan accordingly. The most traditional way of eating these ears is with sprinklings of hot red pepper vinegar.

1 In a large pot or casserole, combine the pigs' ears, onions, celery, carrots, thyme, peppercorns, cloves, bay leaf, and salt, add enough water to cover, and bring to a boil, skimming any scum off the top. Reduce the heat to low, cover, and simmer till the ears are tender, 2 to 2½ hours.

2 Transfer the ears to a large, shallow baking pan, spoon a little clear cooking liquid over the tops, weigh them down with a large, heavy pot, cover with plastic wrap, and let stand till flattened, about 2 hours.

3 Preheat the oven to 400°F.

4 Drain the liquid from the pan and cut the ears in half lengthwise. Brush the ears on both sides with mustard, dip in the melted butter, coat lightly with bread crumbs, and bake till browned and crispy, 15 to 20 minutes, turning once.

5 Serve immediately.

Orlando Stuffed Pork Belly with Cream Gravy

Makes 6 servings

1 cup seedless dark raisins

2 slices day-old bread

¼ cup milk

2 tablespoons bacon grease

1 tablespoon chopped fresh parsley leaves

1 teaspoon dried sage

1 teaspoon dried thyme

Salt and freshly ground black pepper to taste

1 large egg, beaten

2½ pounds fresh pork belly

½ cup water

1 cup beef broth, plus more if needed

½ cup half-and-half

In the flatlands (including many orange groves) around Orlando, Florida, wild razorback hogs proliferate and are trapped by hunters (referred to locally as "crackers") to be slaughtered, processed, and sold to roadside restaurants and for community cookouts across the state. Only once, while judging a March of Dimes Gourmet Gala in Orlando, have I had the opportunity to sample Florida wild pig, but I can report that the stuffed, braised belly with cream gravy I was served was some of the most delicious pork I've ever put in my mouth. Whether it's cut from feral or domesticated hogs, pork belly (composed of layers of fat, meat, and rind from behind the spareribs of the animal) is today not only available in more and more markets but also one of the most popular items on many upscale restaurant menus. Once you've eaten the dish, you'll understand why.

1 In a small bowl, soak the raisins in water to cover for 15 minutes; drain. In another bowl, soak the bread in the milk for 5 minutes; squeeze dry and break up into tiny morsels.

2 Preheat the oven to 425°F.

3 In a skillet, heat the bacon grease over moderate heat, add the bread morsels, and brown lightly. Add the parsley, sage, thyme, and salt and pepper, stir till well blended, and remove from the heat. Add the raisins and egg and stir till the stuffing is well blended.

4 With a sharp knife, cut a large pocket between the layers of lean belly meat, fill with the stuffing, and tie securely with butcher's twine. Place the belly in a large roasting pan, add the water, and roast till browned, about 20 minutes. Add the broth, reduce the heat to 325°F, cover, and braise the belly for 1½ hours, adding a little more broth if necessary.

5 Transfer the belly to a platter, skim fat off the surface of the cooking liquid in the pan, add the half-and-half, and cook over moderate heat till the gravy thickens slightly.

6 To serve, remove the twine from the belly, carve into 6 portions, and serve with the hot gravy.

Palmetto Scrapple

2 meaty pork hocks, dressed

½ pound fresh lean pork belly, rind removed

¼ pound pork liver

1½ quarts water

1 teaspoon dried sage

1 teaspoon salt

½ teaspoon freshly ground black pepper

1½ cups yellow cornmeal

1 medium onion, minced

Bacon grease for panfrying

Originally made from pork "scraps" and served primarily as a breakfast dish, scrapple is generally acknowledged to be a Pennsylvania Dutch creation. Do not, however, tell that to South Carolinians, who've been making their own distinctive mush since colonial days. The differences are noteworthy. Up North, scrapple is usually composed of lean, primal cuts of pork and white cornmeal, while the South Carolina version has more fatty meats, plus liver, and favors yellow cornmeal. Yankee scrapple is fried in butter, South Carolina scrapple in bacon grease. Also, outside the Palmetto State, the same basic concoction found packaged in Southern markets is often simply called "livermush." Personally, I love them all—sliced and fried just like sausage patties and served with fried apples.

1 Place the hocks, belly, and liver in a large, heavy pot and add the water, sage, salt, and pepper. Bring to a boil, reduce the heat to low, cover, and simmer till the meat on the hocks almost falls from the bones, about 2 hours. Remove the meats from the broth, discard the skin and bones of the hocks, and either coarsely grind or mince the meats. Strain the broth into a bowl, let cool, and skim off the fat.

2 Pour the broth into the top of a large double boiler, add the cornmeal, and stir over boiling water till thickened, 10 to 15 minutes, stirring constantly to prevent lumps. Add the meats and onion, cover, and cook over boiling water for 45 minutes. Taste for seasoning, scrape the mixture into a 9 by 5 by 2-inch loaf pan, and let cool. Cover with foil and chill till firm, about 2 hours.

3 To serve, unmold the loaf, cut into medium-thick slices, and panfry the slices on both sides in a little bacon grease over moderate heat till nicely browned. Serve hot.

BRAINS AND EGGS

1 pound hogs' brains

1 tablespoon fresh lemon juice

1 tablespoon white vinegar

1 teaspoon salt, plus more
to taste

6 large eggs

½ cup whole milk

Freshly ground black pepper
to taste

3 tablespoons bacon grease

3 tablespoons butter, cut into
pieces

For generations, hogs' brains and scrambled eggs have been considered a great delicacy in the South, and my own mother still remembers a certain Mr. Norwood including a container of brains in his biweekly house delivery of farm-fresh eggs, butter, milk, sausage, and chickens. Carelessly handled and cooked, hogs' brains can be an objectionable strong jolt to the palate, but when soaked in acidulated water and properly skinned, the texture is soft and tender and the flavor delicious and almost delicate. I have seen packages of frozen hogs' brains in Southern markets, but most likely you'll have to depend on the goodwill of a butcher. In any case, remember that all brains are highly perishable and that they must be handled very gently to prevent mushiness.

1 Rinse the brains carefully under running water, place in a bowl, add enough water to cover plus the lemon juice, vinegar, and 1 teaspoon salt, and let soak for about 1 hour in the refrigerator.

2 Drain the brains and, using a very sharp knife, gently peel off and discard as much of the thin outer membrane as possible. Separate into small pieces and pat dry with paper towels. In a bowl, whisk the eggs, milk, and salt and pepper till well blended; set aside.

3 In a large skillet, heat the bacon grease over moderate heat, add the brains, and brown lightly, turning once very carefully. Add the butter to the skillet, reduce the heat to low, add the beaten egg mixture, and scramble gently just till the eggs are set and still slightly soft. Transfer the brains and eggs to a bowl and serve immediately.

PIG PICKIN'S

The largest pig ever recorded was Big Bell, a Poland China owned by W. C. Chappell of Jackson, Tennessee, in 1933. Bill weighed 2,552 pounds and measured nine feet from snout to tail.

PORK SWEETBREADS, BACON, AND MUSHROOM SKEWERS

MAKES 6 TO 8 SERVINGS

1½ pounds fresh pork sweetbreads

1 tablespoon white vinegar

1 teaspoon salt

8 thick slices bacon, cut into thirds

16 fresh mushrooms, cut in half

8 metal skewers, 4 to 5 inches long (or wooden skewers soaked in water)

Sweetbreads are the rich, creamy, fragile thymus glands of young animals, and while pork sweetbreads are more strongly flavored than veal, lamb, or even beef ones (and more difficult to find), when they're simmered in acidulated liquid, carefully cleaned, skewered with bacon and mushrooms, and lightly browned in bacon drippings, they have an almost nutty flavor that is irresistible. Since they're so rich and filling, not many sweetbreads are required per serving, and since the meat is so perishable, it should be cooked the same day it's purchased. (On rare occasions, I've seen frozen pork sweetbreads in upscale Southern markets, but generally you have to depend on a clever butcher to find fresh ones.)

1 Wash the sweetbreads gently under running water and place in a large skillet with enough water to cover. Add the vinegar and salt, bring to a gentle simmer, cover, and cook for 20 minutes. Drain the sweetbreads, and then, with a very sharp knife, remove all the thin outer membrane. Break the sweetbreads into 24 pieces.

2 Wash and dry the skillet, and fry the bacon pieces over moderate heat till about half-cooked. Drain on paper towels and reserve the fat in the skillet.

3 Thread equal numbers of pieces of bacon, sweetbreads, and mushrooms alternately on the skewers, pushing them close together. Place 4 skewers in the skillet, brown the ingredients lightly on all sides over moderately low heat, transfer to a platter, and keep warm in the oven. Repeat with the other 4 skewers.

4 Serve hot.

PIG PICKIN'S

"Barbecue is a window into the soul of the practitioners . . . and I've learned much about barbecuing in the Carolinas, particularly a regional specialty like pulled pork in Lexington, N. C. or the vinegar splash." —Steven Raichlen, *BBQ USA*

VEGETABLES and RICE

Pole Beans and Potatoes with Side Meat

Streak-o'-Lean Snappies
with Pecan Butter

Specs and Smoked Sausage

Kentucky Shellouts with Smoked Ham Hock

White Beans with Scallions and Bacon

Slab Bacon Hoppin' John

Turnip Greens with Ham Hock

Collard Greens with Pork Belly

Mustard Greens with Streak-o'-Lean

Georgia Okra, Tomato, and Bacon Mull

Smothered Cabbage with Bacon
and Salt Pork

Mushy Turnips with Bacon and Pork

Brussels Sprouts with Slab Bacon

Corn and Bacon Soufflé

Old Dominion Scalloped Potatoes
with Country Ham

Country Ham Spoon Bread

Tennessee Sausage Spoon Bread

Southern Fried Hominy

Bacon- and Mushroom-Stuffed
Vidalia Onions

Damon's Baked Bourbon Wild Mushrooms
Stuffed with Country Ham

Baked Bell Peppers Stuffed with
Sausage, Mushrooms, and Pimentos

Baked Country
Ham-Stuffed Tomatoes

Creole Mirlitons Stuffed
with Ham and Cheese

Polly's Baked Tomatoes Stuffed
with Ground Pork and Rice

Savannah Red Rice

Sarasota Green Rice

Lowcountry Chicken and Ham Perloo

Louisiana Red Beans and Rice
with Pickled Pork

Turkey Wing, Canadian Bacon,
and Lima Bean Bog

Creole Ham, Sausage,
and Shrimp Jambalaya

POLE BEANS AND POTATOES WITH SIDE MEAT

MAKES 6 SERVINGS

¼ pound lean salt pork (streak-o'-lean), sliced bacon, hog jowl, or fatback, diced

1 medium onion, finely chopped

2 pounds fresh pole or other thick-skinned green beans, strings removed

4 cups water

½ teaspoon sugar

Salt and freshly ground black pepper to taste

½ to ¾ pound small new potatoes, lightly scrubbed and quartered

When you hear about notorious Southern string beans that are cooked to hell with a chunk of salt pork or other side meat and served with small new potatoes, the reference is to these broad, flat, tough pole beans, also known as Kentucky Wonders, that require at least an hour of simmering for meltingly tender texture and succulent flavor. Today, even in the South, genuine pole beans are increasingly difficult to find except during the summer months, replaced by the more delicate, stringless Blue Lake hybrid that can be cooked in a matter of 20 minutes or so. Since the whole idea behind this style of beans is to cook them long enough for them to absorb the flavor of the side meat without becoming mushy, when I'm forced to buy the hybrids, I hand-pick the sturdiest, largest, fattest one I can find and boil them at the lowest simmer. Some cooks, my mother included, still follow the old method of simply steaming the whole potatoes on top of the beans during the final 30 minutes of simmering, but I prefer my potatoes cooked directly in the liquid for extra flavor.

1 In a large pot, cook the pork over low heat till it renders a little fat, add the onion, and stir for about 2 minutes. Add the beans, water, sugar, and salt and pepper, bring to a boil, reduce the heat to low, cover, and simmer till the beans are tender, 1 to 1½ hours. Add the potatoes, stir, return to a simmer, and cook till the potatoes are still slightly firm and the beans meltingly tender, about 20 minutes.

2 Serve the beans and potatoes hot with a slotted spoon.

Streak-o'-Lean Snappies with Pecan Butter

Makes 6 servings

2 pounds fresh green beans (not thin French-style)

1 medium onion, finely chopped

One 1-inch-thick chunk lean salt pork (streak-o'-lean)

Salt and freshly ground black pepper to taste

8 tablespoons (1 stick) butter

2/3 cup coarsely crushed pecans

Snappies is a Southern term for any sturdy green beans that are snapped in half or thirds before cooking, and, for the record, I don't ever recall eating in the South a single green bean simmered with side meat that wasn't snapped. As for Southern pecan butter, it's not a "butter" at all but simply crushed pecans that are glazed in butter and used to enhance any number of cooked vegetables. When snappies are combined with this exquisite butter, the dish is worthy of the most refined dinner table or buffet.

1 Remove any tough strings from the beans, pinch off the ends, snap the beans into 1½-inch pieces, rinse well in a colander, and transfer to a large pot. Add the onion, salt pork, salt and pepper, and enough water to cover by 1 inch. Bring to a boil, reduce the heat to low, cover, and simmer the beans slowly for 45 minutes.

2 Shortly before the beans are done, make the pecan butter by melting the butter in a small, heavy skillet over moderate heat. Add the pecans, stir till they are well coated, and cook, stirring, till the pecans are golden brown, about 10 minutes. Season with salt and stir again.

3 To serve, drain the beans, discard the salt pork, and place in a large serving bowl. Pour the pecan butter over the top, toss gently, and serve immediately.

Specs and Smoked Sausage

1½ pounds shelled fresh butter
    beans (or thawed frozen
    Fordhook lima beans)

4 tablespoons (½ stick) butter,
    cut into pieces

½ teaspoon salt

Freshly ground black pepper
    to taste

1 tablespoons peanut oil

½ pound andouille, kielbasa,
    or other spicy smoked sausage,
    cut into ¼-inch rounds

Especially rich and creamy when simmered slowly, "specs" are Southern white butter beans speckled with red and purple, and while the beans are delicious with no more than a little butter (Southerners would never destroy the distinctive flavor by adding herbs or other such seasonings), they're unforgettable when combined with some form of smoked sausage. In the South, specs are usually available at farmers' markets during the summer, but if you can't find them, substitute fresh or frozen Fordhook limas. The ideal sausage with these beans is Cajun andouille, which has a unique spicy flavor and is showing up in more and more delis around the country.

1 In a saucepan, combine the butter beans, butter, salt and pepper, and enough water to just cover. Bring to a boil, reduce the heat to low, cover, and simmer till the beans are almost tender, 15 to 20 minutes.

2 Meanwhile, heat the oil in a small skillet over moderate heat, add the sausage, and brown on both sides, turning frequently. Add the sausage to the beans, stir well, and continue simmering till the beans are tender but not mushy, 5 to 10 minutes longer.

3 Serve hot.

Kentucky Shellouts with Smoked Ham Hock

Makes 4 to 6 servings

1 medium smoked ham hock
(about ½ pound)

3 pounds fresh cranberry beans
(or 1 pound dried beans,
soaked in water overnight)

1 teaspoon salt

¼ teaspoon freshly ground
black pepper

Cranberry beans are large, beige beans splotched with red that have a delectable nutty flavor, and my only guess as to why they're called "shellouts" in Kentucky, where they're so abundant and popular, is that the tough, knobby pods must be removed before the beans can be cooked. The beans are traditionally not only simmered with a smoked ham hock but also always mixed with chopped meat from the hock just before serving. They are available fresh during the summer and dried year-round; the dried variety, often packaged as "shell beans," can be found in most finer markets outside the South and should be soaked in cold water overnight before cooking.

1 Place the ham hock in a large pot with enough water to cover, bring to a boil, skimming any scum off the top, reduce the heat to low, cover, and simmer till tender, about 1½ hours.

2 Just before cooking, shell the beans and add them to the pot along with more water to cover. Add the salt and pepper, return the liquid to a simmer, cover, and cook till the beans are tender, 20 to 25 minutes.

3 Remove the hock from the pot, remove and finely chop the lean meat, discarding the fat and bone, and place the meat in a bowl. Drain the beans, add them to the bowl, and toss till the beans and meat are blended.

4 Serve hot.

WHITE BEANS WITH SCALLIONS AND BACON

MAKES 4 TO 6 SERVINGS

2 cups dried navy beans, rinsed and picked over

1 teaspoon salt

½ teaspoon freshly ground black pepper

6 thick slices bacon

2 scallions, chopped

Prejudices die hard in the South, and none more so than the habit of calling ordinary navy beans "white beans" for the simple reason that the former term is considered "Yankee." In any case, Southerners find the combination of white beans and bacon (both the meat and the grease) to be a culinary marriage made in heaven, and once you prepare the succulent beans in this manner, you'll understand why. If you're finicky about pouring warm bacon fat over the beans, you might as well fix another less sinful (and much less sapid) vegetable to serve with your pork roast or barbecued spareribs.

1 Place the beans in a saucepan with enough water to cover, bring to a boil, remove from the heat, and let stand for 1 hour.

2 Add the salt and pepper to the beans, bring to a boil, reduce the heat to low, cover, and simmer till tender but not mushy, about 1 hour.

3 Meanwhile, fry the bacon in a skillet over moderate heat till crisp, drain on paper towels, pour off all but about 3 tablespoons of fat, and keep warm.

4 Drain the beans, place in a serving bowl, and pour the warm bacon fat over the top. Add the scallions, crumble the bacon over the top, toss till well blended, and serve warm.

SLAB BACON HOPPIN' JOHN

MAKES 6 TO 8 SERVINGS

¼ pound slab bacon (rind removed), cut into ¼-inch cubes

1 small onion, finely chopped

1 celery rib, finely chopped

1 garlic clove, minced

2 pounds black-eyed peas (fresh or frozen)

Salt and freshly ground black pepper to taste

Red pepper flakes to taste

3 cups water

Hot cooked rice

3 large ripe tomatoes, chopped or stewed

For centuries, this dish of black-eyed peas and rice has been religiously eaten all over the South on New Year's Day to bring good luck, and while debate can rage over whether tomatoes should be included or the peas should be firm or mushy, everybody agrees that no hoppin' John is genuine unless it's flavored with some form of bacon, salt pork, or fatback. Personally, I find it a pain to have to soak dried black-eyed peas before cooking and have little use for the canned variety (which can have a metallic taste), but I do consider frozen peas to be just as good as the fresh. Hoppin' John is wonderful with any pork dish—especially baked spareribs and fried chitlins.

1 In a large saucepan, fry the bacon over moderate heat till almost crisp; pour off all but about 1 tablespoon of the grease.

2 Add the onion, celery, and garlic and cook, stirring, for 2 minutes. Add the peas, salt and pepper, red pepper flakes, and water, bring to a boil, reduce the heat to low, cover, and simmer till the peas are tender but not mushy, about 1 hour.

3 Drain the peas, and then serve them in small bowls over mounds of hot rice with a few spoonfuls of tomatoes on top.

Turnip Greens with Ham Hock

Makes 6 to 8 servings

3 to 4 pounds fresh turnip greens

1 medium ham hock, skin removed

1 tablespoon sugar

2 teaspoons salt

2 medium onions, coarsely chopped

1 cup cider vinegar

Freshly ground black pepper to taste

Sometimes referred to as "Southern penicillin" because of their restorative value, turnip greens are always boiled to death with at least one ham hock in the South, and it's virtually unheard-of not to serve cornbread with the greens for dunking into the some of the delectable, nutritious cooking liquid (pot likker). Never underestimate the amount of dirt and grit on turnip greens, meaning they must be swished around repeatedly in several changes of fresh water before cooking till the leaves are impeccably clean. If you love plenty of meat in your greens the way I do, you'll use two ham hocks.

1 Remove and discard the stems and ribs of the greens, place the leaves in a sink or large pot of cold water, and swish around to remove all the dirt and grit, repeating the procedure with more fresh water if necessary. Tear the leaves into several pieces each and set aside.

2 Place the ham hock in a large pot with enough water to cover, bring to a boil, skimming any scum off the top, reduce the heat to low, cover, and simmer for about 30 minutes. Add the sugar and salt, return to a boil, and gradually add the torn leaves. Reduce the heat to low, cover, and simmer the greens till soft and tender, 1 to 1½ hours.

3 In a bowl, combine the onions, vinegar, and pepper and stir till well blended.

4 Remove the hock from the pot with a slotted spoon, cut off and chop the lean meat, and discard the fat and bone. Drain the greens well in a colander, transfer to a large serving bowl, add the chopped meat, top with the onions and vinegar, and toss well. Serve the greens with small bowls of pot likker and cornbread on the side.

PIG PICKIN'S

The first recorded barbecue "social" in this country took place outside of Jamestown, Virginia a few years after the first settlers arrived. Wild boar was the guest of honor.

Collard Greens with Pork Belly

3 pounds fresh collard greens

¼ pound lean pork belly

8 cups water

¼ cup cider vinegar

1 tablespoon salt

1 teaspoon freshly ground
    black pepper

Tabasco sauce to taste

Stronger in taste than turnip greens but milder than mustard greens and kale, collard greens are cooked in the South with every type of pork side meat imaginable and are believed by many to produce the most flavorful cooking liquid (pot likker) for dunking cornbread. The peak season for collards is January through April, when the leaves are bright and crisp with little evidence of yellowing, wilting, or insect damage. Like all tough Southern greens, collards must be cooked slowly for at least an hour to attain perfect tenderness and to absorb the flavor of the pork. If you want something really special, toss the greens with about a cup of chopped pecans that have been slightly browned in butter.

1 Remove and discard the ribs of the collards, tear the leaves into bite-size pieces, and place in a large stainless-steel or enameled pot. Add the pork belly, water, vinegar, salt, and pepper, bring to a boil, reduce the heat to low, cover, and simmer till the collards are very tender, 1 to 1½ hours.

2 Remove the pork belly, cut off and discard any rind, cut the meat into small pieces, and return the pieces to the pot. Add the Tabasco, reheat till the collards and pork are piping hot, and serve in small bowls with pot likker spooned over the top.

Mustard Greens with Streak-o'-Lean

Makes 6 servings

1 cup white vinegar

1 tablespoon red pepper flakes

3 pounds fresh mustard greens

1 pound lean salt pork
   (streak-o'-lean), cut in half

2 tablespoons sugar

Salt and freshly ground black
   pepper to taste

6 cups water

Because of their pungent flavor, dark mustard greens have as many detractors as champions throughout the South, which explains why they're usually tamed in cooking not only with a sturdy chunk of pork but also with substantial amounts of white vinegar, sugar, and hot red pepper flakes. The best greens (crisp young leaves with a rich green color) are marketed during the winter months, and beware of any that are yellowed and flabby, with thick, fibrous stems. Frozen mustard greens are an acceptable substitute for the fresh, but stay away from the canned. If you don't have a slab of streak-o'-lean on hand for this dish, use thin bacon slices cut in half.

1 In a jar, combine the vinegar and red pepper flakes, screw on the lid tightly, shake well, and let stand overnight for the flavors to develop.

2 Remove and discard the stems and thick veins of the greens, shred the leaves, and place in a large pot. Add the pork, sugar, salt and pepper, and water, bring to a boil, reduce the heat to low, cover, and simmer till the greens are completely withered and tender, 1½ to 2 hours.

3 To serve, remove the streak-o'-lean, cut off and discard any rind, and cut the meat into thin slices. Divide the greens between 6 serving bowls, add equal amounts of pork to each portion, spoon a little cooking liquid (pot likker) over the top, drizzle with the spicy vinegar, and serve with cornbread.

Georgia Okra, Tomato, and Bacon Mull

MAKES 6 SERVINGS

- 2 pounds fresh, firm, small okra, rinsed and stems removed
- 6 slices lean bacon, cut into small pieces
- 2 medium onions, chopped
- 6 large, ripe tomatoes, peeled and chopped
- 1 tablespoon fresh thyme leaves
- 2 teaspoons salt
- Freshly ground black pepper to taste
- Tabasco sauce to taste

My best guess is that the term *mull* can be traced back to an early colonial beverage that was heated with herbs and spices and gradually evolved to denote various seafood and vegetable mixtures found mainly in coastal Virginia, the Carolinas, and Georgia. Okra and tomatoes, of course, are today simmered with herbs all over the South, but in Georgia it's almost obligatory to add some form of pork and serve the mull as a side dish to barbecue or any meat cooked on the grill. While frozen okra can be used, nothing is more toothsome than small, firm, fresh pods that are slightly fuzzy and not in the least spotted.

1 Place the okra in a large saucepan with enough water to cover, bring to a boil, reduce the heat to moderately low, and simmer till tender but not slimy, about 10 minutes. Drain the okra in a colander.

2 In a large skillet, fry the bacon over moderate heat till crisp; drain on paper towels. Pour off all but 2 tablespoons of the grease, add the onions, and stir for 10 minutes. Add the tomatoes, thyme, and salt, season with pepper and Tabasco, stir well, reduce the heat to low, and simmer till the tomatoes are soft, about 20 minutes. Add the okra and bacon, stir gently, and simmer for about 10 minutes longer.

3 Serve hot.

Smothered Cabbage with Bacon and Salt Pork

1 firm head green cabbage
   (3 to 3½ pounds)

½ pound lean bacon, cut into
   small pieces

¼ pound salt pork, cut into
   small pieces

1 medium onion, chopped

2 small fresh red chile peppers,
   seeded and finely chopped

Freshly ground black pepper
   to taste

1 teaspoon sugar

In Southern lingo, any vegetable that is steamed in its own moisture is often referred to as being "smothered," and when it comes to cabbage, it is almost inconceivable to cook it without at least one form of fatty pork to melt into the leaves and give them succulent flavor and an unctuous texture. In Creole Louisiana, pickled pork would most likely be substituted for the salt pork in this recipe, but, in either case, note that no salt is needed. Also, be sure to choose a fresh, young, firm head of cabbage that still has plenty of natural moisture and is not in the least wilted and dried out.

1 Remove and discard any discolored outer leaves from the cabbage, cut the head into large wedges, core them, rinse under cold running water, and set aside.

2 In a large, heavy pot or casserole, fry the bacon and salt pork over moderate heat till half-cooked, add the onion, and stir till softened, about 5 minutes. Add the cabbage wedges and stir well. Add the remaining ingredients, reduce the heat to low, cover, and cook slowly and gently till the cabbage is very tender, about 1 hour, stirring from time to time and adding a few sprinkles of water if the cabbage seems too dry.

3 Serve hot.

MUSHY TURNIPS WITH BACON AND PORK

MAKES 4 TO 6 SERVINGS

3 thick slices bacon, diced

1 pound pork loin, cut into
   1-inch cubes

2 medium onions, chopped

2 pounds small to medium
   turnips (about 8 to 10),
   peeled and diced

1 tablespoon sugar

Salt and freshly ground black
   pepper to taste

Cayenne pepper to taste

¼ cup chopped fresh parsley
   leaves

In the South, turnips have been relished for centuries (despite Scarlett O'Hara's disparaging proclamation), and while the root vegetable is often simply boiled and mashed with butter just like potatoes, those who prefer more flavor and textural contrast add one or two forms of pork and simmer the turnips till they're delectably mushy. If you can use small, young, heavy turnips that have a delicate, slightly sweet taste (available during the winter months), no sugar is necessary in this recipe, but older, coarser turnips that have developed a stronger savor need to be sweetened.

1 In a large, heavy saucepan, fry the bacon over moderate heat till crisp; drain on paper towels. Add the pork to the bacon fat and brown on all sides, scraping the browned bits from the bottom. Add the onions and turnips, stir well, cover the pan, reduce the heat to low, and cook for 30 minutes, stirring from time to time. Sprinkle the sugar over the top, season with salt, pepper, and cayenne, add the bacon and parsley, cover, and continue cooking till the turnips are very soft, about 30 minutes, stirring often and making sure the turnips don't burn.

2 Serve hot.

Brussels Sprouts with Slab Bacon

MAKES 6 SERVINGS

1 pound Brussels sprouts, fresh
   or thawed frozen

¼ pound smoked slab bacon
   (rind removed), coarsely
   chopped

1 tablespoon butter

1 teaspoon chopped fresh thyme
   leaves

Pinch of ground nutmeg

Salt and freshly ground black
   pepper to taste

Contrary to popular opinion, Southerners do eat and like Brussels sprouts, so long, that is, as their pungent aroma and flavor are tamed with various herbs and spices, cheese, sour cream, peanuts, and, above all, some form of smoky bacon. One problem, of course, has always been that Southern cooks have overcooked the sprouts the way they tend to do most vegetables, apparently unaware that nothing intensifies the strong flavor more. While today modern cooks are learning the advantages of not only buying superior, firm, fresh sprouts in the fall but also preparing them so that they're crisp-tender, so closely is bacon identified with the vegetable that, blessedly, I can't imagine the classic combination disappearing anytime soon.

1 If the Brussels sprouts are fresh, remove any withered leaves and trim off the stems. Cut the sprouts in half through the root ends and place in a saucepan with enough water to cover. Bring to a low boil, cover, and cook till crisp-tender, about 15 minutes; drain well.

2 Meanwhile, fry the bacon in a large skillet over moderate heat till almost crisp, and pour off all but about 1 tablespoon of the fat. Melt the butter in the skillet, add the sprouts, thyme, nutmeg, and salt and pepper, and stir just till the edges begin to brown.

3 Serve hot.

CORN AND BACON SOUFFLÉ

MAKES 4 SERVINGS

½ pound sliced hickory-smoked bacon

6 tablespoons (¾ stick) butter

¼ cup grated Parmesan cheese

1 medium onion, finely chopped

1½ cups whole corn kernels, fresh or thawed frozen

3 tablespoons all-purpose flour

2 cups milk, heated

6 large eggs

Salt and freshly ground black pepper to taste

Cayenne pepper to taste

Never mind that in the South the term *soufflé* normally refers to any baked vegetable dish that contains eggs. Over the years, I've come up with dozens of ways to highlight the first luscious fresh corn of July and August, but no preparation makes a bigger hit on summer buffets than this golden corn soufflé enhanced with smoky bacon, meat from a smoked ham hock used to flavor a stew or casserole, or even spicy Cajun andouille sausage. If absolutely necessary, frozen (no canned) corn can be used, but, in either case, test the soufflé with a skewer or knife after about 30 minutes of baking to make sure the interior is still soft and slightly moist.

1 In a large skillet, fry the bacon over moderate heat till crisp. Drain on paper towels and crumble. Pour off all but about 1 tablespoon of fat from the skillet.

2 Grease the bottom and sides of a 1½-quart soufflé or baking dish with 1 tablespoon of the butter, coat the surfaces with half the grated cheese, and set aside.

3 Add 2 tablespoons of the butter to the skillet and melt over moderate heat. Add the onion and corn, stir for 3 minutes, and set aside.

4 Preheat the oven to 375°F.

5 In a saucepan, melt the remaining 3 tablespoons of butter over low heat, add the flour, and whisk till golden, 2 to 3 minutes. Remove the pan from the heat, add the milk, and whisk till thickened and smooth. Cool the mixture slightly, then whisk in the eggs one at a time till well blended. Add the corn mixture, bacon, salt and pepper, and cayenne and blend thoroughly. Scrape the mixture into the prepared soufflé dish, sprinkle the remaining cheese over the top, and bake till golden brown, 30 to 35 minutes.

6 Serve hot.

Old Dominion Scalloped Potatoes with Country Ham

MAKES 6 SERVINGS

4 medium russet potatoes (about 2 pounds), peeled and sliced ⅛ inch thick

1 cup finely diced cooked country ham

½ cup chopped fresh chives

Salt and freshly ground black pepper to taste

¾ cup grated Parmesan cheese

3 tablespoons butter, cut into pieces

1 cup half-and-half

Scalloped potatoes with lots of butter and cheese have been a staple in Southern homes for centuries, but only in Virginia have I encountered the dish made with the state's incomparable country-cured ham—simply called "Virginia ham" in the Old Dominion. Do remember that you need to use dry russet potatoes for any gratin, and if the potatoes seem to be drying out after 35 or 40 minutes, just add a little whole milk, basting them slightly to produce a golden crust.

1 Preheat the oven to 375°F.

2 Butter a 1½ to 2-quart gratin or baking dish and arrange alternate layers of overlapping potato slices and ham, sprinkling a few chives over each layer and seasoning with salt and pepper. Sprinkle ¼ cup of the cheese over the top, dot with the butter, pour the half-and-half over the top, and bake till the potatoes are tender, about 45 minutes, basting from time to time with the liquid. Sprinkle the remaining cheese over the top and bake till golden brown, about 10 minutes longer.

3 Serve piping hot directly from the dish.

Country Ham Spoon Bread

Makes 6 servings

3 cups milk

1½ cups white cornmeal

8 tablespoons (1 stick) butter, softened and cut into pieces

2 teaspoons baking powder

5 large eggs, separated

1 cup diced cooked country ham

Served either at breakfast or as a side dish for roasted meats and poultry, spoon bread is an elegant, pudding-like Southern specialty that can be made simply with cornmeal or enhanced with anything from various pork products to cheese to nuts. Since this particular spoon bread is flavored with cured country ham, no salt is needed, and while many Southern cooks wouldn't dream of adding sugar to any spoon bread (or cornbread), you do have the option of using one or two tablespoons, if desired. And yes, this version should remain moist enough to be eaten with a spoon or small fork.

1 Preheat the oven to 350°F. Butter a medium casserole or baking dish and set aside.

2 In a large saucepan, bring the milk to a low boil and gradually add the cornmeal, stirring rapidly with a spoon as you slowly pour it in. Reduce the heat to low and cook, stirring constantly, till the mixture is thick, about 10 minutes. Remove the pan from the heat, add the butter and baking powder, stir till the butter has melted, and set aside to cool.

3 In a small bowl, beat the egg yolks with a fork till light, and then stir them into the cooled cornmeal mixture. Add the country ham and stir till well blended. In a large bowl, beat the egg whites with an electric mixer till stiff peaks form, and then fold them into the mixture till all traces of white have disappeared. Scrape the mixture into the prepared casserole and bake till nicely set but still very moist, 30 to 35 minutes.

4 Serve hot.

Tennessee Sausage Spoon Bread

MAKES 6 SERVINGS

½ pound bulk pork sausage

3 cups whole milk

2 teaspoons sugar

1 teaspoon salt

1 cup yellow cornmeal

4 tablespoons (½ stick) butter, cut into pieces

5 large eggs, separated

1 cup fresh or frozen corn kernels

Not all Southern spoon breads are necessarily limpid and delicate, as exemplified by this sturdier version I once encountered at a diner on the road to Memphis and asked the cook about. Not only does it have whole kernels of corn, a tablespoon of sausage grease, and no baking powder, but the texture is much more like a baked bread than a pudding. This is definitely not a breakfast spoon bread but rather one intended to be served with broiled fish, barbecued pork chops, or maybe a platter of chitlins. It's so good that, personally, I could eat it by itself for lunch with no more than a few ham biscuits. By no means make this spoon bread with reduced-fat milk.

1 Preheat the oven to 350°F. Butter a 2-quart casserole and set aside.

2 In a skillet, break up the sausage and fry over moderate heat till well browned. Drain on paper towels and reserve 1 tablespoon of the grease.

3 In a large, heavy saucepan, combine the milk, sugar, and salt, bring to a low boil, and gradually add the cornmeal, stirring constantly, till the mixture thickens, about 10 minutes. Remove the pan from the heat, add the butter and reserved sausage grease, and stir till well blended.

4 In a bowl, beat the egg yolks with a fork till light, and then stir into the cornmeal mixture. Add the sausage meat and corn kernels and stir till well blended. In another bowl, beat the egg whites with an electric mixer till stiff peaks form, and then fold them into the mixture. Scrape the mixture into the prepared casserole and bake till the spoon bread is golden brown and puffy, about 45 minutes.

5 Serve hot directly from the casserole.

PIG PICKIN'S

Probably the largest and most important barbecue cook-off in America is the annual Memphis in May competition that takes place the first week in May on the banks of the Mississippi.

SOUTHERN FRIED HOMINY

4 slices lean bacon, diced

1 small onion, minced

½ small green bell pepper, seeded and minced

2 cups canned hominy, drained

Salt and freshly ground black pepper to taste

Tabasco sauce to taste

Hominy is dried corn kernels from which the outer hull and germ have been removed, and while today the delicacy is used mainly to make all sorts of casseroles, breads, and savory puddings, nothing is better and more unusual with fried chicken, baked ham, or roast pork than hominy that is simply stir-fried with smoky bacon till meltingly soft and golden. If you prefer more textural contrast, fry the bacon fully and crumble it over the cooked hominy.

1 In a large skillet, fry the bacon over moderate heat till half-cooked, add the onion and bell pepper, and stir till softened, about 5 minutes. Add the hominy, salt and pepper, and Tabasco and continue to stir-fry till the hominy is golden, about 10 minutes.

2 Serve hot.

Bacon- and Mushroom-Stuffed Vidalia Onions

4 Vidalia onions

4 thick slices hickory-smoked bacon, finely chopped

½ pound mushrooms, finely chopped

½ cup fresh bread crumbs

¼ pound aged Swiss cheese, grated

2 tablespoons chopped fresh parsley leaves

Salt and freshly ground black pepper to taste

½ cup chicken broth

Frankly, these noble stuffed Vidalia onions are so succulent that I often prefer to build a meal around them and serve them as a main course. I might also vary the stuffing, substituting about ¼ pound of cooked finely chopped country ham, bulk pork sausage, or ham hock for the bacon and experimenting with various full-flavored cheeses. Another idea is to serve the onions with a large platter of cold cuts and a loaf of crusty country bread with plenty of sweet butter.

1 Peel the onions, cut off the root ends, and, with a sharp paring knife, hollow out each one to within ¼ inch of the sides, trimming the edges to make a wide, even opening. Arrange the onion shells in a medium baking dish, finely chop the onion pulp, and set aside.

2 Preheat the oven to 400°F.

3 In a large skillet, fry the bacon over moderate heat till almost crisp, add the chopped onions and mushrooms, and stir till the vegetables are golden, about 10 minutes. Add the bread crumbs, 2 tablespoons of the cheese, the parsley, and salt and pepper and stir till the cheese begins to melt, about 5 minutes.

4 Stuff the onion shells with equal amounts of the mixture, pour the broth into the bottom of the dish, cover with foil, and bake for 20 minutes. Uncover, sprinkle the tops with the remaining cheese, and bake till golden brown, about 20 minutes longer.

5 Serve hot.

Damon's Baked Bourbon Wild Mushrooms Stuffed with Country Ham

½ ounce dried cep (porcini) mushrooms

12 large fresh cremini mushrooms, rinsed and wiped dry

5 tablespoons butter

2 garlic cloves, minced

¼ cup minced cooked country ham

2 tablespoons chopped fresh parsley leaves

½ cup dry bread crumbs

Freshly ground black pepper to taste

3 tablespoons bourbon

This is a brilliant creation of my friend/colleague Damon Lee Fowler in Savannah, Georgia, the result of his effort to produce stuffed mushrooms that, for once, have some real flavor. Dried cep mushrooms are readily available today in most markets and should be pale brown in color and not crumbly. Since fresh cremini mushrooms are in good supply almost everywhere, I use those for the recipe, but if your market also carries fresh portobellos or shiitakes, they too are wonderful for stuffing. The earthy mushrooms are sublime with virtually any pork chops, steaks, or cutlets, and I also like to serve them with barbecued spareribs or kabobs. (Damon strongly discourages using large, ordinary button mushrooms for this dish since the bland flavor just does not hold up to the assertive stuffing.)

1 Place the dried cep mushrooms in a small bowl, add enough boiling water to cover, and let soak for 30 minutes. Chop the stems of the cremini mushrooms finely and set aside.

2 Preheat the oven to 375°F. Butter a large baking dish and set aside.

3 Place the soaked mushrooms in a medium skillet and strain the soaking liquid through a paper towel over them. Bring the liquid to a low boil and cook till the liquid has evaporated. Chop the mushrooms finely and set aside.

4 Melt 3 tablespoons of the butter in the skillet over moderate heat, add the garlic, and stir till golden, about 5 minutes. Add the chopped cremini stems, stir for 5 minutes, add the ham and parsley, stir well, and remove from the heat. Add the bread crumbs and pepper and toss till the stuffing is well blended.

5 Arrange the cremini caps stem side up in the prepared baking dish and fill with equal amounts of the stuffing. Sprinkle the bourbon over the tops, dot each with some of the remaining butter, and bake till the caps are tender and the tops lightly browned, about 20 minutes.

6 Serve the mushrooms immediately.

Baked Bell Peppers Stuffed with Sausage, Mushrooms, and Pimentos

6 large green bell peppers

1 pound hot bulk pork sausage with sage

1 pound fresh mushrooms, finely chopped

2 large onions, finely chopped

1 garlic clove, minced

One 4-ounce jar pimentos, drained and chopped

1 cup finely chopped fresh parsley leaves

2 large eggs, beaten

2 cups fresh bread crumbs

Salt and freshly ground black pepper to taste

4 tablespoons (½ stick) butter, melted

Stuffed and baked green bell peppers have been a lunch and light supper staple throughout the South since at least the nineteenth century, and while stuffings made with ground beef and onions, flavored rice or macaroni, and various cheese concoctions are forever popular, perhaps the most beloved is an eggy mixture of spicy bulk sausage, onions, and mushrooms enhanced with garlic and pimentos. Do check the peppers after about 30 minutes of baking to make sure they're not overcooked; the texture should be fully tender but not in the least mushy. In the South, the peppers are always served as a main course with sides like pickled peaches and sesame sticks.

1 Cut the peppers in half lengthwise, remove and discard the seeds and veins, and set aside.

2 Preheat the oven to 350°F. Butter a large baking dish or shallow casserole and set aside.

3 In a large, heavy skillet, break up the sausage and fry over moderate heat till cooked through, stirring. Add the mushrooms, onions, and garlic, stir till softened, about 10 minutes, and transfer to a bowl. Add the pimentos, parsley, eggs, 1 cup of the bread crumbs, and salt and pepper and mix till the stuffing is well blended. Fill the pepper halves with equal amounts of the stuffing and arrange in the prepared baking dish. Sprinkle the remaining bread crumbs over the tops, drizzle the butter over the crumbs, and bake till the peppers are soft and the tops nicely browned, 35 to 40 minutes.

4 Serve piping hot.

BAKED COUNTRY HAM-STUFFED TOMATOES

8 large, firm, ripe tomatoes

8 tablespoons (1 stick) butter

2 medium onions, finely chopped

1 cup finely chopped lean
   country ham

2 tablespoons finely chopped
   fresh basil leaves

Freshly ground black pepper
   to taste

½ cup fine dry bread crumbs

Come summertime, Southerners love to stuff large, ripe, home-grown tomatoes with everything from shrimp or chicken salad to herbed rice and meat mixtures to fresh corn and other relishes, but one of the most unusual and delicious versions I ever tasted is this baked one with country ham and fresh basil, created by my own mother. To prevent the stuffing from being too juicy, just make sure to cook the tomato pulp till it loses most of its liquid. Mother has always served these tomatoes as a side dish to large pork roasts, but I find they make a perfect luncheon dish with deviled eggs and a basket of beaten biscuits.

1 Core the tomatoes, carefully scoop out a wide, shallow pocket on the cored end of each, and arrange the tomatoes in a large baking dish or on a heavy baking sheet. Chop the scooped-out flesh and set aside.

2 Preheat the oven to 400°F.

3 In a medium skillet, melt 4 tablespoons of the butter over moderate heat, add the onions and country ham, and cook, stirring, till the onions are very soft but not browned, about 7 minutes. Add the basil, pepper, and reserved tomato pulp and continue to cook, stirring, till the pulp loses most of its liquid, about 8 minutes. Divide the mixture evenly among the pockets in the tomatoes and spread it out to the edges with a fork, pressing down slightly. Sprinkle the tops with the bread crumbs. In a small saucepan, melt the remaining butter, drizzle it over the breadcrumbs, and bake till the tops are nicely browned, about 20 minutes.

4 Serve hot.

CREOLE MIRLITONS STUFFED WITH HAM AND CHEESE

3 large mirlitons (chayotes), about 1 pound each

½ pound extra-sharp cheddar cheese, grated

½ pound cooked ham, finely chopped

1 small onion, finely chopped

2 garlic cloves, minced

1 large egg, beaten

Salt and freshly ground black pepper to taste

Cayenne pepper to taste

1½ cups fresh bread crumbs

4 tablespoons (½ stick) butter, melted

Also called "vegetable pears," pale-green mirlitons are actually a gourd-like fruit harvested in late summer and autumn in Louisiana and usually marketed elsewhere as chayotes. The flavor is mild and delicate, so much so, in fact, that mirlitons almost demand either assertive seasoning as a side vegetable to counter the blandness or a sturdy meat and cheese stuffing before being baked as a main course. In Louisiana, diced andouille sausage, cooked pig's belly, or smoked ham hock might well be used in the stuffing, but I've learned that this is also still another way to use up ordinary leftover smoked ham to great advantage when it's blended with a well-aged cheese.

1 Cut the mirlitons in half, remove the seeds, and place the halves in a pot with enough water to cover. Bring to a boil, reduce the heat to low, and let simmer just till tender, about 15 minutes (do not overcook). Drain and, when cool enough to handle, scoop out most of the pulp, chop finely, and set the shells aside.

2 Preheat the oven to 350°F. Butter a large, heavy baking pan and set aside.

3 In a bowl, combine the mirliton pulp, cheese, ham, onion, garlic, egg, salt and pepper, cayenne, and 1 cup of the bread crumbs and stir till the stuffing is well blended. Fill the mirliton shells with equal amounts of the stuffing and arrange on the prepared baking pan. Sprinkle the tops with the remaining bread crumbs, drizzle the butter over the crumbs, and bake till lightly browned, about 30 minutes.

4 Serve hot.

PIG PICKIN'S

"There has always been a connection between country sausage and country music. The Louvin Brothers recorded the theme song for Tennessee Pride brand almost 50 years ago. In 1969, Jimmy Dean . . . started selling his own sausage, which quickly became the nation's number one brand."

—Julia Reed, *Queen of the Turtle Derby*

POLLY'S BAKED TOMATOES STUFFED WITH GROUND PORK AND RICE

MAKES 6 SERVINGS

6 medium ripe tomatoes, cored

6 tablespoons (¾ stick) butter

1 pound ground pork

6 scallions (part of green tops included), finely chopped

1 celery rib, finely chopped

1 garlic clove, minced

2 cups cooked rice

¼ cup finely chopped fresh parsley leaves

2 large eggs, beaten

½ teaspoon powdered sage

Salt and freshly ground black pepper to taste

½ cup fresh bread crumbs

When my friend Polly entertained a large gathering at her cottage on Chesapeake Bay just south of Annapolis, Maryland, we could usually count on a huge picnic table overflowing with boiled blue crabs, bowls of red cabbage coleslaw and potato salad, and beaten biscuits. But when it was a question of only a small, casual summer supper, she loved nothing more than to stuff home-grown tomatoes with a well-seasoned rice and meat mixture and bake them till the tops were a crusty brown. Since those days, I've made the stuffing with sausage, regular or Canadian bacon, and various types of ham, but what guests seem to enjoy most is this one with sagey ground pork (preferably shoulder with sufficient fat for both flavor and moistness).

1 Preheat the oven to 350°F.

2 Cut the tomatoes in half lengthwise, create wide indentions in each half by cutting out about half of the pulp, reserve the pulp, and arrange the tomatoes in a large, heavy baking pan.

3 In a small skillet, melt 2 tablespoons of the butter over moderate heat, break up the pork in the fat, and stir till browned. Add the scallions, celery, and garlic and stir for 5 minutes longer. Add the reserved tomato pulp, stir for 5 minutes longer, and transfer the mixture to a large bowl. Add the rice, parsley, eggs, sage, and salt and pepper, stir till the stuffing is well blended, and fill each tomato half with equal amounts of the stuffing. Sprinkle the tops with the bread crumbs. In a small saucepan, melt the remaining butter, drizzle it over the bread crumbs, and bake the tomatoes till the tops are golden brown, about 1 hour.

4 Serve 2 hot tomato halves per person.

Savannah Red Rice

½ pound double-smoked sliced bacon

2 medium onions, finely chopped

One 6-ounce can tomato paste

2 cups water

2 teaspoons salt

2 to 3 teaspoons sugar

Freshly ground black pepper to taste

Tabasco sauce to taste

2 cups long-grain rice

Only recently did I learn that Savannah Red Rice did not originate in Savannah and was popular throughout the Carolinas and Georgia and actually called "Tomato Pilau" by Savannahians long before the city's legendary Pirate's House Restaurant added the tag *Savannah* on its menu some fifty years ago. No matter. Red rice, so called by virtue of the tomato or tomato paste that gives the dish its ruddy color, is a Southern classic, and to prepare it without some form of bacon or salt pork to contribute to its unique flavor would be inconceivable. The texture of the spicy rice should be dry and fluffy, meaning it must be stirred repeatedly while cooking till the grains are virtually separate. In the Georgia Lowcountry, the rice is standard fare at all oyster roasts and other outdoor affairs, but, otherwise, it's delicious with any seafood or roasted meat.

1 In a large skillet, fry the bacon over moderate heat till crisp. Drain on paper towels and crumble. Pour off half the fat from the skillet and reserve. Add the onions to the remaining fat in the skillet and stir for 2 minutes. Add the tomato paste, water, salt, sugar, pepper, and Tabasco, stir well, and cook for 10 minutes.

2 Transfer the contents of the skillet to a large saucepan, add the reserved bacon fat, and bring to a boil. Add the rice, reduce the heat to moderately low, stir, cover, and cook till the rice has absorbed most of the liquid, 25 to 30 minutes, stirring frequently with a fork. Remove the pan from the heat, add the crumbled bacon, stir well with the fork, and let the rice stand for about 5 minutes to dry slightly.

3 Fluff again with the fork and serve immediately.

PIG PICKIN'S

"The Pig: mogul of appetite, lord of misrule, the king who must die." —John Thorne, *Serious Pig*

SARASOTA GREEN RICE

¼ pound lean slab bacon (rind removed), finely diced

2½ cups cooked rice

1 small onion, minced

¼ pound sharp cheddar cheese, grated

½ cup finely chopped fresh parsley leaves

3 tablespoons butter, melted

Salt and freshly ground black pepper to taste

1 cup whole milk

1 large egg

Taking its name from the parsley responsible for its distinctive color, green rice may not be unique to Sarasota, Florida, but that's the only place I've ever encountered the delightful ring—served at a sumptuous cookout that featured huge barbecued shrimp. Be sure to use a quality bacon for this dish (artisanal or double smoked, if possible), and check the rice after about 45 minutes of baking to make sure it's not too dry. If you like, you can decorate the ring with a few chopped pimentos.

1 Preheat the oven to 350°F. Butter a medium ring mold and set aside.

2 In a skillet, fry the bacon over moderate heat till almost crisp; drain on paper towels.

3 In a bowl, combine the rice, bacon, onion, cheese, parsley, butter, and salt and pepper and stir till well blended. In a small bowl, beat together the milk and egg till frothy, add to the rice mixture, and stir till well blended. Scrape into the prepared mold, cover with foil, and bake till firm, about 1 hour.

4 Unmold the rice onto a platter and serve hot.

Lowcountry Chicken and Ham Perloo

One 3- to 3½-pound chicken (giblets included), cut up

8 tablespoons (1 stick) butter

2 medium onions, chopped

2 celery ribs, chopped

1 medium green bell pepper, seeded and chopped

2 large ripe tomatoes, chopped, juice reserved

1 pound cooked ham, cut into cubes

1 teaspoon dried sage, crumbled

1 teaspoon dried tarragon, crumbled

1 small fresh red chile pepper, seeded and minced

Salt and freshly ground black pepper to taste

2 cups long-grain rice

While coastal Carolina rice perloos can be made with anything from tiny river shrimp to spicy sausages to wild game, none is more popular than this traditional herby one featuring both chicken (with its giblets) and either regular smoked or country ham. Just remember that the rice in a genuine perloo, unlike that in a much more liquidy bog, must be cooked till all the broth is absorbed and the texture is dry and fluffy— much like a Creole jambalaya.

1 Place the chicken plus the giblets in a large pot and add enough water to cover. Bring to a boil, reduce the heat to moderate, cover, and cook till the chicken is tender, about 30 minutes. With a slotted spoon, transfer the chicken and giblets to a plate and reserve the stock in the pot. When cool enough to handle, skin and bone the chicken, cut the meat into cubes, and set aside. Coarsely chop the giblets and set aside.

2 In another large pot, melt the butter over moderate heat, add the onions, celery, and bell pepper, and cook, stirring, till the onions are golden, about 10 minutes. Add the tomatoes plus their juice, the chicken and giblets, ham, sage, tarragon, and chile pepper, season with salt and pepper, and stir well. Add the rice and 1 quart of the reserved chicken stock, stir, and bring to a low boil. Reduce the heat to low, cover, and simmer till the broth is absorbed and the rice is tender and dry, 35 to 40 minutes. Fluff the perloo with a fork before serving hot in a large pottery casserole or on a handsome serving platter.

Louisiana Red Beans and Rice with Pickled Pork

Makes 6 servings

1½ cups dried kidney beans, rinsed and picked over

3 tablespoons vegetable oil

1 medium onion, chopped

2 celery ribs, chopped

½ small green bell pepper, seeded and chopped

1 garlic clove, minced

½ pound pickled pork (page 315), thinly sliced

1 small fresh red chile pepper, chopped

¼ teaspoon dried thyme, crumbled

¼ teaspoon dried oregano, crumbled

1 bay leaf

Salt and freshly ground black pepper to taste

1 tablespoon cider vinegar

1 cup long-grain rice

2 cups chicken broth

½ cup diced smoked ham

1 red onion, finely chopped

For generations, red beans and rice has been almost a ritual on Mondays in homes and restaurants throughout the Louisiana Delta and in New Orleans, a hefty dish that depends for distinctive flavor as much on various pork products as on the two starchy main ingredients. On home territory, the spicy, packaged Cajun ham called tasso would most likely be used in place of regular smoked ham, but since it's easy enough to make your own pickled pork (page 315), there's really no excuse for substituting ordinary salt pork for the much more aromatic and delectable side meat. It would be unthinkable to serve red beans and rice without a bowl of chopped red onions to sprinkle over the top.

1 Place the kidney beans in a large, heavy pot with enough cold water to cover by 3 inches and let soak overnight. Pick out any shells, drain the beans in a colander, and dry the pot.

2 Heat the oil in the pot over moderate heat, add the onion, celery, bell pepper, and garlic, and stir till the vegetables soften, about 5 minutes. Return the soaked beans to the pot and add the pickled pork, chile pepper, thyme, oregano, bay leaf, salt and pepper, vinegar, and enough water to cover by 1 inch. Bring to a low simmer, cover, and cook till the beans are tender and most of the liquid has been absorbed, 35 to 40 minutes.

3 Meanwhile, in a medium saucepan, combine the rice, chicken broth, ham, and salt to taste and bring to a boil. Reduce the heat to moderate, cover, and cook till all the liquid has been absorbed, about 15 minutes.

4 In a large serving bowl, combine the beans-and-rice mixture, stir well, and serve with chopped red onion sprinkled over each portion.

PIG PICKIN'S

Every winter in Broussard, Louisiana, there is a Louisiana Boudin Festival where young Cajun men and women compete to see who can eat the most pork and rice sausage.

Turkey Wing, Canadian Bacon, and Lima Bean Bog

Makes 4 to 6 servings

2 large turkey wings
  (2 to 2½ pounds)

¼ cup peanut oil

2 medium onions, coarsely
  chopped

2 medium carrots, scraped and
  coarsely chopped

2 garlic cloves, minced

2 large, ripe tomatoes, coarsely
  chopped

½ teaspoon dried tarragon,
  crumbled

2 bay leaves

Salt and freshly ground black
  pepper to taste

5 cups water

½ pound Canadian bacon,
  cut into thin strips

2 cups fresh or frozen lima beans

3 to 4 cups boiled rice
  (fairly wet)

Nineteenth-century plantation culture in the coastal Carolinas produced numerous culinary concepts based on the grain known as "Carolina gold," but surely none were more distinctive than the soupy bogs enriched with regional shellfish, cured country ham, various vegetables, and countless other ingredients. This particular bog was inspired by one that used to be on the menu of the gracious Olde Pink House restaurant in Myrtle Beach, South Carolina, the most unusual ingredient being a highly smoked Canadian bacon that was cut into thin strips. Although sweet chicken wings (simmered no longer than one hour) could be used, I find that turkey not only has much more flavor but also provides a sturdier texture to contrast with the soft rice. The main point is that, unlike a fluffy perloo or jambalaya, the rice in a bog must be wet and almost soggy.

1 Cut off and set aside the turkey wing tips and cut the wings in half at the joint. In a large, heavy pot, heat the oil over moderately high heat, add the wings including the tips, and brown lightly on all sides. Add the onions, carrots, and garlic and cook, stirring, till the onions are soft, about 5 minutes. Add the tomatoes and stir for 1 minute. Add the tarragon, bay leaves, salt and pepper, and water and bring to a boil. Reduce the heat to moderately low, cover, and simmer till the wings are tender, about 2 hours.

2 Discard the wing tips and bay leaves, transfer the wings to a bowl, remove and discard the skin and bones, and cut the turkey meat into 1½-inch strips. Pour off all but about 2 cups of the cooking liquid, add the turkey strips, Canadian bacon, and limas to the pot, return the mixture to a simmer, and cook till the limas are tender, about 15 minutes. Add the rice, stir till well blended, and heat till the mixture is piping hot but the rice is still quite wet.

PIG PICKIN'S

"We talk a lot about being a 'barbecue man.' You got to be able to man the pits but also work the grounds and wait tables and work the cash register— that's being a real barbecue man." —Chip Stamey, Stamey's Barbecue, Greensboro, North Carolina

CREOLE HAM, SAUSAGE, AND SHRIMP JAMBALAYA

MAKES 6 SERVINGS

2 ounces salt pork, cut into pieces

4 medium onions, chopped

2 celery ribs, chopped

1 small green bell pepper, seeded and chopped

2 garlic cloves, minced

1 pound cooked ham, chopped

½ pound spicy smoked sausage links, cut into ½-inch slices

2 teaspoons salt

½ teaspoon freshly ground black pepper

¼ teaspoon dried thyme

¼ teaspoon cayenne pepper

2 bay leaves

2½ cups uncooked long-grain rice

5 cups water

1 pound fresh shrimp, shelled and deveined

Tabasco sauce

Since Gonzales, a small Cajun town between New Orleans and Baton Rouge, Louisiana, proclaims itself "The Jambalaya Capital of the World" and sponsors a major festival and cooking competition every June, don't even suggest to any of the locals that this legendary rice dish is considered by many to be a hallmark of Creole cookery. What matters is that the name itself derives from the French *jambon*, and that some form of ham continues to be the main ingredient of jambalaya even when crawfish or shrimp, poultry, or even game is added to the elaborate dish. Cajuns will tell you that no jambalaya is authentic unless it contains tasso, a highly seasoned local ham rarely found outside Louisiana. Nor are you likely to encounter any jambalaya in the region that doesn't also boast a spicy, smoked pork sausage such as andouille or kielbasa. The best I can determine is that my jambalaya would be classified as Creole by virtue of the fact that it has no tomatoes.

1 In a heavy 8-quart pot or casserole, cook the salt pork over low heat till all the fat is rendered, add the onions, celery, bell pepper, and garlic, and stir till the vegetables soften, 8 to 10 minutes. Add the ham, sausage, salt, pepper, thyme, cayenne, and bay leaves and continue stirring for about 10 minutes longer. Add the rice and water, bring to a boil, reduce the heat to low, cover, and simmer for about 45 minutes. Add the shrimp, stir well, increase the heat to moderate, and stir with a fork till the rice begins to dry out and is fluffy, about 15 minutes.

2 Serve the jambalaya hot with Tabasco on the side.

BREADS

Skillet Cornbread with Cracklin's

Ole Miss Sausage and Black-Eyed Pea Cornbread

Lard Hoecakes

Bacon Corn Sticks

Bacon Corn Pones

Bacon Grease Hush Puppies

Piggy Spoon Bread

Tennessee Cracklin' Cloud Biscuits

Sausage-Olive Biscuits

Bacon-Cheddar Biscuits

West Virginia Ham and Grits Biscuits

Alabama Biscuit Muffins

Bacon-Peanut Butter Muffins

Bacon, Herb, and Poppy Seed Yeast Rolls

Shenandoah Smoked-Pork Bread

Bacon-Pimento Cheese Bread

Country Ham Potato Bread

Sausage and Walnut Bread

Baltimore Bacon and Cheese Yeast Bread

Old-Fashioned Ham and Cheese Pie Bread

SKILLET CORNBREAD WITH CRACKLIN'S

MAKES 6 TO 8 SERVINGS

½ pound pork fatback
　or salt pork

1½ cups yellow cornmeal
　(preferably stone-ground)

¼ cup all-purpose flour

1 teaspoon baking powder

¼ teaspoon baking soda

½ teaspoon salt

1½ cups buttermilk

1 large egg, beaten

4 tablespoons (½ stick) butter

Ideally in the South, cracklin's are made by rendering nuggets of fresh pork fat at hog-killing time in the fall, and then used to flavor any number of stews, vegetables, and breads, like this popular skillet cornbread. While there's nothing like fresh cracklin's (I can eat them out of my hand like peanuts), practicality almost demands that you substitute either fatback or salt pork, both of which are widely available in most markets. (Even if you can find them, I do not advise using packaged, store-bought cracklin's, which can have a strange artificial flavor and texture.) This cornbread can be made with either butter or lard (the former providing more flavor, the latter a lighter texture), but by no means prepare it in anything but a heavy cast-iron skillet, which maintains steady, even heat like no other equipment.

1　To make the cracklin's, cut the fatback into small cubes, arrange the cubes in a small cast-iron skillet, and barely cover with water. Bring to a boil, cook till all the water evaporates, and continue cooking till the pieces are totally rendered of fat and are crisp, taking care not to burn. Drain on paper towels and set aside.

2　Preheat the oven to 425°F.

3 In a bowl, whisk together the cornmeal, flour, baking powder, baking soda, and salt. Whisking, gradually add the buttermilk till well blended, add the egg, and stir till well blended. Add the cracklin's and stir till well blended.

4 In a 9-inch cast-iron skillet, melt the butter over moderate heat, pour about half into the batter, and stir till well blended. Scrape the batter into the hot skillet, place on the center rack of the oven, and bake till golden brown, about 35 minutes.

5 Serve the cornbread hot in wedges.

PIG PICKIN'S

In 1976, the Southern supermarket chain Winn Dixie ran an ad for "An Easy and economical way to have your own neighborhood or family pig pickin': Whole Pigs—Ready to Eat— 36-46 lb. Average—99 Cents Per Pound"

Ole Miss Sausage and Black-Eyed Pea Cornbread

Makes 6 to 8 servings

½ pound bulk pork sausage

1 small onion, chopped

2 cups white cornmeal

1 cup all-purpose flour

1 teaspoon salt

½ teaspoon freshly ground black pepper

½ teaspoon baking soda

1 cup buttermilk

½ cup vegetable oil

2 large eggs

1 cup grated aged Colby or Swiss cheese

One 15-ounce can black-eyed peas, drained

½ cup canned chopped green chiles

Encountered at a tailgate feast on the campus of the University of Mississippi at Oxford, this rugged cornbread, contributed by an alumna, remains one of the most unusual and delicious Southern breads I have ever put in my mouth. Since the batter should be slightly lumpy, do not overmix it, and do feel free to experiment, as I have countless times, with various full-flavored cheeses.

1 Preheat the oven to 375°F. Grease a large baking dish or pan and set aside.

2 In a skillet, break up the sausage, add the onion, and stir over moderate heat till the meat is browned, about 10 minutes. Drain the sausage and onion on paper towels.

3 In a large bowl, whisk together the cornmeal, flour, salt, pepper, and baking soda. In another bowl, whisk together the buttermilk, oil, and eggs till frothy, add to the dry mixture, and stir just till the dry mixture is moistened. (Do not overmix; the batter should be slightly lumpy.) Add the cheese, black-eyed peas, and chiles and stir till the mixture is well blended. Scrape the batter into the prepared dish and bake till golden brown, 40 to 50 minutes.

4 Allow to cool for about 10 minutes before serving.

LARD HOECAKES

MAKES ABOUT 8 HOECAKES

1 cup white cornmeal

1 teaspoon salt

1 tablespoon chilled lard

½ to ¾ cup boiling water

3 tablespoons bacon grease

Who knows whether the early Southern colonial settlers actually cooked these crisp corn cakes on the metal ends of hoes over open fires? What matters is that today the toothsome griddle cakes, slathered with butter and fruit preserves for breakfast or served plain with soups, gumbos, stews, boiled greens, or elaborate salads, are a hallmark of Southern cornmeal baking and worthy of the finest dinner tables and buffets. Some cooks leaven their hoecakes (like ashcakes and johnnycakes) with baking powder and eggs; I find that a little lard is all that's needed to lighten the cakes and produce just the right crispy texture. As for the sublime flavor, don't even consider frying the cakes in any fat but bacon grease.

1 In a bowl, combine the cornmeal, salt, and lard and rub with your fingertips till the lard is well incorporated in the meal. Gradually add enough boiling water to the meal to make a batter that is soft but not too wet, mixing as rapidly as possible. Flour your hands lightly, form the batter into thin cakes about 3 inches in diameter, and place on a plate.

2 Brush a heavy cast-iron griddle with a thick coating of bacon grease, heat till very hot but not smoking, add the hoecakes a few at a time, and fry till golden brown and crisp, about 2 minutes on each side. Repeat with the remaining grease and cakes, transferring them to a platter and keeping them as hot as possible till serving time.

BACON CORN STICKS

4 slices lean hickory-smoked bacon

1 cup yellow cornmeal

½ cup all-purpose flour

2 teaspoons sugar

2 teaspoons baking powder

½ teaspoon baking soda

½ teaspoon salt

1 large egg, beaten

½ cup buttermilk

2 tablespoons vegetable shortening, cut into bits and at room temperature

In the South, bacon, lean salt pork (streak-o'-lean), fatback, and country ham are regularly used to flavor all sorts of breads, and none is so beloved as these crusty corn sticks served with soups, stews, and fried fish. Genuine corn sticks must be baked in special seven-stick cast-iron molds (available in most cookware shops and home stores), which, like new cast-iron skillets, should be initially "seasoned" by rubbing the surfaces with cooking oil and leaving them in a 300°F oven for at least one hour. For the corn sticks to come out soft on the inside with crispy tops, the seasoned molds must be heated till scorching hot and the sticks must be baked at a high temperature. The corn sticks are almost as good made with whole milk as with buttermilk, in which case the baking soda is not needed.

1 In a skillet, fry the bacon over moderate heat till crisp. Drain on paper towels and crumble finely, reserving the fat in the skillet.

2 In a large bowl, whisk together the cornmeal, flour, sugar, baking powder, baking soda, and salt till well blended. Add the egg and buttermilk and stir till well blended. Add the shortening and bacon, stir till well blended, cover the bowl with plastic wrap, and chill the batter for 1 hour.

3 Preheat the oven to 475°F.

4 Grease a 7-stick cast-iron corn-stick mold with some of the bacon fat from the skillet and place in the oven till very hot, about 10 minutes. Spoon the batter into the mold and bake till the tops are golden brown and crisp, 10 to 12 minutes.

5 Serve piping hot.

PIG PICKIN'S

"No one can outperform a gifted Southerner when it comes to such activities as curing hams and barbecuing pork shoulders." — John Egerton, *Southern Food*

BACON CORN PONES

¼ pound sliced bacon

3 cups yellow cornmeal

1 teaspoon baking powder

½ teaspoon baking soda

1 teaspoon salt

1¼ cups buttermilk

Traced back to colonial days, Southern corn pone (derived from the Indian *suppone*) is the earliest and crudest form of cornbread and was originally made with nothing more than cornmeal, water, salt, and either bacon or bear grease. After the introduction of baking soda and powder in the nineteenth century, the pones baked over open fires or fried became considerably lighter in texture, but even today no authentic corn pone contains eggs, and cooks still have to make sure the batter is stiff enough so that the oval patties don't spread too much on the baking sheet on in the skillet. Pones fried in bacon grease (about five minutes on each side over moderate heat) are just as delicious as the baked ones, and all corn pones can be served in place of cornbread, corn sticks, or hoecakes.

1 Preheat the oven to 400°F. Grease a large baking sheet and set aside.

2 In a large skillet, fry the bacon over moderate heat till crisp. Drain on paper towels and crumble finely, reserving the fat in the skillet.

3 In a large bowl, combine the cornmeal, baking powder, baking soda, and salt and stir till well blended. Add the crumbled bacon, 3 tablespoons of the bacon fat, the buttermilk, and just enough water to form a stiff batter when well stirred. Let the batter stand for about 5 minutes.

4 With your hands, form the batter into small oval patties, place the patties 1 inch apart on the prepared baking sheet, and bake till lightly browned and crisp, about 20 minutes.

5 Serve the pones hot with plenty of butter.

PIG PICKIN'S

Abraham Lincoln's two favorite breakfasts were fried apples with salt pork, and ham with cream gravy and biscuits.

Bacon Grease Hush Puppies

1 cup yellow cornmeal

½ cup all-purpose flour

1 teaspoon sugar

½ teaspoon baking powder

½ teaspoon baking soda

½ teaspoon salt

1 large egg, beaten

1 tablespoon bacon grease

2 tablespoons minced onion

1 cup buttermilk

Corn oil for deep frying

St. Marks, Florida, a small fishing village south of Tallahassee, lays claim to being the original home of hush puppies, but given the much greater popularity of the wonderful cornmeal dodgers in the coastal Carolinas ever since the Civil War (during which cooks allegedly shouted "Hush, puppies!" to barking dogs being tossed scraps at fish camps), I have my doubts. For years, I was convinced that the best hush puppies on earth were those served at the Center Pier Restaurant at Carolina Beach, North Carolina. Then I tasted these made with buttermilk and flavored with bacon grease at a seafood house in Calabash, North Carolina, and I couldn't quiz the savvy waitress fast enough. Just remember that nothing is worse than a cold hush puppy, and that the question of whether hush puppies should be buttered is a highly debated one that you'll have to answer for yourself.

1 In a bowl, combine the cornmeal, flour, sugar, baking powder, baking soda, and salt and stir till well blended. Add the egg, bacon grease, onion, and buttermilk and stir till the batter is well blended and thick.

2 In a deep-fat fryer or deep cast-iron skillet, heat about 3 inches of oil to 375°F on a thermometer, drop the batter in batches by teaspoons into the fat, and fry till the hush puppies are golden brown and crisp, about 3 minutes. Drain on paper towels briefly and serve immediately in a covered bread basket.

PIGGY SPOON BREAD

½ pound lean salt pork
   (streak-o'-lean), finely diced

2 cups water

1 cup yellow cornmeal

1 cup whole milk

3 large eggs, separated

1 teaspoon baking powder

1 teaspoon salt

½ teaspoon freshly ground
   black pepper

Unlike most puddinglike spoon breads that can literally be eaten with a spoon, this one flavored with salt pork is firm, like bread, and intended to be eaten with a mess of boiled turnip greens or collards and dipped into the cooking liquid (pot likker). Not that the spoon bread isn't also delicious at breakfast sopped in country ham red-eye gravy or runny fried egg yolks. In fact, the dish can be just as successful made with diced cooked country ham or pig belly and served with anything from greens to eggs to black-eyed peas.

1 Preheat the oven to 350°F.

2 In a 2-quart ovenproof casserole, fry the salt pork over moderate heat till crisp; drain on paper towels. Tilt the casserole back and forth to coat the sides with fat, pour off the excess fat, and set the casserole aside.

3 In a large, heavy saucepan, bring the water to a boil, gradually add the cornmeal, reduce the heat to moderate, and stir till thickened, 10 to 15 minutes. Remove the pan from the heat, add the milk, and stir till well blended. In a small bowl, beat the egg yolks till frothy, add to the cornmeal mixture along with the salt pork, baking powder, salt, and pepper, and stir till well blended. In another bowl, whisk the egg whites till stiff and fold them into the mixture till well blended. Scrape the mixture into the prepared casserole and bake till fully set, firm, and well browned, about 1 hour.

4 Serve hot.

TENNESSEE CRACKLIN' CLOUD BISCUITS

MAKES ABOUT 1 DOZEN BISCUITS

½ envelope active dry yeast

2 tablespoons warm water

¼ cup finely diced salt pork

2¼ cups unbleached all-purpose flour

1 teaspoon baking powder

¼ cup chilled vegetable shortening

1 cup whole milk

In various areas of the South, biscuits made with yeast are called everything from "angel" to "fluff" to "bride's" to "cloud" biscuits, and these Tennessee cloud biscuits with cracklin's are some of the most feathery and wondrous I've ever tasted. Bits of fried bacon or country ham could be substituted for the cracklin's, but, in any case, note that no salt is needed and also that once the yeast mixture and milk are added, the dough should be stirred only till the dry ingredients are moistened—not a second longer. Any leftover biscuits are also delectable when split, toasted, and served with fruit preserves or honey for breakfast.

1 In a small bowl, combine the yeast and water and let proof for 10 minutes.

2 In a small, heavy skillet, fry the salt pork over moderate heat till well browned and crisp, about 10 minutes; drain the cracklin's on paper towels.

3 In a large bowl, whisk together the flour and baking powder. Add the shortening and rub it into the flour with your fingertips till the mixture is mealy. Add the cracklin's and stir till well blended. Make a well in the dry ingredients, pour the yeast mixture and milk into the well, and stir gently just till the dry ingredients are moistened and the dough is soft. Cover with a towel or plastic wrap and let rise in a warm area for about 1 hour.

4 Preheat the oven to 425°F.

5 Transfer the dough to a lightly floured surface and knead about 8 times. Roll out about ½ inch thick and cut out rounds with a 2½-inch biscuit cutter. Roll the scraps together and cut out more rounds.

6 Arrange the rounds on a baking sheet about 1 inch apart and bake in the upper third of the oven till golden brown, about 15 minutes.

7 Serve hot.

Sausage-Olive Biscuits

½ pound fresh bulk pork sausage
(page 248)

1 cup finely chopped pimento-
stuffed olives

1½ cups all-purpose flour

2 teaspoons baking powder

½ teaspoon baking soda

½ teaspoon salt

3 tablespoons chilled vegetable
shortening

¾ cup buttermilk

Southerners never stop coming up with ways to flavor biscuits, and while the sausage-olive combination in these is delightfully compatible and unusual, you might well substitute finely chopped bell pepper, scallions, mushrooms, or pecans for the olives—with or without a teaspoon of a dried herb. If at all possible, I do recommend making your own sausage meat for these biscuits, since you never know how the lean-to-fat ratio of commercial products might affect the texture. The biscuits are great with cocktails, soups, or salads, or just for nibbling.

1 In a skillet, break up the sausage meat and fry over moderate heat till all pink color has disappeared, stirring. Drain on paper towels. Place the sausage in a bowl, add the olives, toss till well blended, and set aside.

2 Preheat the oven to 450°F.

3 In a large bowl, whisk together the flour, baking powder, baking soda, and salt. Add the shortening and rub with your fingers till the mixture is mealy. Add the sausage-olive mixture, stir, and then gradually add the buttermilk, stirring till the dough is soft.

4 Transfer the dough to a lightly floured surface and knead briefly with your fingertips. Shape the mixture into balls about 1 inch in diameter, rolling between the palms of your hands. Arrange the balls on one or two baking sheets, press them down slightly with your fingertips, and bake till lightly browned, 12 to 15 minutes.

5 Serve hot or at room temperature.

PIG PICKIN'S

Southern Living magazine once published a recipe for a "Barbecue Sundae": pulled pork, baked beans, and creamy slaw layered in a Mason jar and garnished with a dill pickle.

BACON-CHEDDAR BISCUITS

½ pound sliced lean applewood-smoked bacon

2 cups all-purpose flour

2 tablespoons baking powder

½ teaspoon salt

Cayenne pepper to taste

⅓ cup chilled lard

½ pound extra-sharp cheddar cheese, grated

1 cup milk

These are the type of flavored biscuits that Southerners like to keep on hand for cocktail parties, bridge luncheons, and afternoon teas. Feel free to experiment with various styles of bacon and cheeses, but if you want the biscuits to be particularly light and crispy, be sure to use the lard in place of butter, margarine, or vegetable shortening. Also, by no means handle the dough too much: Stir in the milk mixture just till the dry ingredients are moistened, knead the dough no more than a few times, and pat (don't roll) it out gently with your fingertips.

1 In a large skillet, fry the bacon over moderate heat till crisp. Drain on paper towels and crumble finely.

2 Preheat the oven to 425°F. Lightly grease a large baking sheet and set aside.

3 In a large bowl, whisk together the flour, baking powder, salt, and cayenne. Add the lard and cut it into the flour with a pastry cutter till the mixture is mealy. Add the bacon, cheese, and milk and stir just till the dry ingredients are well moistened.

4 Transfer the dough to a lightly floured surface and knead 4 to 5 times—no more. Pat out the dough about ½ inch thick and cut out rounds with a 2-inch biscuit cutter. Pat the scraps together and cut out more rounds. Arrange the rounds on the prepared baking sheet about ½ inch apart and bake in the upper third of the oven till golden, 12 to 15 minutes.

5 Let cool, and then store in an airtight container for up to 2 weeks.

WEST VIRGINIA HAM AND GRITS BISCUITS

½ cup regular grits (not instant)

2 cups all-purpose flour

4 teaspoons baking powder

3 tablespoons chilled lard

½ cup whole or 2 percent milk, or as needed

¼ cup finely diced cooked country ham

I still don't know if the cook at a sleek diner outside Charleston, West Virginia, cooked grits from scratch (as he claimed) or used leftover ones (perfectly permissible) to make these memorable biscuits at breakfast, but since I noticed a couple of sacked country hams hanging from hooks just outside the kitchen, I had no reason to doubt the pedigree of the zesty ham that flavored the hefty wonders. The trick to making this style of biscuit, of course, is leavening the dough with enough baking powder and lard (not butter), and because the biscuits are not intended to be light and fluffy, the dough can be kneaded till pliable. I've also made these biscuits with up to ½ cup of fried and crumbled lean bacon. And, once again, ½ cup or more of leftover grits at room temperature works just as well in this recipe.

1 Preheat the oven to 400°F.

2 Cook the grits according to package directions and let cool.

3 In a large bowl, whisk together the flour and baking powder. Add the lard and rub it into the flour till the mixture is mealy. Stir in the milk, then beat in the grits and ham with a wooden spoon till well blended, adding more milk if necessary for a smooth dough.

4 Transfer the dough to a lightly floured surface and knead till pliable. Pat the dough out about ½ inch thick and cut out rounds with a 2-inch biscuit cutter. Pat the scraps together and cut out more rounds. Arrange the rounds on a baking sheet about 1 inch apart and bake in the upper third of the oven till golden brown, 12 to 15 minutes.

5 Serve hot.

PIG PICKIN'S

Queen Victoria of England had a standing order for Virginia's Smithfield ham.

Alabama Biscuit Muffins

2½ cups all-purpose flour

1 tablespoon sugar

2 teaspoons baking powder

1 teaspoon salt

10 tablespoons chilled lard, cut into bits

1 tablespoon bacon grease

1 cup whole milk

I've never encountered biscuit muffins (a misnomer, since the sturdy muffins bear little resemblance to genuine biscuits) outside the Deep South, and while Mississippians I've known claim the distinctive bread to be a specialty of their state, where I've eaten them mostly is in Alabama. "They put sugar in their muffins over in Alabama," Craig Claiborne used to grumble disapprovingly, "and in Louisiana they use lard instead of butter." Such biases prevail about hundreds of regional dishes all over the South, but despite the various perceptions of what does and does not constitute an authentic biscuit muffin, I can say that I've never found one that wasn't flavored with a little bacon grease. No bread is simpler to make, and the light muffins are not only ideal with rich stratas, savory puddings, seafood stews, and the like but also sumptuous spread with jams, jellies, or molasses at breakfast.

1 Preheat the oven to 350°F. Grease a 12-cup muffin pan and set aside.

2 In a large bowl, whisk together the flour, sugar, baking powder, and salt. Add the lard and rub it into the flour with your fingertips till the mixture is mealy. Add the bacon grease and milk and stir till the dough is slightly firm. Spoon the mixture into the prepared muffin pan and bake till the muffins are browned and crusty, 40 to 45 minutes.

3 Serve hot.

Bacon–Peanut Butter Muffins

4 slices lean hickory-smoked
   bacon

2 cups all-purpose flour

1 tablespoon sugar

2 teaspoons baking powder

1 teaspoon baking soda

1 teaspoon salt

1 cup buttermilk

2 large eggs

¼ cup smooth peanut butter

What Southern child didn't grow up eating peanut butter and bacon sandwiches, a flavor memory that lingers well into adulthood and one that no doubt inspired my sister to come up with these nostalgic muffins for her children (one of whom, by the way, now bakes them for her children). The muffins are rich but remarkably light in texture, and they're not only perfect for picnics and cookouts but also an unusual treat at afternoon teas. Since the bacon provides plenty of crunch, be sure to use smooth peanut butter for these muffins.

1 Preheat the oven to 375°F. Grease a 12-cup muffin pan and set aside.

2 In a skillet, fry the bacon over moderate heat till crisp; drain on paper towels and crumble finely. Pour off all but about 2 tablespoons of grease from the skillet and set the skillet aside.

3 In a large bowl, combine the flour, sugar, baking powder, baking soda, and salt and stir till well blended. In another bowl, whisk together the buttermilk and eggs till frothy, stir in the crumbled bacon and reserved bacon grease, add to the flour mixture, and stir just till a moist batter forms. Fill about one-quarter of each cup of the prepared muffin pan with batter, spoon about 1 teaspoon of peanut butter into each cup, and fill each cup about two-thirds full with the remaining batter.

4 Bake the muffins till puffy and golden brown, 25 to 30 minutes. Let cool on a wire rack.

Bacon, Herb, and Poppy Seed Yeast Rolls

Makes 1 dozen or more rolls

2 tablespoons butter, melted

¼ cup poppy seeds

5 slices lean bacon

1 envelope active dry yeast

¼ cup warm water

1 cup milk

½ cup vegetable shortening

1 tablespoon sugar

1 teaspoon garlic salt

¼ teaspoon dried thyme, crumbled

¼ teaspoon dried oregano, crumbled

3 cups all-purpose flour

2 large eggs, beaten

Southerners love dinner yeast rolls about as much as biscuits and cornbread and take as much pride in creating new flavored versions as in conceiving different styles of muffins and hush puppies. I've never figured out when and why poppy seeds began to play such an important role in Southern cookery (poppy seed wafers, poppy seed noodles, poppy seed chicken, poppy seed cake), but there can be no doubt that the nutty, silver-blue seeds meld with the bacon and herbs in these rolls to produce a flavor sensation that couldn't be more distinctive. Since the rolls should be more a firm bread than a puffy muffin, make sure the dough is not too moist, adding a little more flour with the bacon, if necessary, before the first rise.

1 Prepare a 12-cup muffin pan by spooning ½ teaspoon of melted butter into each cup and sprinkling poppy seeds over the tops. Set aside.

2 In a large skillet, fry the bacon over moderate heat till crisp; drain on paper towels and crumble.

3 In a small bowl, combine the yeast and water and let proof for about 10 minutes.

4 In a large saucepan, scald the milk over high heat, reduce the heat to moderate, add the shortening, sugar, garlic salt, thyme, and oregano, and stir till the shortening melts and the ingredients are well blended. Transfer to a large bowl and let cool to lukewarm. Gradually add the flour and beat with a wooden spoon till well blended. Add the eggs and yeast mixture and beat till the dough is smooth. Add the bacon, stir till well blended, cover with a towel or plastic wrap, and let rise in a warm area till bubbly, about 1 hour.

5 Stir the dough down, fill the prepared muffin cups half-full of dough, cover, and let rise again till doubled in bulk, about 45 minutes. Meanwhile, preheat the oven to 425°F.

6 Bake the rolls till lightly browned, about 20 minutes. Serve hot.

SHENANDOAH SMOKED-PORK BREAD

MAKES 2 LOAVES

2 envelopes active dry yeast

2 teaspoons sugar

2½ cups warm water

6 to 7 cups all-purpose flour

2 teaspoons salt

2 cups cooked, diced, smoked pork loin chops

I must drive down the Shenandoah Valley of western Virginia at least four times a year, and never do I make the trip and not look for this yeasty smoked-pork bread (plain or braided) that I once found at a bakery in Harrisonburg and was later served at a nondescript family restaurant outside Roanoke. According to a waitress at the latter locale, it's a bread that farm wives in the region have been making for generations with smoked pork chops, belly, ham hocks, and who knows what other cuts, and, evidently, the ways some loaves are braided is a matter of great pride for many. If you care to try your hand at braiding (I've never mastered the knack), do so before the second rise after you've divided the dough. In addition to the wonderful flavor, a real plus about this yeast bread is that it doesn't take much more than two hours to prepare. Since the bread freezes beautifully, it's almost a sin not to make two loaves.

1 Grease two 9 by 5 by 3-inch loaf pans and set aside.

2 In a large bowl, combine the yeast, sugar, and water, stir, and let proof for about 10 minutes. Add 3 cups of the flour and the salt and beat well with a wooden spoon till smooth. Gradually add just enough of the remaining flour to make a soft dough, stirring steadily. Turn out onto a lightly floured surface and knead till the dough is no longer sticky, about 2 minutes. Place in a large oiled bowl, turn to coat lightly, cover with a towel or plastic wrap, and let rise in a warm area till doubled in bulk, 30 to 45 minutes.

3 Transfer the dough back to the floured surface, add the diced pork, and knead just till the pork is well incorporated. Divide the dough in half, place each half in one of the prepared loaf pans, cover, and let rise again till doubled in bulk, 30 to 45 minutes. Meanwhile, preheat the oven to 400°F.

4 Bake the loaves in the center of the oven till the tops are nicely browned and crusted, 30 to 40 minutes. Turn out onto a wire rack and let cool.

BACON-PIMENTO CHEESE BREAD

4 slices bacon

1 envelope active dry yeast

2 tablespoons warm water

3½ cups plus 3 tablespoons all-purpose flour

2 teaspoons sugar

1 teaspoon salt

1 cup milk

1 tablespoon minced fresh chives

2 ounces sharp cheddar cheese, shredded

¼ cup finely chopped pimentos

1 tablespoon butter, melted

I couldn't agree more with the distinguished Southern novelist Reynolds Price that pimento cheese is the most sublime spread ever conceived, and if you think a plain pimento cheese and bacon sandwich is something to whistle "Dixie" about, wait till you try this incredible bread enriched with both crumbled bacon and bacon grease. One word of warning, however: Do not try to simply substitute prepared pimento cheese spread for the individual cheese and pimentos indicated in the recipe; all the mayonnaise in the spread will distort the bread.

1 In a medium skillet, fry the bacon over moderate heat till crisp. Drain on paper towels, crumble, and reserve the grease in the skillet.

2 In a small bowl, combine the yeast and water and let proof for about 10 minutes.

3 In a medium saucepan, combine the 3 tablespoons of flour, reserved bacon grease, sugar, and salt, gradually stir in the milk, and cook over moderate heat, stirring constantly, till thick and smooth, about 10 minutes. Remove the pan from the heat, add the chives, cheese, and pimentos, stir till the cheese melts, and let cool slightly.

4 Add the yeast mixture to the cheese mixture, stir, and gradually add the 3 cups of flour, beating with an electric mixer till smooth and adding enough extra flour to make a firm dough. Turn the dough out onto a lightly floured surface and knead till smooth and elastic, about 8 minutes. Place in an oiled bowl, turn to coat the surface, cover with a towel or plastic wrap, and let rise in a warm area till doubled in bulk, about 1 hour.

5 Punch the dough down, transfer to a 9 by 5 by 3-inch loaf pan, cover, and let rise again till doubled in bulk, about 1 hour. Meanwhile, preheat the oven to 350°F.

6 Brush the top of the loaf with melted butter and bake till the loaf sounds hollow when tapped, 35 to 40 minutes. Turn out onto a wire rack and let cool.

Country Ham Potato Bread

Makes 3 small round loaves

For the Starter:

2 cups peeled and diced russet potatoes

3 cups water

2 cups all-purpose flour

2 tablespoons sugar

For the Bread:

1 cup warm cooked mashed potatoes

1½ cups water

1 cup starter

1 envelope active dry yeast

2 tablespoons sugar

2 tablespoons vegetable oil

1 teaspoon salt

5½ to 6 cups all-purpose flour

2 cups finely diced cooked country ham

Since this exceptional yeast bread requires a potato starter that must be made two to three days in advance, as well as two risings, it can be a test of patience. Southern potato bread, however, which is traditionally made with leftover mashed potatoes and usually flavored with diced cooked bacon, salt pork, pig belly, or country ham, is a special treat, and serious cooks are as prone to keep (and continuously "feed") a starter in the refrigerator as to routinely collect (and maybe filter) bacon grease in a coffee can above the stove. So long as you're going to the trouble to make this bread, it's almost ridiculous not to make three small loaves—which do freeze beautifully when wrapped tightly in plastic.

1 To make the starter, combine the potatoes and water in a large saucepan, bring to a boil, reduce the heat to low, cover, and cook slowly till the potatoes are very tender, 20 to 25 minutes. Strain the mixture through a sieve into a bowl, mashing down on the potatoes with a heavy spoon. Let the potato water cool, and then discard the potatoes. Add the flour and sugar to the water, stir well till a wet dough forms, cover with plastic wrap, and let ferment at room temperature for 2 to 3 days. Cover the starter and refrigerate till needed.

2 To make the bread, combine the mashed potatoes, 1 cup of the water, and the starter in a large bowl and let stand for 1 hour. Meanwhile, combine the remaining water and yeast in a small bowl and let proof for about 10 minutes.

3 Add the yeast mixture to the potato mixture and stir well. Add the sugar, oil, salt, 2 cups of the flour, and the ham, stir till well blended, and then gradually add enough of the remaining flour to form a soft, smooth dough. Transfer the dough to a lightly floured surface and knead till very smooth. Place in a large greased bowl, turn several times, cover with plastic wrap, and let rise in a warm area till doubled in bulk, about 1 hour.

4 Punch the dough down, shape it into 3 round loaves, place each loaf in a small greased round pan, cover, and let rise till doubled in bulk, 40 to 45 minutes.

5 Preheat the oven to 375°F.

6 Bake the loaves till golden brown and crusty, about 45 minutes. Let cool on wire racks.

SAUSAGE AND WALNUT BREAD

½ cup currants (you may use raisins, but currants plump better)

1 pound Neese's red-hot sausage (I like this brand best)

1½ cups brown sugar

1½ cups white sugar

2 eggs

1 cup chopped walnuts (you may use pecans, I never have)

3 cups flour

1 teaspoon spice blend*

1 teaspoon baking powder

1 teaspoon baking soda

1 cup cold coffee (for goodness sakes, don't consider instant!)

½ cup chopped fruit (I almost forgot this)

*Spice blend consists of cinnamon, coriander, nutmeg, allspice, powdered cloves, ginger, and mace in decreasing quantities. Mix this up to your pleasure.

Before his untimely death, Bill Neal, owner and chef at Crook's Corner restaurant in Chapel Hill, North Carolina, gave me a taste of this unusual "bread," the recipe for which came from a friend in Winston-Salem who, in turn, got it from a friend of his (just the way so many recipes in the South circulate among families and friends). I found the bread utterly sumptuous, baked up a loaf using pecans instead of walnuts, and served it to great acclaim at breakfast with various homemade fruit preserves. Since the old-fashioned style of the original recipe exemplifies so quaintly (yet clearly) the way many Southerners write recipes, I reproduce it here verbatim—as Bill did when he shared the recipe—and if I can follow it, you can. As for the Neese's sausage, that's one of the fresh (never frozen) North Carolina commercial bulk sausages I grew up eating and still buy in large quantities when I'm home. Jimmy Dean bulk sausage, readily available around the country, is the only brand I know that comes close to approaching the quality of Neese's. This bread is also delicious served at social coffees and teas.

Simmer the fruit—all of it, currants, too—in enough water to cover for five minutes to plump it up. Five minutes should do. Drain it. Mix up the sausage, sugars, and eggs. Stir in the nuts and fruits. Mix up the flour, spices, and baking powder. Stir the baking soda into the coffee. Blend the coffee and flour mixture into the sausage mixture. Pour all of this into a greased, floured nine inch tube pan. (I always use a bundt pan.) Bake this at 350 degrees for an hour and a half. Oh, yes, I forgot one thing, add a good shot of Jack Daniels or bourbon if you prefer. This goes in with the fruit right after you drain it.

PIG PICKIN'S

"If the country ham is an endangered species, it is not the fault of anyone in Smithfield, Virginia. It is the result of changes in the outside world, of a new national taste formed by square, water-cured ham in cans, and of naïve people who throw away gift Smithfield hams because they find them too salty." —Raymond Sokolov, *Fading Feast*

Baltimore Bacon and Cheese Yeast Bread

¼ pound lean sliced bacon

1 envelope active dry yeast

3 tablespoons warm water

1 cup whole milk

2 large eggs

8 tablespoons (1 stick) butter, melted and cooled

¼ cup sugar

1 teaspoon salt

5 cups all-purpose flour

1 pound aged Swiss cheese, grated

1 large egg, beaten

I don't know when, why, or how this venerable, beguiling yeast bread came to be identified with Baltimore, but even today in some of the city's finer seafood and family-style restaurants, the bread with a twisted top might be proudly placed on the table even before menus are distributed. The bread is time-consuming to make, and dealing with the twisted folds of dough can be tricky, but whether it's served with crab cakes, grilled fish or poultry, or simply a platter of cold cuts and fresh fruit, guests will rave about it. Although aged Swiss cheese seems to be a standard ingredient with Baltimore cooks, feel free to experiment with other full-flavored cheeses—as well as with various artisanal bacons.

1 In a large skillet, fry the bacon over moderate heat till crisp; drain on paper towels and crumble.

2 In a small bowl, combine the yeast and water and let proof for about 10 minutes.

3 In a large bowl, beat together the milk and eggs till frothy. Add the butter, sugar, and salt and beat till well blended. Add the yeast mixture, stir, add 2 cups of the flour, and stir till a sticky dough forms. Add another 1½ cups of flour, stir well, transfer the dough to a work surface, and knead in enough of the remaining flour to make a very soft dough. Knead the dough till it is smooth and satiny, about 15 minutes. Place in an oiled bowl, turning it, cover with a towel or plastic wrap, and let rise in a warm area till doubled in bulk, about 1½ hours.

4 Grease a 9-inch pie pan. Punch down the dough, roll it out on a lightly floured surface into a 16-inch round, and center the dough in the pan with the edges hanging over the sides. In a bowl, mix together the crumbled bacon and cheese, mound the mixture in the center of the dough, and gather the edges of the dough in folds up over the filling, twisting the ends tightly together on top. Brush the surface of the dough with the beaten egg, cover lightly with a towel or plastic wrap, and let rise again till doubled in bulk, about 1 hour.

5 Preheat the oven to 325°F.

6 Bake the bread till golden brown and hollow-sounding when tapped, about 1 hour. Let cool for 15 minutes, remove from the pan, and let stand for another 30 minutes before slicing.

Old-Fashioned Ham and Cheese Pie Bread

Makes 6 servings

2 cups all-purpose flour

2 teaspoons baking powder

½ teaspoon salt

3 tablespoons chilled vegetable shortening

1 cup milk

1 large egg, beaten

1 cup chopped cooked smoked ham

2 scallions (white parts only), chopped

6 ounces sharp cheddar cheese, shredded

1 teaspoon prepared mustard

2 tablespoons corn oil

3 tablespoons butter, melted

2 tablespoons sesame seeds

Once was the time when elaborate pie (or pan) breads were baked in rural homes and at diners all over the Deep South and served in wedges in place of ordinary cornbread. Today, it's rare to find an old-fashioned pie bread, and this recipe for one passed down from a great aunt in Macon, Georgia, must be at least a hundred years old. There's certainly nothing delicate about the bread, but it's nonetheless delicious with bowls of hot soup or a large, tart luncheon salad. Note that chopped cooked bacon or country ham can be substituted for the regular smoked ham and that you can freeze the bread after the initial 30-minute baking and reheat it with the remaining cheese and sesame seeds when ready to serve.

1 Preheat the oven to 375°F. Grease a 10-inch pie pan and set aside.

2 In a large bowl, combine the flour, baking powder, and salt and stir till well blended. Add the shortening and work with your fingertips till the mixture is mealy. Add the milk and egg and stir till a batter forms. Add the ham, scallions, half the cheese, the mustard, and the oil and mix till well blended. Scrape the batter into the prepared pie pan, drizzle the butter over the top, and bake till firm, about 30 minutes. Sprinkle the remaining cheese over the top, scatter the sesame seeds over the cheese, and bake till the cheese melts and the top is golden, about 10 minutes longer.

3 To serve, cut the bread into wedges.

Acknowledgments

One does not simply do lots of research, test multiple recipes, sit down, and write a long cookbook on Southern Pig. You have to be virtually weaned on the meat and spend almost a lifetime sharing its glory with numerous family members, friends, colleagues, and often total strangers, all of whom somehow enrich the passionate experience that only intensifies as time moves on.

It would be impossible to thank literally everyone who, over the years, has contributed to my knowledge and appreciation of pork, introduced me to countless other enthusiasts, producers, organizations, and restaurants, and generously provided me with facts, ideas, and treasured recipes. At the top of the list, however, would have to be three Southern food experts and close friends: Jean Anderson, Kathleen Purvis, and Damon Lee Fowler. Thanks, too, is due to Peter Kaminsky, John and Dale Reed, Louis Osteen, John Edge, Emeril Lagasse, Julia Reed, John Thorne, Jeffrey Steingarten, Leah Chase, Fred Thompson, Mildred "Mama Dip" Council, Sylvia Woods, James Lasyone, Paul Prudhomme, Ella Brennan, "Hoppin'" John Taylor, my sister Patricia Royal, and the late Craig Claiborne, Eula Mae Doré, Jeanne Voltz, Bill Neal, Edna Lewis, and, above all, my beloved and gifted mother, Martha Pearl Villas.

Deepest thanks also to my veteran independent country ham producer, Clayton Long in Glendale Springs, North Carolina, as well as to the specialty ham producers in Smithfield, Virginia, Wayco Ham Company in Goldsboro, North Carolina, B & B Food Products in Cadiz, Kentucky, and G & W Hamery in Murfreesboro, Tennessee; to Neese's sausage company in Greensboro, North Carolina; and when it comes to genuine Southern barbecue, to the helpful folks at the North Carolina Barbecue Society in Winston-Salem, North Carolina, Big Bob Gibson's in Decatur, Alabama, Piggy Park in Columbia, South Carolina, Goldies Trail in Vicksburg, Mississippi, Corky's in Memphis, Tennessee, Johnny Harris in Savannah, Georgia, Wilber's in Goldsboro, North Carolina, and Mallard Creek Presbyterian Church in Charlotte, North Carolina.

Fellow Southerners and various locales are mentioned throughout the book, but to those nameless waiters and waitresses who have jotted down recipes on paper napkins, butchers who have patiently explained different cuts of meat to me, farmers who have allowed me to roam their pig pens, and gracious hosts and organizers who have invited me to pig pickin's, barbecues, roasts, festivals, benefits, and cook-offs, I can only offer a heartfelt "Thank you" for all their generous help and friendship.

Finally, I'm indebted to my loyal and ever-vigilant agent, Jane Dystel, for staying on top of this book every step of the way; to my long-time, dedicated, savvy editor at Wiley, Justin Schwartz, for always going the extra mile to make things right; and to my publisher, Natalie Chapman, for her strong encouragement, support, and faith in me.

INDEX